Solaris™
Security

Solaris™ Security

Peter H. Gregory

Sun Microsystems Press
A Prentice Hall Title

Library of Congress Cataloging-in-Publication Data

Gregory, Peter H.
    Solaris security / Peter H. Gregory.
       p.   cm.
    ISBN 0-13-096053-5
    1. Computer security.   2. Solaris (Computer file) I. Title.
  QA76.9.A25G75   2000
  005.8—dc21   99-26686
                                                        CIP

Editorial/production supervision: *BooksCraft, Inc., Indianapolis, IN*
Acquisitions editor: *Gregory Doench*
Editorial assistant: *Mary Treacy*
Marketing manager: *Bryan Gambrel*
Manufacturing manager: *Alexis R. Heydt*
Art director: *Gail Cocker-Bogusz*
Interior designer: *Meg VanArsdale*
Cover director: *Jerry Votta*
Cover designer: *Anthony Gemmellaro*
Project coordinator: *Anne Trowbridge*

Sun Microsystems Press
Marketing manager: *Michael Llowyd Alread*
Publisher: *Rachel Borden*

© 2000 by Prentice Hall PTR
Prentice-Hall, Inc.
Upper Saddle River, New Jersey 07458

10 9 8 7 6 5 4 3 2 1

ISBN 0-13-096053-5

Sun Microsystems Press
A Prentice Hall Title

*To Corinne and Laney,
without whom life would lack
meaning and joy.*

---

*To the memory of Melanie Baker-Bowman,
friend and colleague.*

CONTENTS

Part Two: *The Standalone System*   21

3 The PROM, OpenBoot, and Physical Security   23

14 Name Services   181

15 NFS and the Automounter   203

Part Four: *Disaster and Recovery*   215

16 System Recovery Preparation   217

F Implementing C2 Security   259

G Verifying the Integrity of Public-Domain Software   265

LIST OF FIGURES

LIST OF TABLES

FOREWORD

The other day, there was a news story about hackers who took over some U.S. government Web sites. Most people probably thought one of two things about this event: that the hackers were very good, or that the government was really incompetent. And the story undoubtedly confirmed a widespread fear: that cyberspace is a very bad neighborhood where lawlessness abounds and no one is safe.

Are any of these beliefs accurate? Are all of them accurate? As is generally the case, none is completely correct, but all have an element of truth.

We can address the first belief easily enough. Yes, some hackers are excellent. They can take a new application or protocol and find holes that have completely eluded the designers. But such hackers are a small minority. Most are copycats—so-called "script kiddies"—who run canned programs that exploit known flaws. A large part of running a secure system rests on this point; as we shall see, this is a very important matter.

But if typical hackers aren't that good, is the government—more accurately, the system administrators who run the various machines affected—that bad? Again, this will become clear later.

The last point—the notion that the Internet is inherently very dangerous—is the most interesting. Translated into technical language, the same idea will be expressed somewhat differently—that the protocols used on the Internet are flawed and that, if the designers had paid proper attention to security, we wouldn't have any problems today. The corollary is that, with a bit of will-power, we could deploy newer and better protocols and fix the problem. As this quote from a popular Web page indicates, many businesses appear to support the idea.

> *Our secure server software (SSL) is the industry standard and among the best software available today for secure commerce transactions. It encrypts all of your personal information, including credit card number, name, and address, so that it cannot be read as the information travels over the Internet.*

The context of this quote is an explanation of why it's safe to shop on this particular Web site. The page goes on to cite the large numbers of people who have shopped there without any problems. The implication is that cryptography is both necessary and sufficient to resolve all security concerns.

That cryptography is needed is almost beyond argument. Given the so-called "password sniffers"—eavesdropping programs that pick up passwords in transit—there is little doubt that analogous programs would have been developed to steal credit card numbers. In fact, it's a simpler problem; passwords are generally sent a character at a time, whereas credit card numbers are easily recognized and are likely to be contained in a single large packet. But to claim that the cryptography is sufficient is an exaggeration.

Ignoring the flaws in typical Web cryptography—those are inherent in the nature of the human interactions when using the Web; it's doubtful that any other designers could have done better—the real threat comes from the company's very success: the company has many credit card numbers stored on its site. Anyone who successfully penetrates it can steal them by the millions. In other words, the use of encryption and authentication—which is about all that better network protocols could do for us—protect the data in transit, but leave it unprotected on the destination host. Only if other forms of cryptography can prevent *all* ways to hack into that host can we say that better network protocols would do the trick. In other words, from a security perspective the Internet protocols are designed about as well as they could be; any other network of comparable power would have very similar security issues.

But if the Internet is a dangerous place, and the problem isn't with its design, what *is* the problem? What is wrong with our network security? That's a trick question, though; the right question is, what is wrong with our *hosts*? While there are problems attributable to the network itself—and these are the problems most easily fixed by cryptography—what we generally see is the use of the Internet to exploit host security problems. The distinction can be seen most easily by asking this question of any security hole: if the Internet did not exist, could a local user exploit that hole to gain privileges? In most cases, the answer is yes. In other words, the Internet has provided the access, rather than being an inherent part of the problem.

This realization—that host security is the real issue—is the key to achieving security on the Internet. All the cryptography in the world won't protect a machine that is insecure. The trick, then, is knowing how to protect hosts—and it's not trivial.

One solution, of course, is limit what a host can do. If a program isn't available, it isn't a security risk. But deciding what programs should and shouldn't run on a given computer is a delicate task; one has to balance functionality against security. Indeed, given the intertwined nature of services on a modern operating system, many programs you need won't run without other programs you regard as more dubious. Thorough knowledge is necessary when making such trade-offs.

The purpose of a firewall—the primary Internet security device in use today—is now clear. A firewall shields risky services from hostile outsiders, while permitting their use by presumably trustworthy insiders. In other words, it eases the problem by limiting access, hence changing the risk/benefit equation. Firewalls, then, are not about network security; rather, they are communications interrupters. They limit access to risky host services.

From this, we see the fundamental limitation of firewalls: since they don't provide security per se, anyone who can bypass them—an insider or an outsider who has found some way around or through the firewall—can still exploit residual problems on nominally protected machines. Firewalls are quite valuable, but they are not panaceas, and they must be properly placed to be useful.

One more point must be raised before we can answer the questions posed at the beginning of this discussion: what is the nature of these security holes? It turns out that virtually all of them are bugs, either in code or in system configuration. If we could eliminate bugs, we could eliminate almost all security problems, and most of the rest could be fixed by cryptography.

Of course, we can't prevent bugs, especially in code supplied to us by others. But we can apply patches as they are developed. Most successful attacks, it turns out, rely on *known* holes, holes for which patches and workarounds already exist. Certainly, that is the case for virtually all of the attacks launched by the script kiddies.

Beyond that, system configuration can make a big difference. This is especially true for containing penetrations. For example, suppose that an intruder has somehow gained access to a system. Can he or she be stopped at that point, before further damage is done? That generally depends on whether or not the intruder can obtain *root* privileges, which in turn is critically dependent on local system configuration.

Host security, then, rests on four legs: bug-free code and application design, up-to-date system patches, good configuration, and the proper balance between functionality and security. Three of these four are the responsibility of the system administrator. *You cannot have a secure system without good system administration.*

Good system administration is not easy, however. Apart from internal pressures—there is a perpetual tension between security on the one hand and functionality and ease of use on the other—reliable information is hard to come by. Too many references are too vague and general or try to cover too many different platforms. But the devil is in the details, and a routine vendor-supplied upgrade can overwrite carefully tuned security mechanisms.

Were the system administrators to blame for the break-ins we described earlier? We don't know. But if they were, it was not because they were bad. Rather, it takes great system administration to keep a machine secure, and even good system administration is *hard*.

—Steven M. Bellovin
AT&T Labs Research

PREFACE

Who Should Read This Book

Solaris™ Security has two audiences—IS/IT and security managers and UNIX administrators.

The content for IS/IT and security managers appears primarily in

- Chapter 1, "The Security Problem"
- Chapter 2, "The Security Paradigm"
- Chapter 10, "Network/System Architecture"
- Chapter 16, "System Recovery Preparation"

The remaining chapters in the book are primarily technical and written for the UNIX administrator. However, any IS/IT or security manager who needs to learn more about UNIX technology (in the security context) will find all of the technical chapters easy to read. Most chapters open with "What's in this chapter" and "Why this is important" sections. This allows you to choose whether any particular chapter needs immediate attention or whether it can or should be considered in the future.

A Quick Look at the Contents

This book discusses the physical, logical, and human-factor aspects of computer and network security in the specific context of Solaris 2.x and Solaris 7 running on Sun Microsystems computers. There are five parts.

- **Introduction.** The computer security problem is dramatically illustrated in chapter 1, "The Security Problem." Chapter 2, "The Security Paradigm," is a principle-based prescription recommended for use by all UNIX administrators, but also applicable to those managing computers of other vintages.

- **The standalone system.** This part focuses on the computer itself and covers all aspects of security. Regardless of whether or not it is connected to a network, every system is also a standalone system. Chapter 3, "PROM, OpenBoot, and Physical Security," covers one of the least-known vulnerabilities of a Solaris system, as well as practical means for securing a Sun on a desktop or in a data center. Chapter 4, "The Filesystem," is a comprehensive review of file and directory security, and includes sections on filesystem auditing tools and suggestions for UNIX administrators. Everything about user accounts is discussed in chapter 5, "User Accounts and Environments." The intricacies of system booting are covered in Chapter 6, "System Startup and Shutdown." Chapter 7, "*cron* and *at*," and chapter 8, "System Logs," provide a thorough look at those respective areas.

- **The network-connected system.** This part of the book is dedicated to the role and place of a Sun system on a network. Most severe vulnerabilities of a system are related to its being connected to a network. Chapter 9, "Network Interfaces and Services," discusses the logical attachment of Sun systems to the network and its vulnerable services. The principles of network and system architecture are covered in chapter 10, "Network/System Architecture." "Electronic Mail" is the topic of chapter 11. Chapter 12 reveals vulnerabilities with printing. Chapter 13, "Network Access Control," describes the best means for controlling access to a system via the network. DNS, NIS, and NIS+ are discussed in chapter 14, "Name Services." Chapter 15, "NFS and the Automounter," dissects these services and offers ways of improving their security.

- **Disaster and recovery.** Disasters, whether caused by human error, malice, or natural events, will occur. Chapter 16, "System Recovery Preparation," gives a detailed look at the measures to be taken before a disaster strikes to ensure a rapid, accurate, and complete recovery.

- **Appendices.** Appendix A, "Online Sources for Security Information," is a thorough review of web sites, FTP sites, and mailing lists. Likewise, a comprehensive list of security tool sources is found in appendix B, "Online Sources for Public-Domain Security Tools." Complete information on Solaris patches is found in appendix C, "Obtaining and Applying

Solaris Patches." Appendix D, "Suggested Reading," refers the reader to online and in-print publications of further interest. Sun's Solaris security products are discussed in appendix E. The steps required to implement and manage C2 security are found in appendix F. Appendix G explains how to verify the integrity of public-domain software. A glossary of attacks appears in appendix H. Appendix I is a secure system checklist.

Technical Prerequisites for the Practitioner

Solaris™ Security is written for the intermediate to advanced UNIX administrator who needs a thorough understanding of the Solaris operating system from a security perspective. If you are a technical reader, you should have the following tools and experience:

- A C compiler—either one furnished by Sun or the Gnu C compiler. This is because most public-domain tools are packaged in source form only and require compilation.
- Some experience with building public-domain tools on a UNIX system. This is not as critical a requirement as it was during UNIX's first decade, when public-domain tools were not as portable, where they required a *lot* of modification before they would compile (much less *work* properly). Further, advances in the configuration tools that accompany most public-domain packages permit those with little or no experience with the C language to get even the most complex public-domain tools up and running.

Conventions Used in This Book

Commands and Filenames

I emphasize commands and filenames within paragraphs with italics. For example, the file */etc/passwd* contains system password information. The *trap* command is used to prevent premature exit.

Commands and filenames outside of paragraphs are set in Courier font; for example

```
share -F NFS -o rw=homeusers -d "Home Directories" /export/home
```

Portions of commands indicating syntax (vs. the actual intended content) are set in italics, as follows.

```
share -F FStype -o options -d description path
```

In the example above, *FStype*, *options*, *description*, and *path* are to be replaced with actual values appropriate in practice (I will always point this out in the text where such examples occur in the book).

File Contents and Scripts

Shell scripts and the contents of computer files are set apart from paragraphs and are set in Courier font. The following example user's *.profile* file illustrates.

```
# .profile file for application users
trap exit 1 2 3 15
PATH=/export/app/bin
exec /export/app/bin/application
exit
```

A sample */etc/default/passwd* file appears as follows.

```
#ident "@(#)passwd.dfl 1.3 92/07/14 SMI"
MAXWEEKS=4
MINWEEKS=1
WARNWEEKS=3
PASSLENGTH=6
```

Computer Sessions

Examples of sessions with the computer are set apart from paragraphs and set in Courier font. Input from the user is <u>underlined</u> to distinguish it from computer output. An example session follows.

```
% id
uid=1001(jim) gid=101(users)
% su bob
Password: ********
% id
uid=1004(bob) gid=102(cust)
% lp -d localprinter /home/bob/eom.prt
request-id is localprinter-87 (1 file(s))
%
```

Also note from this example that the user-entered password is represented by a string of underlined asterisks. In reality, Solaris does not echo any actual characters typed when a user enters a password; the underlined asterisks signify a user entering non-echoed text.

Note: Some commands include the underscore (_) character, which is obscured in underlined text. Commands with underscores are *not*

underlined in this book, and all such examples are footnoted. An example command with an underscore follows.

```
# ndd -set /dev/ip ip_forwarding 0
```

Cautions and Warnings

Special notes and cautions are set apart, like this.

> Caution: */usr/bin/su* has the SetUID bit turned on. *Su* will no longer work if this bit is turned off.

Sources for Information

This book references several information sources. Each chapter ends with a section entitled "Where to Go for Additional Information" in which one or more of the following types of references are cited.

- **AnswerBook.** This is an online reference provided by Sun and included with the Solaris 2.x release media. AnswerBook employs hyperlinks to give you the ability to quickly retrieve documents referenced within other documents. Any user can start a local AnswerBook session with the *answerbook* (Sun's proprietary browser that predates Web technology) or *answerbook2* (Web browser interface) command.

- **Man pages.** This is the original UNIX command reference, useful if you know the command or file name you wish to learn more about.

> Note: Man page references in this book contain the *man page section number* to help differentiate those instances where an entry appears in more than one section. For example, when the *passwd* man page is cited, it may appear as "passwd(1M)" (the passwd *command*) or "passwd(4)" (the passwd *file*). To call up the "passwd(1M)" man page, enter the command *man -s 1M passwd* . To call up the "passwd(4)" man page, enter the command *man -s 4 passwd*.

- **docs.sun.com.** Sun has placed its entire AnswerBook and Man Pages collections on the Internet at *http://docs.sun.com/* .

- **SunSolve.** This is an information service made available to Sun customers on current maintenance or support contracts. SunSolve is periodically distributed to customers on CD-ROM and is also available online at *http://sunsolve.sun.com/* . A userid and password are required to use this site.

- **Web sites.** These are organizations or collections of information useful for the security specialist.

- **Publications.** This ranges from paper to electronic magazines, books, and articles.

Security Remedies and Public-Domain Software

This book illustrates security weaknesses in the Solaris operating system and proposes remedies for those weaknesses. Remedies take the form of

- System configuration changes. Frequently, a security weakness can be mitigated simply by changing a configuration.

- The use of Sun-supplied software. This book will describe the package name, where it can be found, and where to find installation instructions.

- The use of commercial software. Sometimes, only a commercial software package is available as a security remedy. This book describes such security programs and where they can be found.

- Process and procedure changes. Frequently a system's weakness lies in the action (or inaction) of users and administrators. This book proposes several changes in behavior that are intended to raise system security awareness.

Warnings:

Solaris™ Security **neither warrants nor endorses the use of configuration changes or public-domain or commercial software. It is the final decision of the UNIX administrator or other local site professional to decide what measures need to be taken to remedy security weaknesses.**

All public-domain software tools must be verified for integrity. A well-known security tool was once compromised (fitted with a back door) and distributed to the unsuspecting public for a short time. A UNIX administrator should no longer take the integrity of a security tool for granted just because it is on a respected or well-known web site. Appendix G contains information on how to verify the integrity of software obtained from the Internet.

The term *public domain* **does not necessarily constitute a legal** *right to use* **for all individuals, organizations, or situations. The license agreement for any public-domain software package should first be examined to ensure that its terms and conditions are not in conflict with the package's intended use. Each site's UNIX administrator or other local site professional must exercise sound judgement.**

About Web Sites

Solaris™ Security is full of uniform resource locators (URLs) containing the latest tools and other information. But, on the other hand, nothing dates a book like obsolete, changed, or inoperative URLs. In the short space of time between final draft and publication of this book, some URLs are certain to become outdated or the Web site restructured, rendering complex URLs inoperative.

Consider the following URL:

> ftp://ftp.win.tue.nl/pub/security/tcp_wrappers_7.6.tar.gz

This URL, because it contains a tool's version number, has a fairly high likelihood of becoming obsolete. If the tool is upgraded, this URL may be deactivated. If something like this happens, try the URL but without the last element, as follows:

> ftp://ftp.win.tue.nl/pub/security/

Examine the contents of this page to determine what data should be retrieved. To continue this example, if even the preceding URL is invalid, truncate the last remaining element

> ftp://ftp.win.tue.nl/pub/

and so forth, until information can be found that will indicate what happened to the desired content. Most responsible Web and file transfer protocol (ftp) sites will deposit a *README* file stating that tools or other information are at another site or no longer available.

If all of the above fails, then information about the desired tool or publication may be found from one of the general security Web sites listed in appendix A, "Online Sources for Security Information," or appendix B, "Online Sources for Public-Domain Security Tools."

Acknowledgments

Solaris Security owes its existence to the influence, ideas, and contributions of several individuals and organizations.

Liz Suto introduced me to the publishing business when she asked me to review her book, *Informix-Online Performance Tuning*. Liz introduced me to Mark Taub, one of Prentice Hall's acquisition editors, with whom I have worked on several book reviews in the years since. Mark in turn introduced me to other editors at Prentice Hall, exposing me to several more reviewing projects.

I would also like to thank John Hedtke, an accomplished technical author and local acquaintance, for sage advice about writing technical books—not only how to approach the book itself, but also its impact on one's life.

Jeff Gitlin (Lucent) reviewed an early version of the manuscript and offered numerous ideas. John Gray (University of Hartford) reviewed an early version of chapters 1–5 and likewise provided invaluable feedback.

As the manuscript matured, some of my AT&T colleagues assisted: Ken Jacob with Solaris patches; Gordon Marler with NIS, NIS+, NFS, and Automounter; Patrick Olney on PGP, system logs, secure system checklist, and glossary of attacks; Rani Sandoy-Brown on *logcheck* and the *proc* commands; and Robert Olson on PROM security, Mike Cattolico (Tigerscience) helped with *IPsec* and *SKIP*. Thanks also to Doug Hughes (Auburn University) for some clarification on some of the content at his NIS security site and to Wietse Venema (IBM) for some helpful PGP information and permission to use his site as an example.

Near the manuscript's completion, Gordon Marler (AT&T) and Armoun Forghan (AM Technologies) did a lot of QA and editing in a short space of time. Gordon QA'd all of the URLs—itself a daunting task. I thank my wife, Corinne Gregory, for the developmental edit of the entire manuscript (while eight months pregnant!). This important step greatly enhanced the book's readability.

The run level state-transition diagram was added at the last minute. Thanks go to Ken Jacob, Rani Sandoy-Brown, Eric Andrews, and Roger Santo for helping to make it understandable.

Special thanks to Steven M. Bellovin, co-author of *Firewalls and Internet Security: Repelling the Wily Hacker*, for writing the Foreword. His pioneering work with UNIX security may be his greatest legacy.

And thanks to my acquisitions editor, Greg Doench. Greg's been a great individual to work with, on prior book and book proposal review projects as well as with this book. Greg's greatest virtue is patience (trust me). And thanks, too, to Mary Treacy, Greg's assistant, for helping Greg help me.

Thanks to Ian Meldrum of Sun Microsystems for acquiring a Sun workstation and Solaris releases 2.5.1, 2.6, and Solaris 7, as well as several SunSolve and AnswerBook collections. And thanks to Jim Barbuscia at Sun, who helped chase down some vital pieces of information.

Finally, I thank my wife, Corinne, for helping me get up at 4 A.M. on weekdays so that I could spend time researching and writing without adversely affecting family time.

———

Special thanks go to Melanie Baker-Bowman, in whose memory I dedicate this book. Melanie was a career tech writer and communications master who really knew the writing business. She was one of my best friends and a colleague at AT&T. We worked together helping to get AT&T's Project Angel off the ground in its early days. She offered encouragement and ideas during the book's proposal and early writing stages. She offered to review the entire first draft of the manuscript for wide-audience readability. Coincident to my sending her the manuscript's first draft, Melanie was diagnosed with advanced cancer of the pancreas. Undaunted, Melanie marked up a few chapters, and we discussed them on the phone. Ultimately, the cancer prevailed and Mel passed away a week before final manuscript submission.

I learned a great deal about writing to a diverse audience during the many writing projects that Melanie and I worked on at AT&T. She lives on throughout this book on every page.

Melanie was best known for kayaking in Puget Sound; I'll always be reminded of her when I see a kayak atop a car or in the Sound. Hence the kayak on the dedication page.

Feedback

Despite much research, experimentation, and QA, it is possible that there are mistakes in this book. Further, progress and technology march on: even before this book goes to press, Web sites referenced herein will rise and fall, security tools will fall into and out of favor, hackers will find brand-new avenues of exploitation, and Sun Microsystems will add and change features in Solaris. Please send me feedback about any mistakes or ideas for future editions:

> Prentice Hall PTR
> Att.: Gregory Doench
> One Lake Street
> Upper Saddle River, NJ 07458

Disclaimer

The opinions, examples, and dramatizations in this book are my own and do not reflect those of my employer, AT&T, or any prior employer or client.

Part One

Introduction

Part 1 illustrates just how large the computer security problem is today. Chapter 1 introduces a dramatized computer security incident and then explains how advances in technology have increased the complexity of system architectures and how new business paradigms have expanded the interconnectivity of computers and networks. These together have broadened and increased the risk of disruption of business operations due to administrator errors and acts of malice by both insiders as well as those outside the company.

- Chapter 1, "The Security Problem," shows the breadth of the security problem with an illustration and describes the factors responsible for increased risk.
- Chapter 2, "The Security Paradigm," introduces new thought processes that will help the Solaris system administrator "take the blinders off" and operate with security as a part of every procedure and decision.

1

THE SECURITY PROBLEM

Ted's pager started beeping at 6:30 A.M. on the first day of a four-day holiday weekend. Ted was staying in town this year, and was on call for the UNIX engineering team, but didn't expect any users to need help. He searched in the dark for the irritant and silenced it.

Ted started to doze, when his on-call automatic pilot kicked in. He sat up, turned on the light, and read the pager message typed in by the answering service that took after-hours UNIX support calls. The pager's display read

!!!CANNOT LOG IN!!!
DEMO IN 1 HR
PH 011-32-49-476934

Exclamation points always signified an emergency condition that needed immediate attention. Emergencies didn't happen often, but when they did, all other work stopped until the emergency was fixed.

The user was the vice president of engineering, Ted's boss, in Brussels, Belgium, doing an important product demo for a large customer. The company's future was riding on a sale that Ted's boss was trying to close that weekend.

Ted walked across the room to his UNIX workstation connected to the company local area network (LAN) via his frame relay remote access connection. He first was going to *telnet* to the main information server named "linus," a Sun E4000 that ran the company's DNS, NIS+, and remote access authentication services.

```
home # telnet linus
linus: Unknown host
#
```

So that's it, thought Ted, DNS is down. No sweat—I'll *telnet* to *linus's* IP address and restart *in.named*. Ted continued typing.

```
home # telnet 192.168.125.11
Trying 192.168.125.11...
telnet: Unable to connect to remote host: Connection timed out
home #
```

So I can't get in either, Ted whispered under his breath. Rats, I'll have to go into the office to get NIS+ restarted or whatever it is that's keeping us both out.

Ted, knowing what was on the line with the demo in Brussels, raced to work. During the 20-minute drive (thankfully it was a holiday!), Ted mentally reviewed what he would have to check to get to the bottom of this problem and get back to his long, lazy weekend.

A few minutes later, Ted was in the server room. He walked over to the *linus* system console and couldn't believe what he saw: the single line at the top of the screen

```
<#0> ok
```

Linus had been halted and was sitting at the OpenBoot prompt.

Why had *linus* halted and not automatically rebooted, Ted wondered to himself. Instinctively, Ted typed *probe-scsi* at the *ok* prompt. Yep, all of the SCSI devices: boot disk, CD-ROM drive, tape drive—all there.

Well, let's boot this beast and get outta here, Ted thought. He typed *boot* at the OpenBoot prompt, but instead of booting, an error occurred: OpenBoot said there was no operating system to boot from.

Disk crash? Filesystem corruption??

Ted had dealt with these kinds of problems before. It isn't pretty, but it's routinely solved: boot from CD-ROM, repair the root filesystem if possible. If not, reinstall Solaris, the backup program, and restore all of the local customizations from tape, and we're back on the air in two hours.

But Ted didn't have two hours—he now had less than half an hour before his boss's demo was scheduled to begin! He had to think quickly...

The jumpstart server was a DNS secondary and a NIS+ slave and could be given a new IP address in a couple of minutes. Brilliant thinking, Ted thought to himself as he walked across the room to *horace*, the jumpstart server.

The system *horace* was halted, too, just like *linus*.

The backup server *driftnet*, the database server *kermit*, and the home directory server *anytown* were all halted.

Ted needed to get help. Clarke, the genius behind the server/network architecture, was out of town with relatives. What was his cell phone number? Would he have it? Chris, another UNIX admin, was let go last month, so he would be no help. Gary had only been here three months, but was out of town somewhere, and Ted didn't have his pager number. Bill, the other veteran UNIX system administrator (SA), was pretty sharp and could help unravel this.

Bill was home with his family but could be there in 20 minutes. Maybe he knew what was going on.

Ted called his boss and told him that someone had stopped all the servers, and that the first one he had tried to reboot would not reboot.

While waiting for Bill to arrive, Ted made a pot of coffee. It would be a long day. He went back to *linus* and *horace* and tried to boot them again. No luck.

Bill arrived and they went back into the server room. "What's this mean, Bill?" Ted asked.

"There is no kernel image on the boot disk to boot from. Let's check the internal cabling and reseat all the memory SIMMS."

They powered down *linus*, opened it up, reseated its memory, and powered back up. Same error message.

"Let's boot from a Solaris Operating System CD," was Bill's next move. "We need to see what's on the root filesystem. There must be some sort of corruption, or perhaps an OS bug that has affected all of the servers." After all, they were all of the same architecture—UltraSPARC—and at the same OS and patch levels.

They went to the cabinet where all of the release media was stored. The CD drawers were empty. "They must be in someone's office." But wait, it wasn't just a few CDs that were missing—*all* the CDs were gone: the OS, Answer-Books, C compilers, backup software, and even the third-party database and software applications. Every CD was missing.

Ted's heart sank. "Some*one* did this to us," he said to Bill. But who?

The VP's Brussels demo didn't happen. Ted and Bill never could get the DNS, the remote access authentication server, or any other server for that matter, up and running that day. None were bootable, and there were no OS CDs to be found anywhere.

Let's take a look at what happened.

Chris, the UNIX SA who was let go, saw it coming. He wasn't happy—in fact, he was downright mad. A week before he was fired, he took all of the release CDs and threw them in a convenience store dumpster on the way home one night. The next week he was let go.

Then, discouraged from having no job prospects, he logged back in, using administrative passwords that were never changed, and did an *rm -rf /* on most of the production servers, thereby destroying all OSs and the data on them. That was just a few hours before the Brussels demo. Ted's boss was the next person to try to access the servers.

Several steps taken by the UNIX SA team could have prevented—or at least minimized—this situation.

- Copies of all OS CDs could have been stored off-site. This would have mitigated the loss of the CDs in the cabinet since there would have been one or more backup sets.

- All administrative passwords should have been changed immediately upon Chris's termination. Chris would not have been able to access the systems days after his termination.

- There was no procedure document specifying the order for starting the servers.

- There was no contact list of UNIX SAs' names and home, pager, and cell numbers.

Could this incident happen to your organization?

Causes of Security Weaknesses

Growth of Network Connectivity

The primary cause of scenarios such as the one described in the previous section is that UNIX systems (and NT systems, VAX systems, AS/400 systems, and all the rest) are being connected to small and large networks—including the Internet—without adequate consideration for security risks. Networks that were once restricted to closed buildings or campuses are being connected to each other (including the Internet) in order to facilitate must-have or nice-to-have business functions without regard to the risks of doing so. Security has traditionally been an afterthought (if considered at all) throughout the chain of command in information technology (IT) organizations, and those organizations have paid the price for their ignorance.

In the 1980s, companies built Ethernet and Token Ring LANs and connected all of their computers to them. These LANs were information islands that did not need much security beyond userid access controls.

Many organizations had guest accounts without passwords, as well as easily guessed administrative passwords, and they never removed or locked the accounts of departing employees (and why should they—the security guards at the front door would prevent former employees from reentering the building; this effectively prevented their accessing the network). The organization LANs facilitated *intra*business functions such as data transfers between desktop systems and mainframes, file and print services for desktop systems, and electronic mail.

By the 1990s, companies began to see the advantages of connecting their LANs to each other, to their business partners' LANs, and, finally, to the Internet itself. Intrabusiness functions expanded to include *inter*business functions.

The explosive popularity of the World Wide Web (WWW) in the mid-1990s resulted in a vast increase in the number of businesses connecting their LANs to the Internet.

In most cases, businesses were connecting their servers and workstations to LANs and their LANs to wide area networks (WANs), business partner networks, and the Internet without serious thought to the security of their systems. Those unprotected guest accounts were still there. The old accounts belonging to long-departed employees were still there and forgotten.

The Internet Worm Incident in 1988 was proof positive that security at the system level was grossly inadequate. While the Worm gave rise to the Carnegie Mellon Computer Emergency Response Team (CERT) and increased security awareness among system vendors and systems administrators, the state of security awareness and preparedness is still way behind the talent and determination of today's amateur and professional hackers, some of whom may be on your payroll.

Security was not a prime concern in the era when UNIX was developed; its security model was designed for small- and medium-sized workgroups in an *intra*network environment. Fortunately, there exist many OEM add-on security features and third-party products to provide adequate protection to UNIX systems that are exposed to additional risks.

Software Vulnerabilities

System and application software not originally intended to withstand Internet hacker attack are now exposed to the Internet. Client/server applications designed for *intra*net-level security have been connected to the Internet and are now exposed to attack. This is true even in situations where such servers are protected by firewalls and other measures. No matter how secure an application may be, that application, the tools used to develop and run it, or the components protecting it have weaknesses.

Another way to look at software vulnerability is to consider the size and complexity of the programs that are accessible from the Internet. Complex tasks require complex software programs. While it may be difficult enough to prove that a *simple* program is secure, it may be impossible to prove that a complex program is secure. Two popular examples of this software complexity are *sendmail* and Web servers.

- *Sendmail* is a large, complex program used to deliver electronic mail, or e-mail, within corporations and between them on the Internet. Over the years, many design flaws in *sendmail* have been exploited by hackers. As a result, it has been revised and patched numerous times to answer the attacks by the increasingly sophisticated hacker community. The developers and maintainers of *sendmail* have done (and are doing) a gallant job of plugging security holes, but the hackers seem to be right behind them, discovering new weaknesses that heretofore were undiscovered.

- World Wide Web servers—relatively new on the scene—are similarly large and complex. Add to this the fact that Web servers call other programs, such as common gateway interface (CGI) scripts, which execute on Web servers themselves, as well as Java and ActiveX programs which are transmitted to and execute on Web clients. Finally, consider that the information being passed between Web servers and Web clients is going beyond product marketing and pricing, for instance, and is increasingly financial, sensitive, or personal in nature. Financial transactions taking place over the Internet are making the systems controlling and recording them increasingly attractive targets of hackers. Not all of the systems involved are as secure as they could and should be.

Employees and Contractors

According to a Data Processing Management Association (DPMA) study published in 1992, over 80 percent of the perpetrators of computer crime work for the company from which data was stolen or damaged. While hacking incidents are sensational and grab the headlines, these inside jobs (most of which are not publicized) are actually doing the most harm. The dramatic example at the beginning of this chapter points this out.

I should note that the DPMA statistic cited above predates the Web and most companies' Internet connections. Internet connectivity provides a tempting, and too often easy, avenue for attack. Further, Internet connectivity and Web applications are still emerging technologies fraught with security weaknesses. Many of the developers and administrators are unaware of the specific weaknesses that can lead to exploitation.

Far too many information systems (IS) and IT shops look only to technology for answers to their security questions. Technology can only close the security gap so far; the rest is up to policies, procedures, and trust.

Motivated and Resourceful Hackers

Companies are building systems that are more attractive than ever before. Hackers try to break into these systems for thrills, publicity, or financial reward. Often they succeed. The systems belong to banks, insurance companies, telephone companies, public utilities, and high-tech companies. Hackers break in to alter financial transactions for direct or indirect personal gain or to steal information that they later sell to competitors or reveal to the public. More companies are making their computers accessible via remote access for employees and are connecting more computers to the Internet. We're creating ever more opportunities for hackers to exploit.

Hackers have more sophisticated tools at their disposal than ever before. Their most popular tool is the personal computer. Hackers may have as many as a dozen or more computers in their homes, all designed to discover and exploit increasingly complex vulnerabilities.

Hackers give their tools away on their Web sites and share their information at conferences. They're organized and motivated, and there are large rewards (prestige in the hacker community, for one) to be won by those patient enough to discover a weakness.

Whereas many companies remain ignorant and uninformed when it comes to security practices and technologies until it is too late, UNIX systems administrators, network administrators, and security professionals are beginning to organize to share security information. Some of these organizations include the System Administrators Guild (SAGE) and National Computing Security Association (NCSA).

Site Policies

Policies define limits of behavior in an organization. The IS shop in this chapter's example had no policy for storing OS and software media off-site; this proved to be a critical flaw as it most likely added *days* to the recovery time.

2

THE SECURITY
PARADIGM

Most UNIX systems administrators do not know where to begin when it comes to securing their systems. Some begin by installing one or more public-domain security tools on their systems; others modify their systems to make them less vulnerable; and still others have relatively open systems inside a very secure firewall. None of these methods will offer adequate protection by themselves. They are piecemeal; they don't fit into a *strategy*, and they don't reflect an overall *approach* or *design*. Moreover, they don't reflect the attitude required for long-term success.

Before any systems, firewalls, or architectures can be changed, security *principles* must be developed, understood, and embraced by the administrators and managers who are responsible for them. This chapter is devoted to the introduction to and justification for these principles.

Principle 1: The Hacker Who Breaks into Your System Will Probably Be Someone You Know

While many hackers are nameless, faceless individuals in another time zone or on another continent, statistics reveal that most system security incidents are inside jobs.

What is an inside job? It boils down to sabotage in one form or another. Examples include

- Sabotaging backup processes to give the appearance of normal backups (but where future recovery will be impossible)
- Planting *time bombs*—deliberate errors in programs or processes that will cause malfunctions long after the employee leaves the company
- Changing root passwords on critical systems and not telling anyone before leaving the company (another form of a time bomb)
- Deliberately erasing backup media
- Removing OS or product media to make recoveries or future installations more difficult

Never give out root passwords to users.[1] Either use tools to get them what they need or deny them the access or function they are requesting. As a last resort, give users root-level privileges only for those functions they absolutely *must* have in order to do their jobs.

Users with root privileges are potential problems. Users with root privileges may become intoxicated with their newfound power and begin to tinker with things they're unfamiliar with. Or users with root access may accidentally remove or change something that will hinder their ability to carry out their *real* jobs (not systems administration!). Finally, a *diabolical* user will use his power to further his dark aspirations and inflict damage beyond his own system. This all leads to the second principle.

Principle 2: Trust No One, *or* Be Careful About Whom You Are Required to Trust

Breach of trust is the biggest threat to computers and the information stored on them. UNIX systems administrators introduce far too many trust relationships between the machines they're responsible for in order to make their

---

1. I once heard an amusing story about a UNIX systems administrator who had a fairly ignorant user who insisted he needed the root password on his computer. The systems administrator resisted until the user got management involved and made trouble. The sysadmin was forced to give the root password to this user, but he did so in a creative way: he changed the name "root" in /etc/passwd to another name, and then he added a nonprivileged userid called "root" and gave its password to the troublesome user. The user never suspected that he didn't have true root privileges and, wanting to save face, never once called the systems administrator when he ran into filesystem permissions problems.

tasks easier to carry out. Frequently, systems administrators create large, simple webs of trust among their systems using the *root* userid. For instance, the *root* userid (which has complete control over *all* aspects of a system) on all systems on the network will trust the *root* userid on many, if not all, other systems on the network.

Why is this a bad idea? It is these same trust relationships that hackers will discover and exploit. A hacker who breaks into root on a machine will first examine the */.rhosts* and */etc/hosts.equiv* files on that machine to see whom it trusts. If machine *larch* trusts machine *tamarack*, then our hacker will suspect that all machines on the network may trust *tamarack*. Machine *larch* has betrayed one of the weaknesses in the network; once the hacker breaks into machine *tamarack*, all machines on the network are easy prey if they all trust *tamarack*.

Principle 2a: Don't Trust Yourself, *or* Verify Everything You Do

A systems administrator is his or her own worst enemy. Working multiple priorities, deadlines, and long hours all contribute to mistakes. Some of these mistakes will result in simple failures in functionality; others will fill up disks, buffers, queues, or process tables; but the worst will silently open up gaping security holes or damage systems in subtle, hard-to-detect ways. More than 50 percent of data damage or loss incidents is due to human error.[2]

Verify everything you do. It is not sufficient to kill a process, remove or *chmod* a file or directory, or lock an account and move on. Stop, think, and verify. Kill the process and look for it. Remove the file or directory and look for it. *Chmod* the file and *ls* it again. Copy the directory to tape and read it back. Protect the directory and try to remove or change it.

Develop a healthy distrust for everything you tell the computer to do. Be a skeptic. Challenge the computer (or yourself) to prove that it did what you told it to.

Veteran airplane pilots still go through their preflight checklists and read the items out loud. Experienced carpenters measure twice and saw once. UNIX systems administrators likewise ought to verify everything, great and small.

---

2. Source: Data Processing Management Association, 1992.

Principle 3: Make Would-Be Intruders Believe They Will Be Caught

Retail stores vulnerable to shoplifting put up signs that read, "If we catch you, we prosecute you." They erect visible detectors, cameras, and monitors. The message is clear: they are watching for thieves and can catch them.

Information is the merchandise of the computer age and, using means similar to retail stores, our information systems must contain visible warnings, barriers, and detectors that will help to deter, detect, and catch would-be criminals. And since those perpetrators of information thievery are most likely employees or associates of the organization owning the systems, those means must be visible to legitimate system users via good password security and messages that say, "We are watching you."

Principle 4: Protect in Layers

The often-fatal mistake systems administrators, network administrators, or technology architects make is that they rely on a single layer or method of security to protect a system or service. An exploitation of the one mechanism protecting the system or service will expose that system or service.

For example, a corporation allows certain individuals to *telnet* through the Internet to one of its servers inside the corporate network. An access list on the corporation's Internet firewall filters *telnet* sessions so that they can originate only from those known, approved IP addresses. A similar, redundant access control mechanism limiting inbound access is on the server. The server is inside a locked room. All accounts require passwords.

Suppose that a bug in the firewall's access list algorithm is discovered that will allow certain other types of access to those servers. A hacker could take advantage of this bug and gain access to the inside of the corporation's network. Figure 2.1 illustrates the concept.

What this corporation should have done was protect in every layer possible. In addition to the filtering firewall, the Internet router could have been set up to filter out unwanted traffic. Further, a mechanism to control access to every computer could have been implemented. Finally, a method other than plain old *telnet* could have been employed to eliminate the risk of a hacker's eavesdropping and gaining passwords (although this was not part of the exploitation in this example).

This example leads us to the next principle.

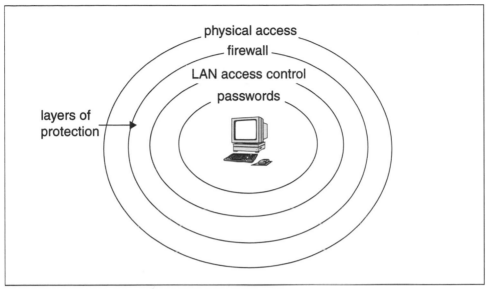

Figure 2.1 *Protecting in Layers*

Principle 5: While Planning Your Security Strategy, Presume the Complete Failure of Any Single Security Layer

A properly designed layer-protected system, application, or service should presume a complete, temporary failure of one layer of security.

Back to our preceding example. This time the same corporation allows inbound *telnet* access and filters access at the network level on both its Internet router and Internet firewall and also implements access lists on its UNIX servers. If any one of these security mechanisms fails, the other two will continue to protect the UNIX servers from unauthorized access. Figure 2.2 illustrates this point.

Hackers are not the only reason to protect in layers. The security mechanisms protecting systems are complex and administered by people. These people, either because they do not understand the site architecture, or because they are not adequately trained on network principles or security tools, can make mistakes resulting in more access than should be allowed (if you have a network engineer who doesn't understand your network or basic network con-

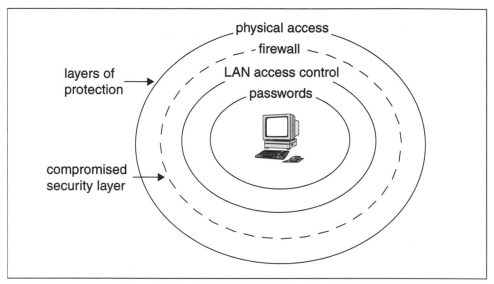

Figure 2.2   *Compromised Security Layer*

cepts administering all of the mechanisms protecting your network, you've got another problem altogether).

Consider the security of your corporate computing assets: the main routers and servers in the data center. While the data center itself is locked and may be entered only by using a magnetic card entry system, many companies' servers in the data center are logged in to highest-privilege accounts, even when unattended. In addition to physical security, consider using automatic/manual locking screen savers and keycard access to privileged accounts. If you're not yet convinced this is necessary, just think back to the last time you saw the data center door propped open by an unescorted tradesman so that he could leave and reenter the data center without having to find a busy systems administrator. Protect in layers.

Principle 6: Make Security a Part of the Initial Design

Most corporate networks were built many years ago before the concept of network security became a topic that anyone talked about. These corporate networks were wholly contained within buildings or groups of buildings when the older physical security paradigm adequately protected them. When this was true, physical access and a userid/password was all it took to acceptably secure an application. Since that time, these relatively unsecure networks have been connected to other similarly unsecure networks, without additions to security at any level.

It is always more difficult to retrofit a feature into any product or system, and this goes for security particularly: adding security features to a system, application, or network after it is built is costly and troublesome. Here are a few reasons why this is so.

- Retrofitted security features often make an application or system more difficult, complicated, or time consuming to access. Users who were able to access an application without having to enter a password will complain now that they must enter a userid and password. They will claim counterproductivity and other half-truths designed to get senior management to think that security only gets in the way.

- It may be necessary to change a system's basic configuration or architecture in order to get the security feature to work. Disks may need to be repartitioned to make room for security software; operating system and/or firmware versions may need to be updated to support security features.

- It may be difficult or impossible to retrofit some devices, systems, or applications with adequate security features, either because they cannot support security extensions or because these extensions may be prohibitively expensive.

How do you get security to be part of a system's plan? By specifying security requirements, policies, and procedures *before* the system is designed or installed. If you allow security features to go in later, you may find that they either never get implemented or the retrofit is poor.

Principle 7: Disable Unneeded Services, Packages, and Features

UNIX systems are shipped with all network services (e.g., *ftp*, *telnet*, *rlogin*, *rsh*, *rexec*, *timed*) activated and ready to go. Each network service is a potential security hole, a possible entry point for a hacker.

This is very simple: if inbound *ftp* isn't needed on a system, turn it off. If inbound *telnet* isn't needed, turn it off. If *rlogin*, *rsh*, and *rexec* aren't needed, turn them off. The remaining services on a system should be *only* those *required* for its function. Note that *required* means *must-have* services, not nice-to-have services.

Chapter 9, "Network Interfaces and Services," describes this topic more fully.

The same principle of removing/disabling unneeded services applies to software packages on a system. If UNIX-to-UNIX copy (UUCP), for instance, is installed on a system, get rid of it. It's consuming space and contains current or future potential security threats.

Another way to consider the reason for removing unneeded services and packages from a system is to examine the risks and benefits for such services. Take, for example, an Internet Web server using trivial file transfer protocol (*tftp*) and *telnet*.

tftp is a dangerous service because it allows any user on another system to transfer files into and out of the system running the *tftp* service. A skilled user may be able to access or replace files he or she has no business manipulating. On our example Web server, *tftp* will not be needed, so there is no benefit from *tftp*. Since *tftp* is dangerous, the risk is high. A package with high risk and zero benefit has no business being available on this particular Web server, so it ought to be disabled.

The *telnet* service would make administration of the Web server easier since the administrator could control the system from the workplace or from home. While *telnet* is not the security risk of *tftp*, it is far from being risk free. In this instance, the benefit is low (measured in convenience only—it is not *required* by the Web server) and the risk is moderately high. *Telnet* is therefore a candidate for removal.

Principle 8: Before Connecting, Understand and Secure

Your customers understandably want the latest and greatest. One of them may be asking you to allow Java, ActiveX, RealAudio, or any of dozens of other Web add-ons. Or possibly they may want you to download and install a new UNIX-based tool or application.

No matter how urgent, the time to make a security assessment is *before* the tool or feature is released to your users. A user who doesn't get to have a requested package because it's a security risk isn't going to be half as upset as the user who had a newly acquired tool taken away. Also, if a tool or feature *is* a security risk, it's better that you find out before the user does (if, indeed, they ever do).

There are all types of UNIX system administrators. Some have a systems programming or software engineering background, but others do not. A UNIX administrator without a programming or software engineering background needs to get some help when assessing public-domain tools being requested by users.

The time to develop a policy that says *someone will make a security assessment of all requested tools, applications, and features before releasing to users* is *now*. Don't wait until the horse is out of the barn.

Principle 9: Prepare for the Worst

While this may sound like a pessimistic approach, it will result in an environment that faces a diminished security risk. Preparing for disaster means preparedness for the day and hour that we all hope will never come.

Assume that hackers are already scheming to break into your site. They may already know a lot about your site's architecture—they may be colleagues who need to settle a score with an insensitive boss or have found a way to pick up some extra spending money by selling information to an unscrupulous competitor.

The Nine Principles: A Way of Life

The nine security principles discussed in this chapter represent a new way of thinking about systems administration and security. A UNIX systems administrator should have a healthy dose of distrust about software, tools, and applications; about some of his customers and about him or herself; and especially about determined, unscrupulous people on the outside who want to get in and play.

Part Two

The Standalone System

Systems must first be physically and logically secure. This applies whether a Sun system is networked or not. Regardless of network connectivity, certain features and characteristics increase the risk of loss or exposure to the person(s) or company using it. Topics covered in this next section include:

- Chapter 3: "The PROM, OpenBoot, and Physical Security"
- Chapter 4: "The Filesystem"
- Chapter 5: "User Accounts Environments"
- Chapter 6: "System Startup and Shutdown"
- Chapter 7: "*cron* and *at*"
- Chapter 8: "System Logs"

THE PROM, OPENBOOT, AND PHYSICAL SECURITY

The SPARC and UltraSPARC PROM and its software, called OpenBoot, are discussed in this chapter, as are issues related to a system's physical security.

What's in this chapter

- What the PROM is
- What OpenBoot is
- How to access OpenBoot
- Why there are security implications to settings in OpenBoot
- Things you need to know about physical security

Why this is important

Someone who can access OpenBoot or its settings can gain complete control of a computer system. There are steps you can take to protect a system from a physical access perspective.

What Is the PROM?

The Sun system PROM (PROM stands for *programmable read-only memory*) is a computer chip containing information and firmware. The information on the PROM includes the system's hostid and several configuration settings such as the boot device and other system boot parameters. The firmware on the PROM is called OpenBoot.

What Is OpenBoot?

OpenBoot is firmware that is part of all Sun SPARC boot PROMs. It contains information about how a SPARC system is booted, plus built-in commands for testing the hardware on a SPARC system.

> **Note: References to OpenBoot commands and features apply to Open-Boot versions 2.0 and later. This book describes OpenBoot version 2.0 (which first appeared on the SPARCStation 2 system) and version 3.0.**

OpenBoot is activated as soon as a SPARC system is turned on. Depending on the configuration settings, the system will either be booted from a local disk (hard disk or CD-ROM) or over the network, or the system will display an OpenBoot prompt and await further instructions. Most systems (and every system's factory-installed default) will automatically boot from an internal hard disk and not stop at or display the OpenBoot prompt at all.

In addition to boot time, OpenBoot can also be accessed while the system is running by pressing Stop-A on the system keyboard (on a system where a Sun keyboard is attached to the keyboard port); by sending a *break* code or power cycling the console terminal (on a system where a terminal is attached to the console serial port); by halting the system; or by running the *eeprom* program.

> **Warning: Administrators must be careful whenever doing a Stop-A on a running system. Pressing Stop-A *stops the system*. Integrity of the system's data is at risk, not to mention availability of its services.**

Why Users Must Be Kept Out of OpenBoot

There are two reasons why no end user should ever have access to OpenBoot:

1. A clever user with access to OpenBoot can boot the system from almost any SCSI device (external hard disk or CD-ROM). A user who can boot a system from his own media can take *complete control* over that system; you might as well give the user the root password.
2. A user who can Stop-A a system can change any of dozens of OpenBoot environment variables, giving the most skilled UNIX administrator a long-term headache.

Protecting OpenBoot by Setting Security Parameters

This section describes the procedure used to password protect a system's OpenBoot. I recommend that all data center systems and end-user systems be protected.

There are three levels of security in OpenBoot: *none, command,* and *full.* Sun systems are shipped with the OpenBoot security level set to *none.* The three levels are explained in Table 3-1.

Table 3-1   *OpenBoot Security Levels*

Mode	Available Commands
none	No password required. All OpenBoot settings can be changed (including the disk partition from which the system is booted) and any OpenBoot command executed. Anyone with physical access to the system has full control over it.
command	All commands except for *boot* and *go* require the password. The system may be booted from the default boot device. The *go* command (continuing system operation after pressing Stop-A or sending the break sequence) is also allowed. The user must enter the OpenBoot password for all other commands.
full	All OpenBoot commands except *go* (continuing system operation after pressing Stop-A or sending the break sequence) require the OpenBoot password.

Recommended Security Level for OpenBoot

Every Sun OpenBoot should be set to *command* or *full,* even if the system is located in a secure data center.

Procedures for Changing OpenBoot Security Levels

The following sections describe the procedure for changing OpenBoot security levels.

How to Set the OpenBoot Password from Solaris

This example sets the OpenBoot password from Solaris (as root).

```
# eeprom security-password
Changing PROM password:
New password:********
Retype new password:********
#
```

How to Set the OpenBoot Password from the OpenBoot Prompt

This example sets the OpenBoot password from the OpenBoot prompt.

```
ok password
ok New password (only first 8 chars are used):********
ok Retype new password:********
ok
```

How to Set OpenBoot Security Levels from Solaris

This example sets the security level to *command* from Solaris (as root).

```
# eeprom security-mode=command
#
```

If the OpenBoot password has never been set, *eeprom* will prompt for it, as in the first example above.

How to Set OpenBoot Security Levels from the OpenBoot Prompt

This example sets the security level to *command*.

```
ok setenv security-mode command
ok
```

This example sets security level to *full*.

```
ok setenv security-mode full
ok
```

Warning: If the OpenBoot password is forgotten when *security mode* is set to *full*, it can be changed only with the *eeprom* command run from user root.

If the PROM and *root* passwords are forgotten (with *security mode* set to *full*), the system's PROM will have to be replaced. This is because it will be impossible to boot the system from CD-ROM (with Solaris OS media in the drive) in an attempt to recover the root password.

Be very careful with *security mode* set to *full*.

All Passwords Lost—Partial Recovery Procedure

This procedure describes the steps used to recover a system where the Open-Boot and root passwords are lost and where the OpenBoot security level is set to full.

Prerequisites: A replacement PROM to be used temporarily; a Solaris-release CD-ROM.

Caveat: This will allow the recovery of the root password, but *not* the PROM password. If the PROM password is forgotten, it cannot be reset or recovered—ever. In this event, replace the PROM as soon as possible.

1. Carefully remove the old PROM from the system. It will be needed later.
2. Insert a new PROM, one with the security mode set to *none*.
3. Follow the instructions in the section on recovering a lost root password (later in this chapter).
4. Shut the system down. Power it off.
5. Switch back to the original PROM removed in step 1.
6. Boot the system.
7. Log in as root using the password set in step 3.

Boot Device Recommendations

A system, even one in a secure data center, should be configured to boot from an *internal* disk rather than an *external* device on a SCSI bus.

In a situation where someone has gained physical access to a data center (but not to the *inside* of a server, for whatever reason), a system configured to boot from an external device could have that external device replaced with another by a simple cable change. Someone can simply attach a different hard disk to the SCSI bus by unplugging the correct device and attaching another one with the same SCSI address. The only clue (which could later be erased) would be a few SCSI device time-out messages. A system booted from this new external device can have a completely altered identity (different node name, network address, password file, access permissions over the network, etc.), thereby compromising any information on the system and possibly on other systems as well.

A system configured to boot from an internal disk must be physically opened in order to change the boot device. This makes it somewhat more difficult for an intruder to take over a system, even one they have physical access to.

Change the OpenBoot Banner

The OpenBoot banner should be changed from the default to some company-specific text. Such text could identify the system as being the property of the company. The following example illustrates a change to the OpenBoot banner.

```
ok setenv oem-banner? true
ok setenv oem-banner "This system property of ABCD Corp"
ok
```

Recover a Lost Root Password

This section describes the procedure used to recover a lost root password.[1] Prerequisites include

- The system must have a CD-ROM drive already installed and configured.
- You must have a Solaris 2.x or Solaris 7 media CD.
- The OpenBoot security level must not be set to *full* (which would prevent the use of the *boot cdrom* command below).

Warning: This is not a risk-free procedure. The system is being *forcibly* halted, resulting in the possible loss of data or filesystem corruption.

Note: This procedure also assumes that the boot disk device (example: /dev/dsk/c0t3d0s0) is known. It is difficult to determine this if the system is halted and cannot be started. Each server's boot device name should be recorded in the event that this type of recovery is required.

The root password recovery procedure outlined in steps 1 through 18 below assumes the system is running *and* that you are logged on (or *can* log in). If the system is halted, skip to step 4.

1. Determine the device name for the partition containing the */etc* directory. Follow this example.

   ```
   # df /etc
   /       (/dev/dsk/c0t3d0s0): 253062 blocks    81357 files
   #
   ```

   In this example, the root partition device is */dev/dsk/c0t3d0s0*; this device is also used in the examples that follow. Substitute the correct root partition device if it is different from the example here.

2. Insert the Solaris 2 or Solaris 7 CD media into the CD-ROM drive.[2]

3. If a prompt is available, flush the filesystem cache by typing *sync*.

4. If the system is running, type *Stop-A*.

5. Type *boot cdrom -s* at the "ok" prompt.

6. At the "#" prompt, type *mkdir /tmp/mnt*, then
   mount /dev/dsk/ c0t3d0s0 /tmp/mnt .
   Note that the following error message may appear:

   ```
   mount: the state of /dev/dsk/c0t3d0s0 is not okay
           and it was attempted to be mounted read/write
   mount: please run fsck and try again
   ```

---

1. Hackers already know how to do this.

2. The OS version of the CD-ROM need not necessarily be the same as the OS version on the system, as long as the CD-ROM being used supports the system's hardware and devices.

If this occurs, it will be necessary to run *fsck* to repair the filesystem. Use the following command: *fsck /dev/rdsk/c0t3d0s0* (note that the device name used with the *mount* command (/dev/dsk/...) is different from the device name used with the *fsck* command (/dev/rdsk/...).

7. Change to the directory containing the root password by typing *cd /tmp/mnt/etc* .

8. Make a backup copy of the */etc/shadow* file, by typing *cp shadow shadowRECOVER* .

9. Get the root password string from the */etc/shadow* file with the *cat* command. For example

```
# cat shadow
root:xd0exJE8X8v2M:6445::::::
daemon:NP:6445::::::
bin:NP:6445::::::
sys:NP:6445:::::
adm:xd0exJE8X8v2M:10473::::::
lp:Rt7ekqsuSIHr2:10473::::::
smtp:NP:6445::::::
uucp:NP:6445::::::
nuucp:NP:6445::::::
listen:*LK*::::::
nobody:NP:6445::::::
noaccess:NP:6445::::::
nobody4:NP:6445::::::
pete:tspx1CqH8igWA:10507::::::
admin:tspx1CqH8igWA:10261::::::
#
```

10. Remove the root password entry from the */etc/shadow* file with the *sed* command. Using the example *shadow* file above, type in the following command:

```
# sed s/xd0exJE8X8v2M// shadow > shadowNEW
#
```

Note: UNIX administrators familiar with operating a system under these conditions can use *vi* instead of *sed* to remove root's password string from */etc/shadow*. There are so many possible scenarios to cover, however (different terminal and console types, for instance), that it is simpler to describe this procedure using *sed*.

11. Check that the *shadowNEW* file created above was properly edited by displaying it again with the *cat* command. Using the example shadow file above, the *shadowNEW* file should appear as follows:

```
# cat shadowNEW
root::6445::::::
daemon:NP:6445::::::
bin:NP:6445::::::
sys:NP:6445::::::
adm:xd0exJE8X8v2M:10473::::::
```

```
lp:Rt7ekqsuSIHr2:10473::::::
smtp:NP:6445::::::
uucp:NP:6445::::::
nuucp:NP:6445::::::
listen:*LK*:::::::
nobody:NP:6445::::::
noaccess:NP:6445::::::
nobody4:NP:6445::::::
pete:tspx1CqH8igWA:10507::::::
admin:tspx1CqH8igWA:10261::::::
#
```

12. If the *shadowNEW* file looks okay, copy it back over the *shadow* file by typing *cp shadowNEW shadow* .

13. Change directory to root by typing *cd /* .

14. Unmount the system's root filesystem by typing *umount /tmp/mnt* .

15. Flush the filesystem cache by typing *sync* .

16. Halt the system by typing *init 0* .

17. Remove the boot CD from the CD-ROM drive.

18. Type *boot* at the "ok" prompt to reboot the system. You should now be able to log on as root without being challenged for a password.

Note: Do not wait for an emergency to test this procedure. Try it on each server (and your own desktop system) and record—in a secure place—system-specific information such as the full device name of the root partition (e.g., */dev/dsk/c0t3d0s0*).

Physical Security Considerations

In keeping with the concept of protecting in layers discussed in chapter 2, I have several recommendations regarding physical security of data center systems. None of these precautions will prevent a determined intruder from accessing or destroying computer equipment, but they will slow them down. The following sections discuss several physical security issues.

Theft and Access Prevention

Physically fasten all systems and peripherals to equipment racks utilizing the locking tabs.

Utilize a physical access mechanism that records who enters the data center at what time. This raises the degree of accountability regarding physical access to data centers by making everyone aware that their entrances to the data centers are controlled and recorded.

Consider the use of surveillance cameras in or near data centers.

Audit PROMs

Periodically audit every system's PROM to ensure that it has not been replaced. This could easily be done by recording all system hostids and then comparing them later to what was recorded earlier.

Do note that this is not a watertight check. An intruder could—given motive, means, and opportunity—physically break into a system, swap a system's PROM for another with different security and boot settings but with the same hostid. So, in and of itself, auditing hostids does not conclusively prove that no tampering has occurred.

OpenBoot Passwords

Password protect OpenBoot on all data center (plus desktop and lab) systems, whether they are in a locked room or not. Assign a different password to each system's OpenBoot, using a nonpredictable password scheme.

Configure automatic, password-protected screen locks. Lock all screens when leaving the room. Chapter 5 will cover procedures for setting up auto screen locks.

The password used to unlock the screen is the login password. To lock the screen, click on the padlock icon on the front panel.

Note: Auto screen locking in the common desktop environment (CDE) works only in Solaris version 2.6 and newer (CDE version 1.2).

CD-ROM Drives

Remove internal CD-ROM drives on systems once the systems are built. An intruder can boot a system from a CD-ROM and make any imaginable alteration to the operating system, including erasing any trace of these alterations. Instead, when you need to boot a system from a CD-ROM, boot it from an external CD-ROM drive.

Keep all peripherals (external CD-ROM drives, external disks, all cables) locked and out of sight. A clever intruder can make good use of them.

Backup Media

Keep all backup and release media locked up and out of sight.

Utilize an off-site media storage vendor. Develop a formal plan to get recently written backup media off-site as soon as possible.

OS Release Media

Keep all Solaris release media locked and out of sight. Together with a CD-ROM drive, an intruder can take complete control of a system in just a few minutes with only these two items.

Send a set of Solaris release media to the off-site storage vendor mentioned in the previous section.

Where to Go for Additional Information

AnswerBook

- AnswerBook 2—OpenBoot Command Reference

Man Pages

- eeprom(1M)
- fsck(1M)
- mount(1M)
- umount(1M)

Publications

- *What to Do If Root Password Is Lost*, SunSolve Infodoc 16786
- Butler, Janet, and Badura, Poul. *Contingency Planning and Disaster Recovery: Protecting Your Organization's Resources.* Computer Technology Research Corp., 1997.

Web Sites

- *Open Firmware Home Page*—http://playground.sun.com/1275/

4

THE FILESYSTEM

In this chapter I describe the basic workings of the UNIX filesystem as it pertains to security.

What's in this chapter

- What the UNIX filesystem is
- How access permissions in the UNIX filesystem work
- How to verify access permissions
- What device permissions are
- How to audit a filesystem

Why this is important

Virtually all information stored on a UNIX computer system is stored in a filesystem. Information can be altered or stolen from a computer system whose filesystem access permissions are improperly set.

What Is the Filesystem?

The filesystem is the part of the computer system used to store and manage the computer's files; it consists of the operating system, system and application programs, and data. Part of managing a system's files includes setting access permissions to control which users of a computer can access what files and by what methods: read-only, read and write, and execute (applies only to system and application program files).

Many UNIX security problems are a direct result of improper understanding and, thus, manipulation of the filesystem. Through misunderstanding or just plain haste, many administrators open potential security holes by modifying ownership or permission settings on files and directories. Changes in permissions are often made to temporarily solve a short-term file or directory access problem. Many times the result is that they leave the door open permanently.

Some Applications Require Open Permissions

Unfortunately, many UNIX-based third-party applications still require that file and/or directory permissions for data stored and managed by the application be kept *wide open* (full read/write access by all system users) in order to function correctly. A UNIX-based e-mail application I used to work with required that all user mailbox directories have global read/write privileges (imagine how easy it would be for one user to access and manipulate another user's mailbox). In another case, an engineering application I supported required that the */tmp* directory have global read/write access *without* the "sticky bit" being set (the use of the sticky bit is discussed later in this chapter). These are just a few examples of how numerous applications still require what should be considered sloppy security settings in order to function correctly.

While troubleshooting an application, UNIX administrators are tempted to set access permissions wide open and leave them that way when an application is being intolerant of standard file or directory access. But all too often, even though a problem may have been isolated to permissions or ownership on a single file or directory (or not a permissions issue at all), a UNIX administrator wants to leave things as they are, call the problem "solved," and move on to another support issue, when, in fact, an even larger problem has been created in its place. This is comparable to propping the office front door open days, nights, and weekends because it's too hard to figure out who has keys and who doesn't.

Some applications mitigate their wide-open permission architecture at the UNIX filesystem level by adding a level of security within the application itself. Application-based security architecture will be specific to each application and is beyond the scope of this book. An example of security within an application is a mechanism where certain users can view or modify certain records or fields in a database. Referring back to the concept of protecting in layers, an application designer should utilize security features wherever possible, including protecting data files at the UNIX filesystem level.

Understanding File and Directory Permissions

Solaris 2.x and Solaris 7 conform to the UNIX System V Release 4 standards for the implementation of the UNIX filesystem permissions structure. This structure controls who can access which information on a UNIX system.

It is necessary to know only two things about file permissions: the **identity of the user** (or defined group of users) attempting to access a file, and the **type of access** required by that user (read, write, search, or execute). Practically everything that may seem complicated (and all too often it *is* complicated) about UNIX file/directory access is derived from these two pieces of information: **who** and **permission** level.

Who: User, Group, and Other

In UNIX, there are three categories of users: an individual *user* (also known as *owner*), a defined *group* of users, and everyone else (also known as *other* or *world*).

Individual users on a system, called *userids*, are defined in the system's */etc/passwd* file or in the NIS *passwd* or NIS+ *passwd.org_dir* databases. People logging onto a UNIX system identify themselves with a *userid* and its corresponding *password*.

Each user is also defined as being a member of a *group*; this primary group is defined in the */etc/passwd* or the NIS *passwd* or NIS+ *passwd.org_dir* databases.

In addition to a user's primary group, a user can belong to secondary groups. These groups of users are defined in the */etc/group* file or in NIS or NIS+ *group* databases. The */etc/passwd* and */etc/group* files (and their NIS and NIS+ counterparts) are described in chapter 5.

Permission Summary: Read, Write, Execute, SetUID, SetGID, Sticky Bit

The basic permissions allowed for a file or directory in UNIX are *read, write,* or *execute* (the term *search* is used in place of *execute* for a directory—more on this later). There are additional special permission parameters known as *Set-UID, SetGID,* and *Sticky Bit*. This section describes in detail the definitions of each type of permission for files and directories.

The terms *read bit, write bit,* and so on refer to the way that UNIX stores information about file permissions. Each item, such as *read file* for a user, is stored as one computer bit. Since a *bit* of computer information can only be 0 or 1, you can think of a bit in this context as a *flag*; either the flag is **on** (bit is set to 1)—permitting access—or the flag is **off** (bit is set to 0)—denying access.

The term *process* refers to any program that can be run on a UNIX system. Programs, or processes, typically read or write files on a UNIX system. The terms *program* and *process* can be used interchangeably here. In the context of filesystem permissions, you can also think of a *process* in terms of a user. A user must run some type of program in order to access a file, even if the program chosen is *cat* (which outputs the contents of a file to the screen) or *vi* (a text editing program used to view or alter the contents of a file).

Permission Details: Read—File   A process will be able to read the contents of a file.

Permission Details: Read—Directory   A *directory* is a special file in a special format, consisting of *filenames* and *inodes*. A process able to list the contents of a directory will be able to see which files reside there. For example, the *ls* program will be able to list the files in a directory with the read bit set.

Permission Details: Write—File   A process will be able to alter or replace the contents of a file. This includes removing the contents of the file by copying */dev/null* to the file. The file cannot be removed—that depends upon the permissions of the *directory* containing the file.

Permission Details: Write—Directory   A process will be able to create or remove files or empty directories or devices residing in the directory. Files in the directory cannot be overwritten (unless *their* permissions allow it), but they *can* be removed and re-created.

More clarification: A process with write access to a directory can remove files from that directory, regardless of whether that process has permission to write (or even read) the files there. Removal of a file is an action taken on the directory containing the file, not on the file itself.

Permission Details: Execute—File   The file can be executed if it is a runnable program. If the file is not a program file, this has no meaning.[1]

Permission Details: Execute—Directory   The read bit is required in order to be able to obtain a list of the files contained in a directory. With only the

---

1. If the file is a *shell script*, removing the execute bit will not prevent it from being run, but will affect only the *way* in which it can be run. A shell script file with an execute bit can be executed directly (that is, by typing its name at a shell prompt). A script file without an execute bit can be read by running the shell itself with the name of the script file as an argument. For example, a shell script called count.sh with no execute bits cannot be run by typing *count.sh* at a prompt, but it *can* be run by typing *sh count.sh* at a prompt.

execute bit set on a directory, it is still possible for a process to open a file or directory *within* that directory as long as the process knows the exact name of the file or directory—and as long as permissions on the file or directory itself permit access.

This characteristic of directory permissions—the capability of allowing a process to open a file or directory while at the same time denying a process the ability to *list* that directory's contents—can be used to effectively hide files, or even entire directory trees, from nonprivileged users. (Since the root userid accesses files and directories without consulting the read or write bits, this method should not be considered hacker-proof, but only as one means for slowing down nonroot users.)

Here's how it's done; consider the directory */home/phil/db/db1998* which contains the files *file1.txt* and *file2.txt* (see Figure 4.1).

Users can *cd* to */home/phil* and see the directory *db*, but users cannot *cd* to *db* nor can they see its contents. However, here they can *cd* through *db* by typing *cd db/db1998*. Once users are in the directory *db1998*, they can see (and read) the two files *file1.txt* and *file2.txt*.

Permission Details: SetUID—File   The SetUID bit for a file is relevant only if the file is a program. SetUID is used to allow a program to assume the identity of a particular user regardless of who is running the program. This is useful in cases where only certain programs should be allowed to access certain information.

As an example, consider this problem: The file */etc/shadow* contains the encrypted passwords for all users on a UNIX system. For obvious security reasons, no user should be able to write to, or even read, this file. How, then, can a user change his or her own password?

The answer: A program that can be run as an ordinary user, but that has the ability to read and write to a file that the user cannot read or write. In this example, the program is the *passwd* program. It is SetUID to root (the SetUID bit is set, and the user root owns the file). Because *passwd* is SetUID

Figure 4.1   *Traversing Directories*

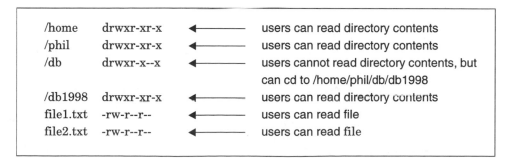

/home	drwxr-xr-x	←	users can read directory contents
/phil	drwxr-xr-x	←	users can read directory contents
/db	drwxr-x--x	←	users cannot read directory contents, but can cd to /home/phil/db/db1998
/db1998	drwxr-xr-x	←	users can read directory contents
file1.txt	-rw-r--r--	←	users can read file
file2.txt	-rw-r--r--	←	users can read file

to root, it is able to read and make the necessary changes to */etc/shadow* when a user needs to change his or her password.

As a security feature, an ordinary user cannot create a SetUID root program. While a user can activate the SetUID bit to any file or program, the *chown* command removes the SetUID bit. This prevents a user from being able to create a SetUID root program. Users can set SetUID only on a program they own; once given away with *chown*, the SetUID bit is cleared.

Permission Details: SetUID—Directory Setting the SetUID bit on a directory has no effect upon that directory.

Permission Details: SetGID—File Just as the SetUID bit allows a program to change its userid to that of another user, the SetGID bit allows a running program to change its groupid from that of the user running it to the groupid of the running program. This gives the program access to all files and directories owned by the group.

Permission Details: SetGID—Directory When the SetGID bit is set on a directory, subsequent files and directories created within this directory inherit the groupid of the directory, not the groupid of the process creating the file or directory.

The following session illustrates this mechanism.

```
% id -a
uid=1001(pete) gid=10(staff) groups=10(staff),8(lp)
% mkdir test
% chgrp lp test
% chmod 777 test
% chmod g+s test
% ls -la
total 32
drwxr-xr-x   8 pete     staff       512 Mar  6 21:03 .
drwxr-xr-x   6 root     root        512 Feb  3 21:37 ..
drwxrwsrwx   2 pete     lp          512 Mar  6 21:03 test
%
% cd test
% touch newfile
% ls -la newfile
-rw-r--r--   2 pete     lp          512 Mar  6 21:04 newfile
%
```

Without the SetGID bit in the directory *test*, the file *newfile* would have had a groupid of *staff*. Instead, *newfile*'s groupid is *lp* because the directory *test* has a groupid of lp, and the directory has the SetGID bit set.

Permission Details: Sticky Bit—File Currently, setting the sticky bit on a file has no effect. Historically, however, setting the sticky bit on a program file caused UNIX to retain the image of that program in memory, thus accelerating subsequent invocations of the program. Memory management changes and improvements in SVR4 and Solaris 2.x have rendered this obsolete.

Permission Details: Sticky Bit—Directory   If the directory is writable and the sticky bit is set, files within the directory can be removed or renamed if at least one of the following conditions is met:

- The file is owned by the user.
- The directory is owned by the user.
- The file is writable by the user.
- The user is root.

Typically, only the */tmp* and */var/tmp* directories on a UNIX system will have the sticky bit set. The reason for this is that */tmp* and */var/tmp* are publicly readable and writable. The sticky bit prevents users from removing files owned by others. Ordinarily, files are allowed to be deleted based upon the permissions of the directory, not the file. Without the sticky bit set in */tmp* and */var/tmp*, anyone would be able to remove any file, since */tmp* and */var/tmp* are world writable. With the sticky bit set in */tmp* and */var/tmp*, the ability to delete a file is based upon whether the process owns the *file*.

Putting It All Together: The Who and the What

The concept of user and group identity and file permissions fits a two-dimensional model as illustrated in Table 4-1.

Table 4-1   *File and Directory Permissions Matrix*

Who	Read	Write	Execute	SetUID	SetGID	Sticky Bit
User	On or Off	On or Off	On or Off			
Group	On or Off	On or Off	On or Off	On or Off	On or Off	On or Off
Other	On or Off	On or Off	On or Off			

How to View File and Directory Permissions

The *ls* command is used to view permissions on a file or directory. The letter *l* option tells *ls* to display the permission fields themselves. Here is an example of *ls* output.

```
% ls -la test
-rwxrwxrwx   1 pete staff      577  Feb 3  20:33   .profile
%
```

These are the elements of the output from the *ls* command.

- *-rwxrwxrwx+*—the permission field that specifies which users have which permissions for reading and writing the file or directory (see Figure 4.2 for a detailed explanation)
- *1*—the number of links (filenames) to the file
- *pete*—the owner of the file
- *staff*—the groupid of the file
- *577*—the size of the file
- *Feb 3 20:33*—the creation/last modification date of the file
- *.profile*—the name of the file

Permissions: Numeric Form

What we have seen thus far is file and directory permissions in *symbolic* form. That is, the position-dependent *rwxrwxrwx* notation of who has what permis-

Figure 4.2 ls *Command File/Directory Permissions*

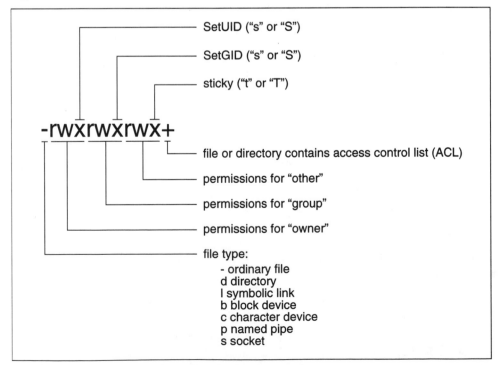

sions. There is also a numeric form that is a bit more shorthand than the symbolic permissions.

It is not only useful but essential that the UNIX administrator understand the numeric form of file and directory permissions. This is because some notations or commands (primarily *umask,* which is discussed later in this chapter) use only the numeric form of permissions. It is therefore important that the UNIX administrator understand both numeric and symbolic permissions.

Numeric permissions employ a *four-digit octal coding system* to represent permissions for read/write/execute for user/group/other, plus sticky bit, Set-UID, and SetGID settings. Incidentally, this numeric system is closer to the way permissions are actually stored and used internally in UNIX.

I will explain the numeric permission system—and how it relates to symbolic permissions—in detail.

The numeric and symbolic systems look like Figure 4.3 side-by-side.

For the *user, group,* and *other* digits, the permission numbers are

- 1—execute
- 2—write
- 4—read

To combine any of permissions 1, 2, or 4, add the values of the digits. For instance:

- 6—read and write (4 + 2)
- 7—read, write, and execute (4 + 2 + 1)

Zero in a field implies *no permission.*

Figure 4.3 *Numeric and Symbolic Permissions*

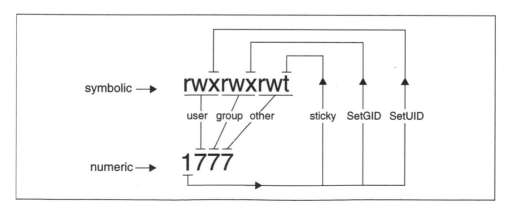

Examples of permissions for *user*, *group*, and *other* are

- 751—7 is the *user* permission (read, write, execute); 5 is the *group* permission (read, execute); 1 is the *other* permission (execute).
- 640—6 is the *user* permission (read, write); 4 is the *group* permission (read); 0 is the *other* permission.

Most of the time, only three digits are used to express permissions. However, a four-number digit (such as 2000) is used to express sticky, SetUID, and SetGID permissions. The permission numbers are

- 1—sticky
- 2—SetGID
- 4—SetUID

Just as with the other three digits, this digit is added to show permissions in combination. For example, a 5 would indicate *sticky* and *SetUID*.

Here is an example using all four digits. A file's permission is 2751. This is broken down as follows:

- 2751—SetGID (2000); user can execute/write/read (700); group can execute/read (50); other can execute (1).

Setting File and Directory Permissions— Numeric

If you're reading this chapter sequentially, then you're just getting used to numeric permissions. We will discuss them first.

The *chmod* command is used to change permissions for a file or directory. The numeric form of *chmod* is

```
chmod nnnn filenamelist
```

where *nnnn* is the numeric permission to apply, and *filenamelist* is a list of one or more files and/or directories. For example, to set a file so that all users (including user and group) can execute a file name *calc* (but *not* read or write its contents), then the command to do so would be

```
chmod 111 calc
```

The command to set the */tmp* directory for read/write/execute for all users, plus the sticky bit,[2] would be

```
chmod 1777 /tmp
```

---

2. This is a typical permission for the */tmp* directory.

Setting File and Directory Permissions— Symbolic

The form of the *chmod* command to set permissions *symbolically* is

```
chmod symbol-list filenamelist
```

where *symbol-list* is three characters: a *who* symbol, an *operator* symbol, and a *what* symbol.

The symbols identifying *who* are

u—user

g—group

o—other

a—all (user and group and other)

The *operator* symbols are

+ —add permissions

– —take away permissions

= —assign permissions

The symbols identifying *what* are

r—read

w—write

x—execute

s—SetUID or SetGID

t—sticky bit

u, g, o—take already-existing permission settings from *user, group,* or *other*

Multiple permission settings can be set in one *chmod* command; entries are separated by a comma (,).

Here are some *chmod* examples.

1. Add write permission for user to file *proc*.

   ```
   chmod u+w proc
   ```

2. Add read and execute permission for all users to file *proc*.

   ```
   chmod a+rx proc
   ```

3. Set user permission to read/write, add read permission to group and other to the file *proc*.

   ```
   chmod u=rw,go+r proc
   ```

umask and How It Works

The *umask* is a value that determines the default permission settings assigned when new files and directories are created.

Each UNIX system has a default *umask* value; each user can change his or her own *umask* value (and usually does so at login time in a *.cshrc*, *.login*, or *.profile* file); each process can also examine or alter its *umask* value with the *umask* command.

umask is an inherited feature. If a process sets a particular *umask*, its children will inherit the same *umask* value.

Here's how *umask* works. Numerically, it specifies which permissions are *not* granted by default when a file or directory is created. For example, a user's *umask* is set to 027. The *umask* 027 is broken down into 0, 2, and 7. The 0 means that the *user* will have all permissions; the 2 means that *group* will not have *write* (2) permissions; the 7 means that *other* will not have *execute* (1), *write* (2), or *read* (4) permissions. This is illustrated in Figure 4.4.

Another way to think about *umask* is to subtract each of its digits from 7; the resulting digits are the permission set up for a file or directory that is created while that *umask* is in effect. This is illustrated in Figure 4.5.

Figure 4.4   umask *Example*

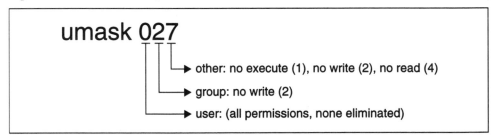

Figure 4.5   umask *Subtraction Example*

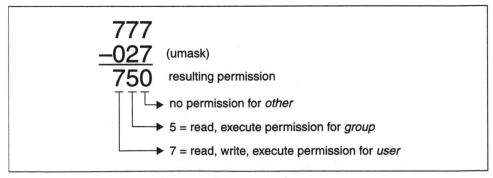

In addition to being set numerically, a *umask* can also be set symbolically, with options similar to *chmod*'s symbolic syntax. For example

```
umask u+rwx,g+rx,o-a   ...is the same as:   umask 027
umask u+rw,g+r,o+r     ...is the same as:   umask 133
```

Ksh and *umask -S*

The Korn shell has a nice feature with its built-in *umask* command. The *-S* option is used to symbolically—rather than numerically—display the user's *umask*. For example

```
% sh
% umask
0027
% ksh
% umask
0027
% umask -S
u=rwx,g=rx,o=
%
```

Default File Permissions and umask

Permissions for files that are created with commands such as *vi*, *cp*, or *touch* or with shell redirection are determined by applying the process's *umask* value to the initial value 666. This is illustrated in the following example.

```
% umask
0027
% touch foo
% ls -ld foo
-rw-r-----   1 pete     staff        0 Oct  1 07:17 foo
%
```

In this example, the file's permissions can be calculated as 666 (initial value) less 027 (*umask*) equals 640 (the file's permissions).

Root User umask

I recommend that root's *umask* be set to 077 or 027. This will result in any file created by root being not readable or writable by others.

Default Directory Permissions and umask

Permissions for directories created with commands such as *mkdir* are determined by applying the process's *umask* value to the initial value 777. The following example illustrates this.

```
% umask
0027
% mkdir foo
% ls -la foo
-rwxr-x---   2 pete      staff        0 Oct  1 07:18 foo
%
```

In this example, the directory's permissions are calculated as 777 (initial value) less 027 (*umask*), giving 750 (the directory's permissions).

How to Find Files with Specific Permission Settings

The UNIX administrator needs to know how to find files with specific security settings. Here are a few examples of the *find* command.

1. Find all SetUID files in and under the current working directory (.).

   ```
   % find . -type f -perm -4000 -print
   ```

2. Find all SetGID files in and under the current working directory (.).

   ```
   % find . -type f -perm -2000 -print
   ```

3. Find all world-writable files in and under the current working directory (.).

   ```
   % find . -type f -perm -o+w -print
   ```

System Device Access Permissions

Solaris is shipped with appropriate permissions assigned to device files such as disk drives, tape drives, and memory. These permissions are discussed here.

A word should be said for Sun's method of indirect references to commonly used devices. For instance, typical disk devices are referenced by SCSI controller and device number, such as

```
/dev/dsk/c0t3d0s0
```

This example signifies a **disk device**, controller 0, SCSI target 3, disk 0, slice 0. But examination of this file shows that it is not a device file, but instead a logical link to the file named

```
../../devices/iommu@f,e0000000/sbus@f,e0001000/espdma@f,400000/esp@f,800000/sd@3,0:a
```

Permissions of this file (in *ls -l* format) are `brw-r----- 1 root sys`.

Warning: Under no circumstance should the permissions of a disk device be changed. A change could result in an entire filesystem being readable or writable by everyone.

Tape drive device permissions are looser, as tape drives are by default considered to be accessible by all users. Permissions of tape drives (in *ls -l* format) are `crw-rw-rw- 1 root sys`. For a production environment, tape device permissions should be tightened so that only the userid actually performing backups will have read and write permissions to relevant tape drive devices.

Solaris **memory devices** are */dev/mem* and */dev/kmem*. These devices are logical links to *../../devices/pseudo/mm@0:mem* and *../../devices/pseudo/mm@0:kmem*, respectively. Permissions for these devices (in *ls -l* format) are `crw-r----- root sys`.

Warning: Under no circumstance should the permissions of a memory device be changed. A change could result in process table and device buffer information being readable or writable by everyone.

The next section describes four tools that will track permissions of all system devices. It is recommended that one or more of these tools be used to ensure that devices are secure.

Filesystem Auditing Tools

There are several tools available that enable the UNIX administrator to audit a UNIX filesystem. The tools that will be discussed in this chapter include Sun Microsystem's Automated System Enhancement Tool (ASET) and the public-domain tools Computer Oracle and Password System (COPS), Tiger, Tripwire, and lsof.

ASET

ASET is a Solaris software package used to enhance security by checking the permissions and contents of system files. ASET can also be used to increase security on a system by tightening up filesystem access permissions.

Where to Find ASET

ASET is included in the standard Solaris 2.5, 2.5.1, 2.6, and Solaris 7 release media. The Solaris package name for ASET is *SUNWast*. Check for ASET on a system with the following command:

```
# pkginfo | grep SUNWast
```

ASET Security Levels

ASET has the following three security levels, each of which is suitable for different environments.

> **Low**—no system behavior is altered. ASET only makes checks and reports weaknesses.
>
> **Medium**—some system files' access permissions are restricted in order to reduce the risk of attack.
>
> **High**—many system files' access permissions are restricted. This setting is the most secure, for use in Internet or Extranet mail, ftp, or Web servers.

Running ASET

A cursory examination can be performed on the system by simply running the *aset* command, as follows:

```
# /usr/aset/aset
======= ASET Execution Log =======

ASET running at security level low

Machine = orion; Current time = 0412_13:11

aset: Using /usr/aset as working directory

Executing task list …
        firewall
        env
        sysconf
        usrgrp
        tune
        cklist
        eeprom

All tasks executed. Some background tasks may still be running.

Run /usr/aset/util/taskstat to check their status:
    /usr/aset/util/taskstat     [aset_dir]

where aset_dir is ASET's operating directory,currently=/usr/aset.

When the tasks complete, the reports can be found in:
    /usr/aset/reports/latest/*.rpt
You can view them by:
    more /usr/aset/reports/latest/*.rpt
#
```

ASET writes its reports into the ASET working directory, usually */usr/aset/reports/latest*. Upon subsequent ASET runs, this directory is renamed to */usr/aset/reports/mmdd_hh:mm*, where *mmdd_hh:mm* is a value coded to the date and time the report was run.

For a complete description of ASET, please refer to the aset(1M) man page.

COPS

COPS is a package from Purdue University that examines a system for a number of known weaknesses and informs the UNIX administrator about them. Some problems can be fixed automatically.

Where to Find COPS

The primary source for COPS is ftp://coast.cs.purdue.edu/pub/tools/unix/cops/ . Look for the latest version and download the tar.Z file. Instructions for unpacking, building, and installing are found in *README* and other documents.

Recommended COPS Tools

- dir.check, file.check—scans system for world-writable system files and directories
- dev.chk—scans system device directories to ensure that hackers won't be able to circumvent filesystem security by writing to disk storage devices directly
- home.chk, user.chk—checks users' home directories for world writability
- root.chk—scans root user login files for world writability; also checks root's paths for sanity, as well as root's *umask* and *hosts.equiv*
- suid.chk—scans system for new SetUID programs

Running COPS

Run COPS regularly, as frequently as once per day (or even more) on servers, and possibly less frequently on desktop systems. COPS detects changes in file and directory permissions from one invocation to the next.

Tiger

Tiger is a package from Texas A&M University that examines a system for known weaknesses and informs the UNIX administrator about those it discovers. Its function is similar to that of COPS.

Where to Find Tiger

Tiger's primary source is ftp://coast.cs.purdue.edu/pub/tools/unix/tiger/TAMU/ . Also needed are signature files for each OS (including Solaris 2.x and Solaris 7) found in ftp://coast.cs.purdue.edu/pub/tools/unix/tiger/TAMU/tiger-sigs/ .

Running Tiger

Tiger can be run by unwrapping the Tiger archive file and running the script *tiger.* It is recommended that Tiger be run as frequently as once per day on servers and perhaps less frequently on desktop systems.

Tripwire

Tripwire, another package from Purdue University, is a sophisticated filesystem auditing tool used to detect signs that a UNIX filesystem has been tampered with.

Tripwire reads a configuration file to find out which files and directories on a UNIX system should be examined. Each file and directory in the configuration file is rigorously examined and the results of that examination are compared against a database containing baseline information about every file and directory to be checked. Differences between the baseline information and what is currently found are listed in a report that the UNIX administrator then can use to determine whether the changes found by Tripwire are legitimate or not.

Where to Find Tripwire

The public-domain version of Tripwire can be found at ftp://coast.cs.purdue.edu/pub/tools/unix/Tripwire/ . A commercial version of Tripwire is available from http://www.tripwiresecurity.com/ .

Setting Up and Running Tripwire

Tripwire comes with a default configuration file that is essentially a list of files and directories that Tripwire should examine. The configuration file should be examined to make sure that all system files and directories are included.

The first time Tripwire is run, it creates a database of complete information for each examined file. Information about each UNIX file is stored in this database. On subsequent runs, information about each file is compared against the values stored in the database. Any files that have been changed (not just the contents, but ownership, permissions, modification/access dates, etc.) will be detected by Tripwire and listed in a report.

I highly recommend that Tripwire be first run on the system immediately after the operating system has been installed. This is because Tripwire, on its initial run on a system, cannot determine whether the system has *already* been compromised.

Run Tripwire at least once a day on servers, and perhaps a little less frequently on desktop systems. Tripwire incurs a great deal of filesystem input/output (I/O), so it would be least intrusive to run Tripwire after hours, started by *cron*.

lsof (list open files)

lsof lists all opened files on a UNIX system and indicates which processes have opened them. This tool can be used to help determine whether hackers are reading or writing files to which they should not have access.

Where to Find lsof

lsof is available at http://sunfreeware.com/ . It is also available at ftp://vic.cc.purdue.edu/pub/tools/unix/lsof/ (this site also has lsof binaries in the event no C compiler is available).

Setting Up and Running lsof

lsof generates a lot of output (a *lot* of files are open on a typically running UNIX system) that only an experienced UNIX administrator can decipher.

Other Security Tools and Techniques

Check /etc Permissions

There are no files in */etc* that need to be group (or other) writable. To determine whether there are any group/other-writable files in */etc*, enter these commands as root:

```
find /etc -type f -perm -g+w -print    (to find group-writable files)
find /etc -type f -perm -o+w -print    (to find world-writable files)
```

Use the *chmod* command to change any errant group/other write permissions as follows:

```
# chmod -R go-w /etc
#
```

Ensure Proper utmp *and* utmpx *Permissions*

The *utmp* and *utmpx* databases contain user access and accounting information for the system. If these files are group- or world-writable, then the record of system accesses can be altered or erased easily.

The file permissions for */var/adm/utmp* and */var/adm/utmpx* should be 644.

Use Fix-modes *Tool to Enhance Security*

The *Fix-modes* tool is used to enhance filesystem security by tightening the security permissions of many Solaris system files. *Fix-modes* creates an audit trail and can be undone.

Fix-modes is available from ftp://ftp.fwi.uva.nl/pub/solaris/fix-modes.tar.gz .

Use the fuser *Command*

The *fuser* command is used to determine which processes, if any, have a particular file or files open. *fuser* can be used to

- See if any process has a file open before removing or renaming the file[3]
- See which processes have files or directories open as part of a troubleshooting process to determine why a filesystem cannot be *umount*ed

Here is an example use of *fuser*.

```
% fuser /tmp
/tmp:      16018c   15218c   14813c   2173o
% fuser /usr/sbin/inetd
/usr/sbin/inetd:     138t
%
```

A letter code follows a process id in *fuser* output. The letter codes are

c—the process's current working directory

r—the process's root directory (this is a mount point directory)

o—an ordinary open file

m—a memory-mapped file

t—a text file (in other words, a currently running program binary file)

Fuser can also be used to list all processes that have any file open in a mounted filesystem and, optionally, kill those processes. This should be used only in emergencies where a filesystem must be unmounted immediately. See the fuser(1M) man page for complete details.

Use the ls *Command to Show Hidden Files and Hidden Characters in Filenames*

The UNIX administrator should always use the *-a* (show hidden files) and *-b* (print nonprintable characters) options when using *ls*.

The *-a* option tells *ls* to show ordinary files and directories *plus hidden* files and directories. A hidden file or directory is one whose name begins with the dot (.) character. This is useful because the UNIX administrator ordinarily should be seeing *all* the contents of a directory with the *ls* command. For

---

3. Note that removing an open file will *not* disrupt a process that has already opened the file. A removed open file will, however, cease to be listed with the *ls* command, but it will still consume disk space. Once a process has closed an open file (presuming that no other processes *also* have the file opened), the file will actually be removed and its space freed.

instance, while troubleshooting a situation where a filesystem has run out of available disk space, the culprit may be a hidden file. If the UNIX administrator does not list hidden files with *ls*, the guilty files will be a little more difficult to find.

The *-b* option tells *ls* to print nonprintable characters in file (or directory) names in octal \bbb notation. Nonprintable characters in filenames? You bet. They can be created by accident or even purposefully by a mischievous user. Consider this example.

```
% touch abc\<backspace>d
% ls
abd
% rm abd
abd: No such file or directory
% ls -b
ab\010d
%
```

Techniques on removing such files are discussed in the next section.

Alias the *ls* Command

The *ls* command can be *aliased* so that the *-a* and *-b* options are used without having to be typed in every time. Procedures for aliasing *ls* follow.

For C shell users, include the following entry in the *login* file.

```
alias ls '/usr/bin/ls -a -b \!*'
```

For Bourne shell and Korn shell users, include the following entry in the *.profile* file.

```
ls() { /usr/bin/ls -a -b $* ; }
```

Alias the rm *Command*

For safety reasons, the *rm* command can be aliased in order to force the UNIX administrator to verify the deletion of each file, preventing accidental deletion. Many UNIX administrators have their personal stories of having removed entire filesystems by accident. The *-i* option tells *rm* to ask for verification of each file being removed. An example of *rm* with the *-i* option is

```
% rm -i *
rm: foo is a directory
rm: gcos.txt (yes/no)? n
rm: hal.doc (yes/no)?
rm: status.out (yes/no)? y
%
```

Some notes about *rm -i*:

- Directories and subdirectories are *not* removed (unless the -*rf* option is also used).
- "No" is the default response (the file *hal.doc* is not removed in the example above).

Randomize Filesystem Inode Numbers with fsirand

The *inode numbers* in a filesystem can be predicted for filesystem files such as / (the root entry for any filesystem), *lost+found*, etc. A clever hacker can attempt to open and alter files by inode number instead of by name. A great way to thwart this vulnerability is by randomizing a filesystem's inode numbers with the *fsirand* command. *fsirand* does not alter the visible filesystem, only its inode numbers.

Filesystems must be unmounted before *fsirand* can be run. Any filesystem altered by *fsirand* first should be backed up and *fsck* run.

Note: *fsirand* functionality is present in *mkfs* in Solaris 2.5 and newer.

Filesystem Quotas

A frequent source of grief for the UNIX administrator is the management of shared disk space. Users all too often consume all available disk space, thus precipitating errors for everyone using that filesystem. Unfriendly users can disrupt other users' work by deliberately filling a shared filesystem with one or more large files. Disk quotas can be used to limit the amount of disk space each user is allowed to use.

This is the procedure for setting up a filesystem for quota use.

1. The mount option *quota* must be added to */etc/vfstab* or the appropriate *automount* map. Here is an example *vfstab* entry.

   ```
   /dev/dsk/c0t1d0s7  /dev/rdsk/c0t1d0s7  /export/home ufs 2 yes (quota)
   ```

2. As root, create a file called *quotas* in the root directory of the filesystem (in this case, */export/home/quotas*). In this example, use the command *touch /export/home/quotas*.

3. Set up a prototype quota entry for a single user with the *edquota* command. An example entry:

   ```
   fs /export/home blocks (soft = 8000, hard = 9999) inodes (soft = 800, hard = 999)
   ```

   In this example, the user's soft disk space limit is 8,000 blocks (times 512 bytes equals 4 MB); the hard disk space limit is 9,999 blocks (5 MB). The soft inode limit (the number of files the user may own) is 800, and the hard limit is 999.

Figure 4.6 *Soft Quota Error*

When a user exceeds a soft limit, a dialogue box is displayed (see Figure 4.6). When a user exceeds a hard limit, the user will not be able to create files. The error message seen is "Disc quota exceeded."

4. Replicate the prototype entry to other users as needed with the *edquota* command. An example command is

```
# edquota -p phil mary john sue rick larry ralph april
#
```

In this example, the quotas values for user *phil* are replicated to users *mary, john, sue, rick, larry, ralph,* and *april.*

5. Activate quotas with the *quotaon* command.
6. Build initial quota statistics with the *quotacheck* command.
7. Create a quota report with the *repquota* command. Here is a sample report.

```
# repquota -a
/dev/dsk/c0t1d0s7 (/export/home):
Block limits                    File limits
User          used  soft  hard  timeleft  used  soft  hard    timeleft
phil   (+-)  17402   999 99999 (7.0 days)  197  9999  9999
#
```

In this example, user *phil* has exceeded his block limit quota; files owned by *phil* are taking too much disk space. This is signified both by the "+ –" symbol and by the "timeleft" field for block limits on the report.

Filesystem Access Control Lists

UNIX system administrators find that the UNIX file and directory permission scheme is insufficient in complex environments. Certain aspects of managing access to files and directories sometimes do not translate well to large environments. Consider the following scenario.

A medium-sized company has several departments. Access control has been set up so that UNIX groups correspond to the different departments. Default file permissions are set up so that only users and groups can read and write to files and directories; thus, files and directories in one department are unavailable to all others. How do users share certain files in their departments with certain individuals in other departments without resorting to setting read or write bits in *other*?

Answer: It cannot be done.

Solaris access control lists (ACLs) can help remedy this problem. The *getfacl* and *setfacl* commands are used to get and set ACL entries for files and directories.

Setfacl, the command to set ACL entries for a file or directory, is used to change ACL permissions. From our example above, consider a specific file *cust.db* that has the following permissions:

```
% ls -la cust.txt
-rw-rw----   1 jsmith  acct        65536 Jan 22  1999 cust.db
%
```

In this example, *cust.db* is owned by user *jsmith*, groupid *acct*. Both user *jsmith* and group *acct* have read/write access to *cust.db*. No other users have access whatsoever to the file.

Consider a situation where user *sjones* needs read/write access to *cust.db*, but where *sjones* is not a member of the group *acct*. A possible solution is to use *setfacl* to add *sjones* as a user with read/write access to *cust.db*. The following session illustrates this situation.

```
% ls -la cust.db
-rw-rw----   1 jsmith  acct        65536 Jan 22  1999 cust.db
% getfacl cust.db

# file: cust.db
# owner: jsmith
# group: acct
user::rw-
group::rw-              #effective:r--
mask:r--
other:---
% setfacl -m user:sjones:rw-cust.db
% getfacl cust.db

# file: cust.db
# owner: jsmith
# group: acct
user::rw-
user:sjones:rw-         #effective:rw-     ← new entry
group::rw-              #effective:r--
mask:r--
other:---
% ls -la cust.db
-rw-rw----+  1 jsmith  acct        65536 Jan 22  1999 cust.db
%
```

Note the "+" on the end of the permission bits in the final *ls* command output. This signifies that there are ACL entries for this file.

Note: Carefully consider the use of ACLs. While ACLs are useful and even necessary in some situations, administering them can become a full-time job.

Where to Go for Additional Information

AnswerBook

- AnswerBook2—System Administration Guide, Managing File Systems
- AnswerBook2—System Administration Guide, Managing System Resources
- AnswerBook2—System Administration Guide, Managing System Security

Man Pages

- aset(1M)
- chmod(1)
- chown(1)
- csh(1)
- edquota(1M)
- fsck(1M)
- find(1M)
- fsirand(1M)
- fuser(1M)
- getfacl(1)
- ksh(1)
- ls(1)
- ls(1B)
- pkginfo(1M)
- repquota(1M)
- rm(1)
- quota(1M)
- quotacheck(1M)
- quotaoff(1M)
- quotaon(1M)
- setfacl(1)
- sh(1)
- umask(1)

Publications

- *How to Set Up Quotas on a File System*, SunSolve SRDB 4652
- *How to Enable User Storage Space Quotas for Solaris*, SunSolve FAQ 1946
- *How to Modify ACLs*, SunSolve Infodoc 12718
- *How to Set ACL Entries on a File*, SunSolve Infodoc 12714
- *How to Delete ACL Entries on a File or Directory*, SunSolve Infodoc 12728

5

USER ACCOUNTS AND ENVIRONMENTS

This chapter describes the basic workings of user accounts on Solaris systems.

What's in this chapter

- What the userid root is and why it needs extra protection
- Ways to respond when a user asks for root privileges
- How the password, shadow, and group files work
- Methods for strengthening account and user environment security
- Auditing tools

Why this is important

User accounts lie at the very heart of UNIX system security. They are the first layer of defense against misuse and attack. It is therefore necessary for a UNIX systems administrator to thoroughly understand what user accounts are and how they work.

Introduction

People identify themselves to a computer via a *userid* (also known as UID). The computer systems we interact with grant or deny access to information based upon our userids.

Computers grant you access to information based upon who they think you are, not upon who you actually are. Take, for example, a financial clerk who has access to bank account information. The clerk is logged into the computer system—that is, the clerk has identified himself by providing a userid and password. The computer then allows the clerk to access and change financial records for its customers.

Now let's say that the clerk gets up to take a five-minute stretch—he just walks away from his terminal. Anyone could sit down at that terminal and enter transactions as though they were the clerk. The computer does not know the difference—it doesn't know whether the person entering transactions is the original clerk who signed on earlier.

User Account Security

The hacker who seeks information from a computer system needs only to find a way to trick either a person or the computer itself about his or her identity. Hackers are interested in the operating system software bugs that permit them to easily assume the identity of a person who is allowed to access or modify the information they seek.

The Root Account

The userid root is the ultimate prize to computer hackers. This account, used by UNIX system administrators, has unlimited access to virtually all programs, files, and resources a computer has to offer. If a hacker can change his identity from that of a normal user to any other user, root is frequently the account of choice because of its unrestricted access.

The root user not only has read access to everything on the computer, but has write access as well. Thus, not only can skilled hackers access any information on a computer, but they can alter it as well. Frequently hackers break into computer systems, get the information (or inflict the damage) they want, and then erase their tracks by removing entries in logs that recorded their presence. All too frequently hackers break into a system, do their dirty deeds, remove traces of their activities on all log files, and quietly sneak away.

The root account is omnipotent not because of its *name*, but because of its *userid*, which is 0. The first line from the */etc/passwd* file is shown in Figure 5.1 to illustrate.

Other accounts can be created with a userid of 0; those other accounts have all the power and privilege that root has. Further, the root account's name could be changed, but as long as its userid number is 0, it is still root.

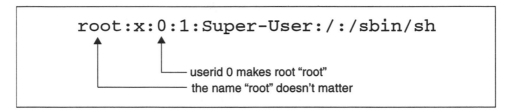

Figure 5.1 *Root Userid Is 0*

Other Administrative Accounts and Groups

Several administrative accounts exist on a Solaris system. While these accounts do not have root privileges, they should be protected as though they did. System processes using these accounts control basic system functions such as electronic mail, relational database access, and printing. A compromise of any of these accounts can result in wholesale exposure and damage to files in its respective subsystem. For example, a compromise in the lp account can result in an intruder's having complete control over the printing subsystem and, hence, the hacker may be able to alter at will the contents of any printout.

Which Administrative Accounts Should Be Locked

Several administrative accounts should be locked so that no one can log in and cause trouble. These accounts include *daemon, bin, sys, adm, lp, uucp, nuucp, listen, nobody,* and *noaccess*. The procedure for locking an account is explained in the shadow file section later in this chapter.

Sysadmin Group

Such vulnerabilities are not limited to user accounts; the sysadmin group (groupid 14) must be similarly protected because members of this group can perform system administration tasks with *Admintool*.

Sys Group

The sys group (groupid 3) must be similarly protected, as it is allowed to run the *ufsdump* command. *ufsdump* is the system backup program; it is possible, then, for a nonroot user to read every file on a system and be able to restore any or all of these files on a system where the user did have root privileges. Such a user would, for example, be able to read the */etc/shadow* file and crack account passwords (*/etc/shadow* is discussed later in the shadow file section; cracking account passwords is discussed in the section on the Crack tool near the end of the chapter).

User Accounts

Except for a few lucky UNIX administrators who get to build the right kind of environment from the ground up, UNIX admins should consider *any* UNIX account as potentially having root privileges. It can be difficult to irrefutably prove that a given account does *not* (or *will not*) have access to a "back door."

When Users Need Root Privileges

Users may legitimately require root privileges if they need to do the following:

- Mount diskettes or CD-ROMs where manual *mount* and *umount* commands are required (the *mount* and *umount* commands can be run only as root) and where Volume Management[1] is not running
- Kill or restart specific processes not belonging to the user; for example, in a software development environment, a user may need to kill and restart a database instance or application (nonroot users can kill only their own processes)

PATH and LD_LIBRARY_PATH

The *PATH* and *LD_LIBRARY_PATH* environment variables must be *safe*, particularly for privileged users such as root. By safe I mean that the referenced directories must have tight permissions (no *group* or *other* write access) and known entities therein. *PATH* or *LD_LIBRARY_PATH* must not contain directories whose contents are questionable or purposes unknown.

Set root's path—defined in /*.profile*—as follows:

```
PATH=/usr/bin:/sbin:/usr/sbin
```

No user's *PATH* or *LD_LIBRARY_PATH* should ever contain "." (search the shell's current working directory for executables or libraries). Otherwise, a user could plant a *Trojan horse*[2] in a directory that he can write to and just sit back and wait until root stumbles into that directory and accidentally executes that program.

---

1. Volume Management is used to facilitate the automatic mounting and unmounting of diskettes and CD-ROMs on the user's behalf without the user needing root privileges.
2. See "Glossary of Attacks" in appendices for a definition and example of the Trojan horse and LD_LIBRARY_PATH attacks.

The Password, Shadow, and Group Files

This section deals with the simplicity of having only direct *passwd*, *shadow*, and *group* files. NIS and NIS+ are dealt with in chapter 14.

Password File

On a UNIX system, user accounts are defined in the system file */etc/passwd*. */etc/passwd* contains the following information about a user: userid, numeric id, numeric groupid the user belongs to, full name, home directory, and login shell. A portion of a */etc/passwd* file is shown here.

```
root:x:0:1:Super-User:/:/sbin/sh
daemon:x:1:1::/:
bin:x:2:2::/usr/bin:
sys:x:3:3::/:
adm:x:4:4:Admin:/var/adm:
lp:x:71:8:Line Printer Admin:/usr/spool/lp:
smtp:x:0:0:Mail Daemon User:/:
uucp:x:5:5:uucp Admin:/usr/lib/uucp:
nuucp:x:9:9:uucp Admin:/var/spool/uucppublic:/usr/lib/uucp/uucico
listen:x:37:4:Network Admin:/usr/net/nls:
nobody:x:60001:60001:Nobody:/:
noaccess:x:60002:60002:No Access User:/:
nobody4:x:65534:65534:SunOS 4.x Nobody:/:
pete:x:1001:10:Peter Gregory:/export/home/pete:/bin/sh
```

The *passwd* file is owned by root and must be readable by all users, but writable only by root. Hence, */etc/passwd* permissions are typically -rw-r--r-- .

Consistency of the *passwd* file can be checked with the *pwck* command.

Shadow File

Unlike UNIX systems in the distant past when the encrypted password string was a part of the *passwd* file and hence readable by all users, the Solaris 2 and Solaris 7 system *passwd* file contains no password information. Instead, the encrypted password information is kept in the shadow file */etc/shadow*. The */etc/shadow* file contains the following information: userid, encrypted password string, and several fields related to the "aging" of each user's password. A sample */etc/shadow* file is shown here.

```
root:tspx1CqH8igWA:6445::::::
daemon:NP:6445::::::
bin:NP:6445::::::
sys:NP:6445::::::
adm:NP:6445::::::
lp:NP:6445::::::
smtp:NP:6445::::::
```

```
uucp:NP:6445::::::
nuucp:NP:6445::::::
listen:*LK*:::::::
nobody:NP:6445::::::
noaccess:NP:6445::::::
nobody4:NP:6445::::::
pete:tspx1CqH8igWA:10261:::::::
```

In this example, several accounts have the string NP or *LK* in the encrypted password file. These codes represent No Password and Locked, respectively. In both cases, the accounts are unusable from a login perspective (the accounts cannot be logged in, as no password can possibly decrypt to the string NP or *LK*).

The */etc/shadow* file is owned by root and readable only by root; no other users on the system can read */etc/shadow*. Its permission settings are -r--------. If */etc/shadow* were readable by anyone, then account passwords could easily be guessed using a password cracking program such as Crack. I'll discuss password cracking later in this chapter.

Password Security

Using Good Passwords

The use of good passwords is the single most important defense against unauthorized system use. Solaris enforces the need for good passwords by requiring a password to have at least six characters, one or more of which is a numeric or special character, such as * or &.

Probably one of the greatest weaknesses in Solaris is that these restrictions are ignored if root is changing a user's password (including its own password!). The rationale behind this lack of restrictions is that the UNIX administrator is assumed to know better than to assign an easy-to-guess password. Still, without constant reminders, UNIX administrators could tend to get sloppy and assign passwords that are too easy to guess.

Password aging is the mechanism that requires that users periodically change their password. Here are some examples.

1. Force the account *jsmith* to change its password every 30 days.

   ```
   # passwd -n 30 jsmith
   #
   ```

2. Force the account *tnguyen* to change its password on the next login.

   ```
   # passwd -f tnguyen
   #
   ```

3. Prevent the user *cowens* from changing its password.

   ```
   # passwd -n 2 -x 1 cowens
   #
   ```

4. Lock the *tbarnes* account, thus preventing login.

```
# passwd -l tbarnes
#
```

See the passwd(1M) man page for additional information.

UNIX Groups

Group Membership

In Solaris 2 and Solaris 7, users have a primary group, defined in */etc/ passwd*, but they can also belong to several other groups, defined in */etc/ group* at the same time. The effect of a user's primary group is the groupid (also known as GID) of files created by the user. Any file created by the user will have a groupid equal to that of the user's primary group.

Two commands are available for displaying group membership: *id* and *groups*. Examples of both follow.

1. Display userid and primary group.

```
% id
uid=1001(phil), gid=10(staff)
%
```

2. Display userid, primary group, and all other groups.

```
% id -a
uid=1001(phil), gid=10(staff), groups=10(staff),20(admins)
%
```

3. Display all group memberships.

```
% groups
staff admins
%
```

The *newgrp* command is used to temporarily change a primary groupid to the groupid of one of the other groups listed in the *id -a* or *groups* command. For example

```
% id -a
uid=1001(phil), gid=10(staff), groups=10(staff),20(admins)
% newgrp admins
% id -a
uid=1001(phil), gid=20(admins), groups=10(staff),20(admins)
%
```

Group File

The */etc/group* file defines the user groups on a UNIX system and the users that are members of these groups. */etc/group* contains the name of the group, the groupid number, and a list of userids that are members of each group. A sample group file is shown here.

```
root::0:root
other::1:
bin::2:root,bin,daemon
sys::3:root,bin,sys,adm
adm::4:root,adm,daemon
uucp::5:root,uucp
mail::6:root
tty::7:root,tty,adm
lp::8:root,lp,adm
nuucp::9:root,nuucp
staff::10:
daemon::12:root,daemon
sysadmin::14:
nobody::60001:
noaccess::60002:
nogroup::65534:
```

The */etc/group* file is owned by root, readable by all users, but writable only by root. */etc/group*'s permissions are -rw-r--r-- .

Consistency of the */etc/group* file can be checked with the *grpck* command.

Group Password

A user can be challenged by a password prompt when changing groups with the *newgrp* command. While no direct tools exist for this purpose, group passwords can be implemented in Solaris 2 and Solaris 7. This is an example *newgrp* session.

```
$ id
uid=1001(phil) gid=10(staff)
$ newgrp sysadmin
newgrp: Password ********
$ id
uid=1001(phil) gid=14(sysadmin)
$
```

Use the procedure in steps 1–6 to set up a group password and enforce its use. In this example, force a user to furnish a password when changing to group *sysadmin*.

1. Remove *phil* from group *sysadmin* (if user *phil* is a member of group *sysadmin*, he will not be required to supply a password when changing to group *sysadmin*).
2. Choose a password; for instance, 5y5*adm1n could be used.
3. Change the password for a normally locked account (e.g., lp) to this password, as follows:

```
# passwd lp
New password: ********
```

```
Re-enter new password: ********
#
```

4. Using *vi*, extract the password string for account *lp* from the file */etc/shadow*. In this example, the */etc/shadow* entry appears as follows:

```
lp:Rt7ekqsuSIHr2:10473::::::
```

5. Using *vi*, insert this string into the password field for the sysadmin entry in */etc/group*. In this example, the */etc/group* entry will appear as follows:

```
sysadmin:Rt7ekqsuSIHr2:14:
```

6. Return the *lp* account to its former locked state; the shadow entry might appear as follows:

```
lp:*LOCK*:10473::::::
```

The /etc/default/passwd *File*

The */etc/default/passwd* file contains several parameters related to account passwords. These are systemwide defaults. A sample */etc/default/passwd* file appears below.

```
#ident "@(#)passwd.df11.392/07/14 SMI"
MAXWEEKS=4
MINWEEKS=1
WARNWEEKS=3
PASSLENGTH=6
```

In this example

- Account passwords must be changed at least every four weeks, but not more than once per week. This prevents a user, having been forced to change his or her password, from immediately changing it back to the familiar old password.
- Users will receive warning messages of upcoming password changes three weeks after changing passwords (and, hence, one week before they are required to change their passwords).
- A user's password must be at least six characters in length.

Root Access

Direct Root Login

For greater accountability, it is advisable that root never log in directly. Instead UNIX administrators should log in using their own unprivileged accounts, and then use the switch user *su* command (explained below) to become root. This provides an audit trail of who became root in the first place.

A system can be configured to restrict locations for which root can log in directly. This is controlled by the CONSOLE= setting in the file */etc/default/ login* (there will be a complete description of */etc/default/login* later in this chapter).

To allow root to log in only at the system console, set CONSOLE=*/dev/console* in the file */etc/default/login*. This would be appropriate in a setting where the system's console is in a locked room. It would be better yet to prevent root from direct login everywhere; set CONSOLE=*/dev/null* in */etc/ default/login*, because every administrator who would need to first be root should log in using his own ordinary account, and then *su* to become root. This forces accountability, since the system records who *su*s to root.

The su *Command*

The switch user or *su* command permits a user to change from one userid to another; *su* prompts the user for the new userid's password. An example session follows.

```
% id
uid=1001(jim) gid=101(users)
% su - bob
Password: ********
% id
uid=1004(bob) gid=102(cust)
% lp -d localprinter /home/bob/eom.prt
request-id is localprinter-87 (1 file(s))
% ^D
% id
uid=1001(jim) gid=101(users)
%
```

In this example, user *jim* changes to user *bob*—*jim* supplied *bob*'s password and then was effectively userid *bob*. User *jim* needed to *su* to *bob*'s account in order to print the report in *bob*'s home directory.

The *su* "-" option in this example causes *jim*'s environment to look just like that of user *bob*'s, as though he had actually logged in as *bob*. Without the "-" *jim*'s environment would have been unchanged (except for the userid itself).

The *su* command is the recommended means for becoming root on a system. This provides needed accountability, since *su* logs all *su* attempts (failed or successful). If one of several UNIX administrators were to log in *directly* as root on a system, it would be impossible to tell which administrator did what.

When a user runs *su*, the userid of the shell running *su* is unchanged; instead, *a new shell is started,* and the userid of that new shell takes the new identity. This is why, in the preceding example, pressing ^*D* returns the user to the former userid.

Restricting Use of *su*

It is possible to restrict use of *su* to a group of users, such as UNIX administrators. This is accomplished with the following commands:

```
% chgrp admins /usr/bin/su
% chmod o-rwx /usr/bin/su
```

In this example, */usr/bin/su* has its groupid changed to *admins*, and *chmod*'d to allow only *su*'s owner (root) and any member of group *admins* to run it. It is assumed that UNIX administrators are already members of the *admins* group.

> **Caution: /usr/bin/su has the SetUID bit turned on; su will no longer work if this bit is turned off.**

su from Root

su does not ask for a userid's password if *su* is running as root. Thus it is possible for the root user to change to any other userid without knowing any passwords (it is presumed that, since the UNIX administrator can *change* any password, he should also be able to *su* to any account without having to provide its password). An example session follows.

```
% id
uid=1008(steve) gid=101(users)
% su - root
Password: ********
# id
uid=0(root) gid=1(other)
# su marty
% id
uid=1015(marty) gid=101(users)
%
```

su Logging

Because it is such a powerful command, *su* can log its attempts in a variety of ways, all of which are controlled by the file */etc/default/su*. Here is a typical */etc/default/su* file.

```
SULOG=/var/adm/sulog
SYSLOG=YES
CONSOLE=/dev/console
PATH=/usr/bin:
SUPATH=/usr/sbin:/usr/bin
```

SULOG defines the *su* logfile for logging all *su* attempts. *SYSLOG*, set to YES or NO, determines whether *su* attempts should also be logged to *syslog*. *CONSOLE* defines to which screen to send *su* messages. *PATH* is the default path for the new user's shell; *SUPATH* is the path set if the new user is root. Note that, for any userid, the *PATH* variable can be changed interactively; the values in */etc/default/su* are merely *initial* values for *PATH*.

Shell and Application Security

Forced Application Startup

As UNIX applications get into the hands of an increasing number of nontechnical users, UNIX administrators are frequently being asked to restrict application users to their applications and to prevent them from being able to reach a UNIX shell prompt. The following example user's *.profile* file illustrates.

```
# .profile file for application users
trap exit 1 2 3 15
PATH=/export/app/bin
exec /export/app/bin/application
exit
```

In this example, the *trap* command is used. This is a safeguard that tells the shell script *.profile* to *exit* (logging the user off) if an interrupt signal is received (such as typing ^C). This is not absolutely foolproof, as a lucky user might be able to interrupt *.profile* before the *trap* command is executed (although this is very unlikely).

If the application permits a user to run a UNIX shell, then this method is not completely foolproof. Another possible option is to change the user's shell to the application itself. An example */etc/passwd* file entry illustrates this approach.

```
bob:x:1018:101:Bob Jones:/home/bob:/export/app/bin/application
```

This may or may not work, depending on whether the application requires that certain environment variables be set prior to execution. The UNIX administrator will have to weigh these options in deciding how to reliably restrict users to an application.

Include System Name in Root Shell Prompt

Many UNIX administrators can attest to having performed the correct operation on the wrong system. Frequently this is because they forgot which system they were on at the time. The system name should be a part of root's shell prompt so that the UNIX administrator will never need to expend extra effort to see which system she is on.

To put the system name in root's shell prompt in Bourne shell (*/bin/sh*) or Korn shell (*/bin/ksh*), add the following to */.profile*:

```
PS1="'uname -n' # "
export PS1
```

To put the system name in root's shell prompt in C shell (*/bin/csh*), add the following to */.login*:

```
set prompt="'uname -n' # "
```

Restricted Shell

There are instances where users need access to a UNIX shell, but where the user's activities on the system need to be restricted. The *restricted shell* may the answer.

The two restricted shells available in Solaris are */usr/lib/rsh* (Bourne shell) and */usr/bin/rksh* (Korn shell). There is no restricted version of the C shell.

The principal features of the restricted shell are as follows:

- User cannot change directory (*cd*).
- PATH variable cannot be changed.
- User cannot specify a path starting with / either in a command or in a filename.
- User cannot redirect output (> and >>).

From these properties, it is possible to restrict a restricted shell user to a subset of commands. This is accomplished by creating a special bin directory and putting that directory in the user's PATH. For example, if a restricted user can run only the *date* and *who* commands, the UNIX administrator would run these commands to set up a bin directory.

```
% mkdir /rusers/bin
% ln /usr/bin/who /rusers/bin/who
% ln /usr/bin/date /rusers/bin/date
```

The user's PATH variable would contain only */rusers/bin*.

> **Note: The UNIX administrator needs to be careful when choosing which commands a restricted shell user can run. For example, *vi* allows a user to launch a normal shell with the *!sh* command.**

Default Login Environment

The */etc/default/login* file contains several parameters related to the user's login environment. Its parameters are

- CONSOLE—if set to console device, then root can directly log in only on that device; if it is not set, root can log in directly on any device or over the network.
- PASSREQ—set to YES if a password is required (recommended).
- PATH—the initial path after logging in; not enforced, since any user can change his path.
- SLEEPTIME—time, in seconds, to sleep between failed login attempts; default is 4, range is 0 through 5.
- SUPATH—the initial path when *su*ing to root; again, not enforced, since root can change its path.
- SYSLOG—if set to YES, all root logins are logged to syslog; default is YES.
- TIMEOUT—time, in seconds, before abandoning a login session; range is 0 through 900.
- UMASK—default login umask; not enforceable since any user can change this.

Writing Directly to the Console

Some environments require the ability to write messages directly to */dev/console* rather than using *syslog* or other more standard message mechanisms.

A UNIX sysadmin will find that, in changing permissions of */dev/console* from its default of 0600 to something like 0620 (*/dev/console* writable by *group*) or 0622 (*/dev/console* writable by *other*), these permissions will "stick" until the current user logs off, at which time */dev/console* permissions revert to 0600. The UNIX sysadmin may be tempted to write some sort of a workaround such as adding a *chmod 0622 /dev/console* to a user's *.profile* or *.login*, but this is a less-than-satisfactory method.

There is an acceptable way of doing this, however. The file */etc/logindevperm* is used by the *login* program to set the permissions of several console devices such as the keyboard, mouse, frame buffer, and sound. An entry can be added to */etc/logindevperm* to allow nondefault permissions for */dev/console*. A sample entry might be

```
/dev/console    0622    /dev/console # change default console mode
```

In this example, *login* will change the permissions of */dev/console* to 0622 (read, write by owner; write by *group* and *other*).

Note: This information is provided only for those canned or preexisting applications that require this functionality. Any new application or tool should not be designed for direct I/O to */dev/console*; use a secure and flexible alternative such as *syslog* instead. Because */dev/console* is not meant to be written to by others, Sun Microsystems cannot support system behavior associated with such a change.

Program Buffer Overflow

One of the common threads in UNIX security bugs has to do with program buffer overflows. Many of the common UNIX commands have been victims of buffer overflow bugs. An intruder will discover a way of overflowing a buffer on a particular command in such a way that executable code is spilled onto the stack. This executable code, written by the intruder, will contain instructions designed to give him root access or to cause some other form of trouble.

Solaris can be configured to prevent stack-based buffer overflows. The procedure is

1. Add the following lines to */etc/system*:

```
set noexec_user_stack=1
set noexec_user_stack_log=1
```

2. Restart the system with the *init 6* command.

Any attempts to execute code in the stack will be logged by *syslog* if *syslog*'s *kern* facility is set to the *notice* (or higher) level. Refer to chapter 8 for more information on *syslog*. An example log message follows:

```
a.out[347] attempt to execute code on stack by uid 555
```

Unfortunately, it's not as simple as this. Some software legitimately tries to run code from the stack, and such software will abort if the protection described above is turned on. This setting should be tried out on a test system before being set on a production server.

Additional Process Information

The process tools collection is a set of commands that can be used to get additional information about processes. These tools reside in */usr/proc/bin*. The commands are described in Table 5-1.

X-Windows Security

One of the greatest security risks a system will face is when a user walks away from a logged-in session. While it may be reasonable to require that

Table 5-1   *Process Tools*

Tool	Description
pcred	View a process's credentials (effective and real userid and groupid)
pfiles	View a process's open files
pflags	View a process's tracing flags and signal status
pldd	View the dynamic libraries linked into a process
pmap	View a process's address space map (a detailed look·at how much virtual memory the process is consuming)
psig	View a process's signal
pstack	View a process's hex/symbolic stack trace
ptime	A high-precision accounting of a process's CPU time; see also the time(1) man page
ptree	Hierarchical view of all of a process's child processes
pwait	Wait for a specified process to terminate
pwdx	View a process's current working directory

users on a "character" terminal or console log off if they leave their systems unattended, X-Windows users will shriek if required to log off. Their arguments are valid: it can take quite a while to set up all of their X-Window programs, windows, and sessions; furthermore, they may be running processes that take a long time (longer than the interval between bathroom breaks) to complete.

X-Windows Screen Lock, Manual

The greatest defense against the risk of abuse of an unattended system is the X-Windows screen lock.

To lock the screen in the common desktop environment (CDE), press the lock symbol on the front panel, as shown in Figure 5.2. To lock the screen in OpenWindows, start the Workspace menu by right-clicking in the window background; then select the Utilities option; then press Lock Screen, as shown in Figure 5.3.

Figure 5.2 *CDE Screen Lock*

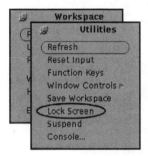

Figure 5.3 *OpenWindows Screen Lock*

X-Windows Screen Lock, Auto

X-Windows can also be configured to automatically lock the screen after a preconfigured period of inactivity. Autolock is both useful and annoying, but it should never be used as the sole means for locking an X-Windows session.

To set autolock in CDE, launch the Style Manager; then select Screen (see Figure 5.4). Turn the Screen Saver and the Screen Lock on, and set the Start Lock slider to the number of minutes desired.

To set autolock in OpenWindows, start the Workspace menu by right-clicking in the window background; then select the Properties option; then select the Miscellaneous category. Set Screen Saver to Auto, and fill in the number of minutes in the field to the right (see Figure 5.5).

X-Windows Display Permissions

The *xhost* command is used to control which systems or users have permission to write to a user's X-Windows display. The following are examples of the *xhost* command.

1. Check to see who has permission to write to this X-Windows display (in this example, no other machines have permission).

```
% xhost
access control enabled, only authorized clients can connect
%
```

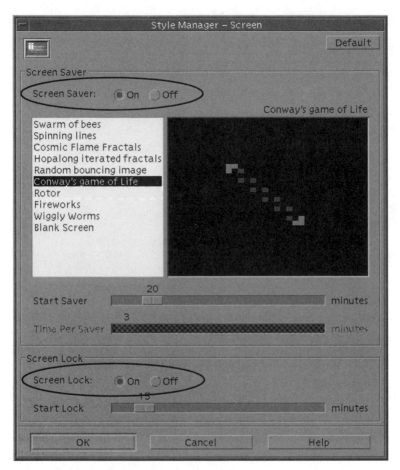

Figure 5.4   *CDE Auto Screen Lock Configuration*

Figure 5.5   *OpenWindows Auto Screen Lock Configuration*

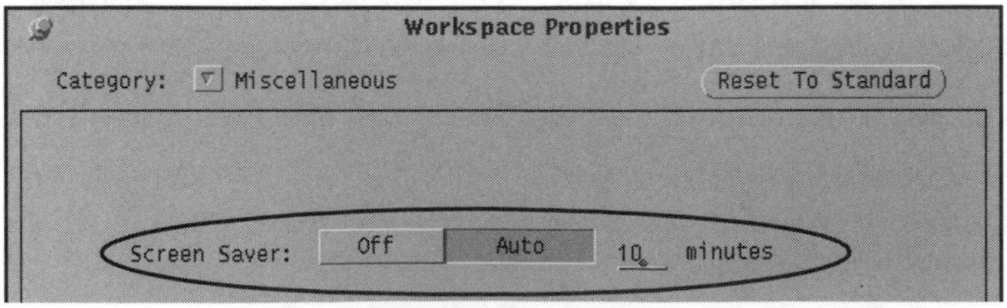

2. Check to see which machines have permission to write to this X-Windows display (in this example, machines *sleepy* and *dopey* have permission).

```
% xhost
access control enabled, only authorized clients can connect
INET:sleepy,dopey
%
```

3. Allow the user *phil* on machine *grumpy* to write to display.

```
% xhost +phil@grumpy
%
```

4. Turn off access control (allow *all* users and machines to write to this display). *This is not a recommended practice!*

```
% xhost +
%
```

Auditing Tools

There are some public-domain auditing tools available that will help to determine what security issues may exist on a UNIX system.

COPS

COPS is an auditing tool used to discover back doors that a user may use as an unauthorized means for gaining root privileges. COPS is discussed in detail in chapter 4.

Crack

Crack is a tool used to guess account passwords on a UNIX system. Crack runs a *dictionary attack* (so named because Crack uses a common word dictionary as its source of passwords to guess) on UNIX system accounts.

A UNIX administrator should periodically run Crack to discover which accounts have passwords that can be easily guessed (such as common words or names). A UNIX administrator would notify users owning cracked accounts by telling them to use better passwords (those not so easily guessed).

Rather than guess passwords by trying to log in, Crack runs the crypt(3C) function and compares the result against the encrypted password string from */etc/shadow*. If the result matches the password string in */etc/shadow*, then Crack has guessed the account's password.

This is the primary reason why password strings were moved from */etc/ passwd* (the globally readable file) to */etc/shadow* (readable only by user root)—to hide these encrypted password strings that could otherwise be cracked. The UNIX administrator can easily run Crack because he has access to the */etc/shadow* file.

Crack can be downloaded from ftp://coast.cs.purdue.edu/pub/tools/unix/ crack/ .

Where to Go for Additional Information

AnswerBook

- AnswerBook2—System Administration Guide, Managing User Accounts and Groups

Man Pages

- crypt(3C)
- group(4)
- groups(1)
- grpck(1B)
- id(1M)
- login(1)
- logindevperm(4)
- passwd(4)
- pwck(1M)
- shadow(4)
- su(1M)

6

SYSTEM STARTUP AND SHUTDOWN

This chapter details the mechanisms controlling system startup and shutdown.[1]

What's in this chapter

- The meaning of system run levels
- The locations and identities of files controlling system startup and shutdown
- Tools and techniques you can use to audit and modify these files

Why this is important

A UNIX system administrator needs to understand the UNIX startup and shutdown mechanisms. Because these mechanisms are not universally understood, they could be the focus of attack or exploitation.

System Run Levels

It is important to be familiar with run levels—what they mean, how to determine a system's run level, and how to change the run level. This is because the tasks of booting and shutting down a system are nothing more than

---

1. For information on boot PROMs and on how information in the PROM controls system startup, see chapter 3.

changing the system's run levels. The active Solaris operating system is classified as running at a particular run level. A run level describes a system's general availability to users—for instance, whether services such as network file system (NFS) would be available. For example, booting a system is a change from level 0 (not running) to level 2 (multiuser mode). Getting a system into maintenance mode is a change from level 2 (multiuser mode) to level 1 (single-user mode). The run levels and their meanings are described in Table 6-1 and illustrated in a state-transition diagram (see Figure 6.1). See the init(1M) man page for additional information.

Determining Current Run Level

Use the *who* command to determine the system's current run level. In the following example, the system is in run level 3.

```
$ who -r
     .      (run-level 3)  Sep 7 15:44      3      0    S
$
```

Table 6-1 *System Run Levels*

Run Level	Description
0	Used to terminate the operating system and bring it to the PROM firmware prompt, where it is safe to power the system down.
1	Single-user administrative/maintenance mode.
2	Multiuser mode; all facilities except NFS are available over the network.
3	Multiuser mode, including NFS.
4	Not currently used by Solaris.
5	Used to bring the system to a state where it is safe to power it down, then power it down automatically on systems that support this.
6	Used to shut the system down, then reboot to the default run state (level 3 by default).
S or s	Single-user mode with all local filesystems mounted.

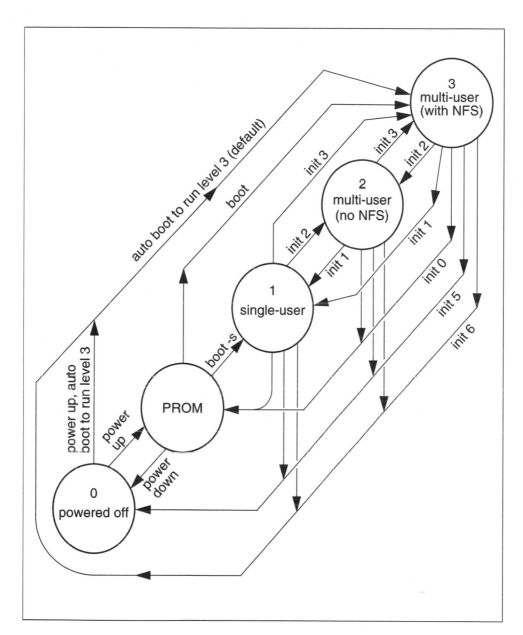

Figure 6.1 *Run Level State Transition Diagram*

System Startup

This section describes the steps that a Sun SPARC system performs during the startup, or boot, procedure.

PROM

The system PROM software and its environment variables load into memory and begin execution. The PROM reads the *auto-boot* and *boot-device* variables in order to determine whether the PROM should attempt a boot and, if so, from which device (*disk* or *net*). See chapter 3 for additional information.

init

The UNIX kernel is loaded, the root filesystem is mounted, and the *init* process is started. If the system is booting to single-user mode, booting stops and the following prompt is displayed:

```
INIT: SINGLE USER MODE
Type Ctrl-d to proceed with normal start-up,
(or give root password for system maintenance)
```

If the root password is entered, a root shell is launched. At this point the UNIX administrator is free to examine the system and perform any maintenance. When complete, the UNIX administrator exits the root shell by typing *exit* or ^D.

Multiuser Mode

When the UNIX system boots to multiuser mode (whether by default or when the administrator exits the root shell in single-user mode), the *init* process reads */etc/inittab* in order to determine what to do next.

The rc Mechanism

The rc mechanism is the collection of scripts that are executed when the system's run level is changed. The rc scripts actually carry out the tasks required to change from one run level to another. This section describes what the rc mechanism does to boot a system to multiuser mode.

The shell script */etc/rc2* is launched. First, */etc/rc2* determines the previous run state of the system. If the previous run state was 0, then each shell script in the directory */etc/rc2.d* that begins with the letter *S* is executed, effectively starting all local and network services except the NFS server.

It is easy to tell what happens when /*etc*/*rc2* runs, by listing the files in the directory /*etc*/*rc2.d*. During the rc2 startup phase, the files in /*etc*/*rc2.d* beginning with the letter *S* are executed in the same order that they appear when listed with the *ls* command. The standard convention for naming files in this directory is *Snndddd*, where *nn* is a two-digit number used to control the run sequence of the files and *dddd* is a string of characters describing the function of the script. A typical list of files in /*etc*/*rc2.d* is as follows:

K20spc	S47asppp	S74syslog	S89bdconfig
K60nfs.server	S69inet	S74xntpd	S91leoconfig
K76snmpdx	S70uucp	S75cron	S92rtvc-config
K77dmi	S71rpc	S76nscd	S92volmgt
README	S71sysid.sys	S80PRESERVE	S93cacheos.finish
S01MOUNTFSYS	S72autoinstall	S80lp	S96ab2mgr
S05RMTMPFILES	S72inetsvc	S80spc	S99audit
S20sysetup	S73cachefs.daemon	S85power	S99dtlogin
S21perf	S73nfs.client	S88sendmail	
S30sysid.net	S74autofs	S88utmpd	

At system startup, all of these files that start with the letter *S* (*S01MOUNT-FSYS*, then *S05RMTMPFILES*, and ending with *S99dtlogin*) are executed in order. The shell scripts are passed the single argument *start*. All other files in the directory are ignored (the files beginning with the letter *K* are run when the run level is changed from 3 to 2. The file *README* is not executed during any run level change.

Next, /*etc*/*rc2* executes all shell scripts found in the /*etc*/*rc.d* directory (this is a historical section which is usually empty). All shell scripts are passed the single argument *start*.

Further, *init* starts /*etc*/*rc3*, which in turn executes all scripts beginning with *S* in the directory /*etc*/*rc3.d*. All shell scripts are passed the single argument *start*.

Next, the service access controller (sac) is started. Sac initiates "port monitors," or processes, which listen on system serial ports in order to control access to the machine.

Finally, the *ttymon* process is started with the express purpose of getting a login prompt on the system console.

System Shutdown

This section describes the steps performed during a system shutdown procedure.

init

When a system administrator shuts the system down with a *shutdown* or *init 0* command, the *init* process first launches the script */etc/rc0*. In a manner similar to system startup, */etc/rc0* executes shell scripts in certain directories. They are as follows:

- */etc/shutdown.d* (this is for historical reasons only, and is usually empty). Shell scripts are passed the single argument *stop*.
- */etc/rc0.d/K**. Shell scripts are passed the single argument *stop*.
- */etc/rc0.d/S** (usually nothing here). Shell scripts are passed the single argument *stop*.

Next, */etc/rc0* attempts to kill all processes with the *killall* command, first by trying to kill all processes "gently," and then more forcefully. Finally, */etc/rc0* dismounts all mounted filesystems (except root).

uadmin

init finally runs the *uadmin* command. *uadmin* performs the following final steps of system shutdown:

- All processes are killed.
- The filesystem buffer cache is flushed.[2]
- The root filesystem is unmounted.
- The processor is halted.

More Information on *rc* Files

Many of the files in the startup and shutdown directories */etc/init.d*, */etc/rc0.d*, */etc/rc2.d*, */etc/rc2.d*, and */etc/rc3.d* are linked together.[3] For instance, */etc/init.d/sendmail*, */etc/rc2.d/S88sendmail*, and */etc/rc0.d/K57sendmail* are all the same file. Likewise, */etc/init.d/lp*, */etc/rc0.d/K20lp*, */etc/rc1.d/K20lp*, and */etc/rc2.d/S80lp* are the same file.

Startup and shutdown scripts are actually the same script. How can one script perform both startup and shutdown duties? Recall that these scripts

---

2. The filesystem buffer cache may contain writes to the disk(s) that have not yet been written to the disk itself. Thus it is important to complete these writes in order to ensure integrity of filesystem information.

3. In the case of rc files, these links are *hard links* as opposed to *symbolic links*. Refer to the ln(1) man page for more information.

are always passed the argument *start* or *stop*. Each script has sections of code
dedicated to startup and shutdown. A functional flow of an rc script follows:

```
initialize common variables
if (argument = "start")
    { startup section }
if (argument = "stop")
    { shutdown section }
if (argument = something else, or if no argument was entered)
    { print error message }
```

These design characteristics were included for the following reasons:

- The complete collection of all startup and shutdown files resides in */etc/
  init.d* (by definition).
- This makes it easier to customize system characteristics by easily modifying the startup and shutdown mechanisms.
- Files with a common purpose are actually the same file, simplifying the
  process of changing system characteristics.

An Example rc File Examined

We will examine the startup file controlling the *syslog* daemon here. This file
has three links:

- */etc/init.d/syslog*
- */etc/rc0.d/K55syslog*—executed by */etc/rc0* with the argument *stop* at
  system shutdown.
- */etc/rc1.d/K55syslog*—executed by */etc/rc1* with the argument *stop*
  when returning to single-user mode.
- */etc/rc2.d/S74syslog*—executed by */etc/rc2* with the argument *start*
  when booting to multiuser mode.

The file appears as follows:

```
#!/bin/sh
#
# Copyright (c) 1991, by Sun Microsystems, Inc.
#
#ident "@(#)syslog1.796/10/02 SMI"
case "$1" in

'start')
    if [ -f /etc/syslog.conf -a -f /usr/sbin/syslogd ]; then
        echo "syslog service starting."
        if [ ! -f /var/adm/messages ]
        then
        cp /dev/null /var/adm/messages
        fi
        /usr/sbin/syslogd 1>/dev/console 2>&1
    fi
    ;;
```

this section is executed by /etc/rc2 at startup

```
'stop')
   [ ! -f /etc/syslog.pid ] && exit 0
   syspid=`cat /etc/syslog.pid`
   if [ "$syspid" -gt 0 ]; then
      echo "Stopping the syslog service."
      kill -15 $syspid 2>&1 | /usr/bin/ro
   fi
   ;;
*)
   echo "Usage: /etc/init.d/syslog { start | stop }"
   ;;
esac
exit 0
```

this section is executed by /etc/rc2 at shutdown

A procedure for locating all of the links to a startup file follows.

1. Determine the inode number of the startup file. For example

```
% ls -li S74syslog
   (37798) -rwxr--r--   4 root     sys          621 Jul 15  1997 S74syslog
   %
```

In this example, the inode number is 37798. This number is used in the next step.

2. Find all other files in */etc* having the same inode number as *S74syslog*. Continuing the example:

```
% find /etc -inum 37798 -print
/etc/init.d/syslog
/etc/rc0.d/K55syslog
/etc/rc1.d/K55syslog
/etc/rc2.d/S74syslog
%
```

Auditing Startup and Shutdown Mechanisms

Because many system safeguards are either not running or are inaccessible during system startup and shutdown, the UNIX administrator must be especially careful to ensure the integrity of the startup and shutdown scripts. Two tools that can be used to audit system startup and shutdown scripts are COPS and Tripwire.

COPS

The *rc.chk* program in COPS is used to audit a system's startup and shutdown programs. rc.chk looks for any world-writable files in the */etc/init.d*, */etc/shutdown.d*, and */etc/rc** directories, as well as in the file */etc/inittab*. (COPS is described in detail in chapter 4.)

Tripwire

Tripwire (also discussed in chapter 4) can be configured to audit a system's startup and shutdown scripts. Make sure that Tripwire is checking the following files and directories.

- */etc* (contains rc scripts and numerous system configuration files)
- */etc/init.d* (contains startup and shutdown scripts)
- */etc/rc0.d* (contains shutdown scripts)
- */etc/rc1.d* (contains shutdown scripts)
- */etc/rc2.d* (contains startup scripts)
- */etc/rc3.d* (contains startup scripts)
- */usr/sbin* (system programs used during startup and shutdown)
- */kernel* (UNIX kernel and device drivers)

Modifying Startup and Shutdown Mechanisms

Adding Startup and Shutdown Scripts

The following procedures will streamline the process of adding startup and shutdown scripts.

- It is easier to copy an existing rc script than to create a new one.
- Rather than combine functions into single scripts, make separate scripts for each function. It will be easier to enable and disable each function independently.
- Using the *ln* command, make hard links to the files in */etc/init.d, /etc/rc0.d, /etc/rc2.d,* and */etc/rc3.d* as appropriate.

Changing Startup and Shutdown Scripts

The following procedures will help with the task of changing startup and shutdown scripts.

- Save a copy of the as-installed script. Make sure the copy does not start with the letter *S* or *K* (if they start with *S* or *K*, the original and copied files will be executed).
- Make liberal comments—details mastered today are often forgotten tomorrow.

Warning: Never have *rc* files execute programs or reference files in world-writable directories (programs or files can be added, removed,

or changed by intruders). Never include world-writable directories in PATH statements. Either practice opens potential security holes, since *rc* files run as root.

Disabling Startup and Shutdown Scripts

This procedure will make the task of removing startup and shutdown scripts easier in the long run.

- Rather than delete a startup or shutdown file, rename it by adding the letter *X* to the beginning of the file's name. This will preserve the file while at the same time preventing it from being executed. For example, rather than remove *S80lp*, rename it to *XS80lp* (this should be done only in */etc/rc0.d*, */etc/rc1.d*, */etc/rc2.d*, or */etc/rc3.d*—never in */etc/init.d*). Always use the *mv* command to rename these files. Using *cp* and *rm* will break the hard link between the files. I'll explain this in the next section.

More on Linked Startup Files

A UNIX administrator must take care when working with linked startup files (refer to the section on *rc* Files earlier in this chapter). For example, if a service needs to be temporarily disabled at system startup, rename the file rather than copying it. Renaming a file will preserve its inode number (and hence its link to the other filenames).

The right way to disable *syslog* at startup is

```
% cd /etc/rc2.d
% mv S74syslog X74syslog
%
```

The wrong way to disable *syslog* at startup is

```
% cd /etc/rc2.d
% cp S74syslog X74syslog
% rm S74syslog
%
```

The reason this second example is wrong lies in the future. The UNIX administrator, having disabled *syslog* with *cp* and *rm*, would probably reenable *syslog* with the following:

```
% cd /rc2.d
% cp X74syslog S74syslog
% rm X74syslog
%
```

The problem with this technique is that, while technically *syslog* startup will work properly, the UNIX administrator's procedures would break the logical link between */etc/rc2.d/S74syslog* and its counterparts */etc/init.d/ syslog*, */etc/rc0.d/K55syslog*, and */etc/rc1.d/K55syslog*. In this situation, modifications made to */etc/rc2.d/S74syslog* will not be reflected in its counterparts (and vice versa) because they are no longer the same file.

Where to Go for Additional Information

AnswerBook

- AnswerBook 2—System Administration Guide, Shutting Down and Booting a System

Man Pages

- boot(1M)
- kernel(1M)
- init(1M)
- inittab(4)
- init.d(4)
- killall(1M)
- ln(1)
- uadmin(1M)
- uadmin(2)

Publications

- *Boot and Run Levels*, SunSolve Technical Bulletin 1077

7

CRON AND *AT*

We will examine the UNIX job scheduling subsystems *cron* and *at* in this chapter.

What's in this chapter

- How *cron* and *at* work and how they are configured
- Common mistakes and pitfalls
- Auditing and mitigating security risks

Why this is important

Because *cron* and *at* are what UNIX administrators tend to use to add their own scheduled jobs to a system, *cron* and *at* tend to be a favorite haunt for hackers. Many UNIX administrators make common mistakes while using *cron* and *at*, and these mistakes can be easily avoided.

cron

What is cron?

cron is a job scheduling system used to execute regularly scheduled commands at predetermined times. Typically, the commands executed by *cron* are batch programs that are used to perform chores such as cycling logfiles, purging old information from files or directories, backing up and cleaning up databases, and so on. A program configured to be run by *cron* is commonly known as a *cron job*.

The UNIX administrator can control which users have access to *cron* (described later on in this chapter).

cron is configured to execute programs at regular intervals. These intervals are measured in minutes, hours, days, weeks, and months. Various simple and complex scheduling schemes can be configured for programs. Examples include

- Every five minutes
- Every day at 4:05 A.M.
- Every Monday at 4:05 A.M., 8:05 A.M., 12:05 P.M. and 4:05 P.M.
- At every hour on the 5th of each month
- Every December 31 at 8 A.M.

A user schedules jobs to run by configuring a *crontab* file. A *crontab* file contains each command a user wishes to run, together with the days and times that each command should be run. The syntax for a *crontab* file is

```
minute  hour  day-of-month  month  day-of-week  command
```

Minute is coded 0–59, *hour* is coded 0–23, *day-of-month* is coded 1–31, *month* is coded 1–12, and *day-of-week* is coded 0–6 (0 = Sunday, 1 = Monday, etc.). A field can have a single number, a list of comma-separated numbers, a range of numbers, or an asterisk.

Lines beginning with the # symbol are comment lines.

Here is an example *crontab* file.

```
#ident  "@(#)root 1.14    97/03/31 SMI"   /* SVr4.0 1.1.3.1 */
#
# root crontab
#
10 3 * * 0,4 /etc/cron.d/logchecker
10 3 * * 0   /usr/lib/newsyslog
45 3,15 * * 0 /usr/lib/fs/nfs/nfsfind
```

In this example, *logchecker* runs on Sundays and Thursdays at 3:10 A.M. *newsyslog* runs on Sundays at 3:10 A.M. *nfsfind* runs on Sundays at 3:45 A.M. and 3:45 P.M.

It is important to understand that there is no intrinsic beginning or end to the intervals described above. When *cron* runs a job every five minutes, it doesn't start tomorrow and end next week—*cron* runs the job every five minutes *forever*. Further, a program started by *cron* cannot tell *cron* to execute it again in five minutes as it is configured to nor can it tell *cron* not to execute it again.

Refer to the crontab(1M) man page for a complete description of *crontab* options.

How cron *Works*

At system startup, the *cron* daemon starts and reads all users' *crontab* files. *cron* also reads the file */etc/default/cron* to determine its generic behavior.

It then does nothing until it is time for the next job to be launched for any userid. *cron* forks (divides into two identical processes) and the *cron* parent process goes back to sleep. The *cron* child process changes its userid to that of the userid for which the job is being launched; the child then executes the job.

How cron *Is Configured*

cron examines the file */etc/default/cron* at system startup in order to determine the values of *CRONLOG, PATH*, and *SUPATH*. These values are shown in Table 7-1.

cron *User Configuration*

Users view and configure *cron* settings with the *crontab* command. The command for viewing a *crontab* file is *crontab -l*.

The recommended procedure for changing a *crontab* file is as follows:

1. *cd* to a directory readable (or searchable) *only* by the userid (this is because the text file generated in the next step might otherwise be readable by other users).

Table 7-1   /etc/default/cron *Settings*

Variable	Description
CRONLOG	*YES* (default)—*cron* will log all commands launched in the file */var/log/cron*. *NO*—*cron* will not log commands launched.
PATH	Default *PATH* for nonroot *cron* jobs. If unspecified, *PATH* = */usr/bin*.
SUPATH	Default *PATH* for root *cron* jobs. If unspecified, *PATH* = */usr/sbin:/usr/bin*.

2. Enter the command *crontab -l > mycronfile*. This causes the user's *crontab* file to be written to the file *mycronfile*.

3. Edit the file *mycronfile*. Make all desired changes.

4. Enter the command *crontab < mycronfile* . This causes the *cron* daemon to copy *mycronfile* to the actual location used by *cron*. The *cron* daemon also rereads the user's new *crontab* file, thereby introducing into its run schedule any changes the user made to his or her *crontab* file. *crontab* performs syntax checking on the *crontab* entry itself, but does not verify the existence or syntax of the command.

5. Enter the command *crontab -l*, in order to verify that the intended changes were made (refer to the second principle in chapter 2).

Note: I do not recommend use of the *crontab -e* command (which is another way to edit a *crontab* file). *crontab -e* places a world-readable copy of the user's *crontab* file in the */tmp* directory. Any user on the system would then be able to see that user's *crontab* file. Refer to the second principle in chapter 2.

User Access to cron *System*

Together, the two files */etc/cron.d/cron.allow* and */etc/cron.d/cron.deny* determine whether any particular user may or may not run the *crontab* command.

The file */etc/cron.d/cron.allow* lists which userids are allowed to use *crontab*. Similarly, */etc/cron.d/cron.deny* lists which userids are not allowed to use *crontab*. A typical *cron.deny* file follows.

```
daemon
bin
smtp
nuucp
listen
nobody
noaccess
```

The userids listed in this example do not have permission to run *crontab*.

A user is allowed to run *crontab* if the user's name appears in *cron.allow*, or if *cron.allow* does not exist and the user's name is not in *cron.deny*. A user is *not* allowed to run *crontab* if *cron.allow* exists and the user's name is not in it, or if *cron.allow* does not exist and the user's name is in *cron.deny*. If neither *cron.allow* nor *cron.deny* exists, a user is not allowed to run *crontab* (except root). See the crontab(1) man page for a complete explanation of the *cron.allow* and *cron.deny* logic.

Note that denial to *crontab* does not imply that a user's *cron* jobs will not be run. In fact, this can be a useful security feature. A system administrator can set up *cron* jobs for particular users, but can forbid the same user from viewing or modifying his or her *crontab* file through the use of */etc/cron.d/cron.allow* and */etc/cron.d/cron.deny*.

at

What Is at?

at is a scheduling system used to execute a command (or series of commands) at a single specified time in the future. The measures of time used are minutes, hours, days, and months. Absolute and relative intervals are allowed. Some scheduling examples include

- Now
- Plus two hours thirty minutes
- Tomorrow at 10 A.M.
- Four hours from now
- Two weeks from now at 4 P.M.

at is distinguished from *cron* primarily in that *cron* is used to execute a command over and over at a specific time, whereas *at* is used to execute a command *one time* at a particular time.

UNIX administrators can control which users have access to *at* in the same way they can control access to *cron*, described earlier.

How at *Works*

At system startup, the *cron* daemon starts and reads all entries in */var/spool/cron/atjobs*. These *at* job entries contain all of the environment information needed to run the *at* job, including the actual *at* job command(s). The names of the *at* job entries themselves tell *cron* when to start the *at* job; the format of the filename is *n.m*, where *n* is the number of seconds since January 1, 1970, and *m* is a sequence digit used to distinguish multiple *at* jobs configured to start at exactly the same second. The sequence digit value is a, b, etc.

The internal mechanism for starting *at* jobs is essentially the same as for *cron* jobs: *cron* forks, the parent process goes back to sleep, and the child process changes its userid to that of the userid for which the job is being launched; the child then executes the *at* job file in */var/spool/cron/atjobs*.

User Access to at *System*

The files */etc/cron.d/at.allow* and */etc/cron.d/at.deny* work exactly like the files */etc/cron.d/cron.allow* and */etc/cron.d/cron.deny* described earlier.

Common Mistakes to Avoid

Failure to Adequately Conceal Programs Launched by cron

Scripts and programs launched by *cron*—particularly for userid root—should not be readable by anyone but the user/owner.

Leaving crontab *Files Lying Around for All to See*

Temporary copies of *crontab* files should not be left in places (like */tmp*) where others can see them and exploit possible weaknesses revealed in *cron* entries.

Unsecure PATH *Elements in Scripts Launched by* cron

The *PATH* statement (whether set in */etc/default/cron* or the launched program itself) should contain no unsecure directories.

For example, *PATH* in a *cron*-launched shell script for user root is set to */tmp:/usr/bin*. A hacker knowing this could create executable programs in the */tmp* directory that were the same name as commands used in the *cron*-launched shell script. Then, when the shell script ran a particular command, the hacker's copy in */tmp* would be run (as root) instead of the correct version in */usr/bin*.

> **Note: If *PATH* were set to */usr/bin:/tmp*, a clever hacker could still have some fun. The intended command used by a *cron*-launched script could be removed from */usr/bin* (*only* if there was already a security problem with permissions incorrectly set in */usr/bin*); this would cause the script to run the hacker's version in */tmp*.**

Indeterminate PATH *Elements in Scripts Launched by* cron

The *PATH* statement should contain no indeterminate directories. *PATH* should not contain any "~" or "." entries, which could be unsecure (readable or—worse—writable by others). "~" or "." in *PATH* open the door to Trojan horse attacks.[1]

---

1. Refer to the Glossary for a definition of Trojan horse.

Use of stdin *and* stdout *in* cron *and* at *Jobs*

Because there is no user terminal or terminal session associated with a *cron* or *at* job, *stdin* and *stdout* must be redirected. Specifically, any command in a *cron* job reading from *stdin* will get an immediate end-of-file (as though the user, if the command were running from a terminal, pressed Ctrl-D).

Any command in a *cron* job writing to *stdout* will have its output sent to the owner of the *cron* job in a mail message. This may or may not be the desired result.

Auditing Tools

Tripwire

Tripwire, described in chapter 4, should be configured to regularly examine the following files and directories:

- */etc/cron.d*—the directory containing *cron* and *at* configuration files and the *logchecker* program
- */etc/default*—the directory containing system default behavior files, including *cron* and *at*
- */var/cron*—the directory containing the *cron* log
- */var/spool/cron*—the directory containing *cron*'s spool area; the *contents* of */var/spool/cron/atjobs* should not be checked unless you do not run *at* jobs, or unless the frequency at which *at* jobs change is low (a yearly job, for instance). This is because the contents of */var/spool/cron/atjobs* will change frequently if *at* is heavily used.
- */etc/cron.d/cron.allow*—one of two files determining access to *cron*
- */etc/cron.d/cron.deny*—one of two files determining access to *cron*
- */etc/cron.d/at.allow*—one of two files determining access to *at*
- */etc/cron.d/at.deny*—one of two files determining access to *at*

COPS

COPS, described in chapter 4, should be set up to run *cron.chk*, the program used to examine *cron* jobs for possible security weaknesses.

Where to Go for Additional Information

AnswerBook

- AnswerBook 2—System Administration Guide, Managing System Resources, Scheduling System Events

Man Pages

- at(1)
- cron(1M)
- crontab(1)
- crontab(4)

Publications

- *Administration and Usage of Crontab*, SunSolve White Paper 918
- *Crontab Administration and Usage*, SunSolve Infodoc 3959

8

SYSTEM LOGS

UNIX system logging capabilities and configuration are described in this chapter.

What's in this chapter

- Description and configuration of *syslog*
- *loginlog*
- *sulog*
- Last log
- Other system logs

Why this is important

UNIX systems record security (and other) events in system logs. UNIX system administrators need to know how these logging mechanisms function so that they can be understood and modified as needed.

What Is a System Log

A system log is a recording of certain events. The kind of events found in a system log is determined by the nature of the particular log and any configurations used to control those events that are logged.

System logs are usually human-readable text files containing a timestamp and other information specific to the message or subsystem.

syslog

syslog is UNIX's general-purpose logging mechanism and consists of the following:

- *syslog()*—an application program interface (API) referenced by several standard system utilities and available to anyone writing software in the C programming language (this topic will not be explored further in this book)
- *logger*—a UNIX command used to add single-line entries to the system log
- */etc/syslog.conf*—the configuration file used to control the logging and routing of system log events
- *syslogd*—the system daemon used to receive and route system log events from *syslog()* calls and *logger* commands

syslog *Facilities and Severity Levels*

syslog system messages are categorized by facility and severity. The facilities are listed in Table 8-1. *syslog* severity categories are listed, in decreasing order, in Table 8-2.

Table 8-1   syslog *Facilities*

Facility	Message Description
user	Generated by user processes. This is the default facility; messages not fitting any of the other listed categories here are classified as facility *user*.
kern	Generated by the system kernel.
mail	Generated by the e-mail system.
daemon	Generated by system daemons, such as *ftpd*.
auth	Generated by the authorization programs *login*, *su*, and *getty*.
lpr	Generated by the printing system.
news	Generated by the UseNet News system.
uucp	Generated by the UUCP system.
cron	Generated by *cron* and *at*.

Table 8-1   syslog *Facilities (Continued)*

Facility	Message Description
local0-7	Generated by up to eight locally defined categories numbered 0 through 7.
mark	Generated by *syslog* itself for timestamping logs.

Table 8-2   syslog *Severity Levels*

Severity	Description
emerg	The most severe messages, such as immediate system shutdown.
alert	System conditions requiring immediate attention.
crit	Critical system conditions, such as failing hardware or software.
err	Other system errors.
warning	Warning messages.
notice	Notices requiring attention at a later time.
info	Informational messages.
debug	Messages for debugging purposes.

syslog *Message Classification Notation*

The notation used to classify *syslog* messages is *facility.severity*. For example, a **warning** message from the printing system would be classified as *lpr.warning*.

For any severity level specified, messages are generated for that and all less-severe levels. For example, *lpr.warning* causes **warning**-, **err**-, **crit**-, **alert**-, and **emerg**-level messages from the lpr service to be generated.

Wild card notation is used in *syslog* notation. For example, **.err* means severity level **err** messages from all facilities (except the mark facility).

syslog *Configuration*

syslog configuration consists of routing error messages from various facilities (and at various severity levels) to one or more of the following destinations:

- Logfiles anywhere on the system
- Another computer running *syslog* with its own *syslog* configuration
- Active users on the system

The notation for *syslog.conf* messages is *selector <tab> action* (note that the character between selector and action *must* be a *tab* and *must not* be one or more spaces). *Action* consists of a system name, pathname, or userid. *Selector* consists of one or more semicolon-separated facility-severity pairs taking the form *facility.level[;facility.level]* . *facility* consists of one or more comma-separated facilities. Here are examples of complete entries.

1. All **debug** (and higher) messages in the mail system are written to the file */var/log/mail.debug.log*.

```
mail.debug          /var/log/mail.debug.log
```

2. **Crit** messages from all facilities are sent to the users *root* and *adm* if they are logged in.

```
*.crit              root,adm
```

syslog is configured in the */etc/syslog.conf* file. A typical *syslog.conf* file follows. First, several comment lines appear.

```
#ident "@(#)syslog.conf 1.4 96/10/11 SMI" /* SunOS 5.0 */
#
# Copyright (c) 1991-1993, by Sun Microsystems, Inc.
#
# syslog configuration file.
#
# This file is processed by m4 so be careful to quote (' ') names
# that match m4 reserved words. Also, within ifdef's, arguments
# containing commas must be quoted.
#
```

The next line directs severity **err** messages from all facilities (*) and severity **notice** messages from the kern and auth facilities to be directed to the device */dev/console*.

```
*.err;kern.notice;auth.notice    /dev/console
```

The next line directs severity **err** messages from all facilities, severity **debug** messages from the kern facility, severity **notice** from the daemon facility, and severity **crit** from the mail facility to all be directed to the */var/adm/messages* file.

```
*.err;kern.debug;daemon.notice;mail.crit    /var/adm/messages
```

The next line directs severity **alert** messages from all facilities and severity **err** messages from the kern and daemon facilities to be directed to the user *operator*.

```
*.alert;kern.err;daemon.err  operator
```

The next line directs severity **alert** messages from all facilities to the user *root*.

```
*.alert  root
```

The next line directs severity **emerg** messages from all facilities to all logged-in users.

```
*.emerg  *
# if a non-loghost machine chooses to have authentication messages
# sent to the loghost machine, un-comment out the following line:
#auth.notice  ifdef('LOGHOST', /var/log/authlog, @loghost)
```

The next line directs all severity **debug** messages from the mail facility to the file */var/log/syslog* if the local system is named *loghost*[1]; otherwise it directs them to the machine loghost as defined in */etc/hosts*, DNS, or NIS.

```
mail.debug  ifdef('LOGHOST', /var/log/syslog, @loghost)
#
```

The next set of lines directs messages from the user facility to the console, to the file */var/adm/messages*, and to the user's root and operator only if the local system is named *loghost*.

```
# non-loghost machines will use the following lines to cause "user"
# log messages to be logged locally.
#
ifdef('LOGHOST', ,
user.err     /dev/console
user.err     /var/adm/messages
user.alert   'root, operator'
user.emerg   *
)
```

Debugging syslog

syslog has a debugging mechanism that allows the UNIX administrator to trace the emergence and flow of *syslog* messages. *syslog* is debugged in two parts:

- On startup, *syslog* displays a two-dimensional matrix illustrating its configuration as defined in the configuration file */etc/syslog.conf.*
- In real time, *syslog* displays inbound *syslog* messages and specifies how the messages are processed.

Follow this procedure to turn on *syslog* debugging.

1. Kill *syslogd* process with a *kill -15 pid* command.

---

1. A system is usually defined as *loghost* in the */etc/hosts* file. For example

```
# /etc/hosts
127.0.0.1     localhost
149.46.23.16  lpserver loghost
```

2. Restart *syslogd* with the command */usr/sbin/syslogd -d*. This will start *syslogd* in debug mode. *syslogd* will first read its configuration file and write output similar to the following:

```
# /usr/sbin/syslogd -d
getnets() found 1 addresses, they are: 0.0.0.0.2.2
amiloghost() testing 127.0.0.1.2.2
I am loghost
amiloghost() testing 127.0.0.1.2.2
nlogs 6
```

The next section is *syslogd* reading from *syslog.conf*.

```
cfline(*.err;kern.notice;auth.notice            /dev/console)
cfline(*.err;kern.debug;daemon.notice;mail.crit /var/adm/messages)
cfline(*.alert;kern.err;daemon.err              operator)
cfline(*.alert                                  root)
cfline(*.emerg                                  *)
cfline(mail.debug                               /var/log/syslog)
```

Here, *syslogd* prints version information.

```
syslogd: version 1.59
Started: Fri May 15 21:07:26 1998
Input message count: system 0, network 0
```

This section is a matrix of inputs and outputs. The *value* in each position represents the minimum severity level (7 = debug, 6 = info, 5 = notice, 4 = warning, 3 = err, 2 = crit, 1 = alert, 0 = emerg, x = nothing). Each *column* is a different service (left to right: kern, user, mail, daemon, auth, lpr, news, uucp, cron, local0–local7, mark). Each *row* represents a different output (a file or user).

```
# Outputs: 6

5 3 3 3 5 3 3 3 3 3 3 3 3 3 3 3 3 3 3 3 3 3 3 3 3 X CONSOLE: /dev/console
7 3 2 5 3 3 3 3 3 3 3 3 3 3 3 3 3 3 3 3 3 3 3 3 3 X FILE: /var/adm/messages
3 1 1 3 1 1 1 1 1 1 1 1 1 1 1 1 1 1 1 1 1 1 1 1 1 X USERS: operator
1 1 1 1 1 1 1 1 1 1 1 1 1 1 1 1 1 1 1 1 1 1 1 1 1 X USERS: root
0 0 0 0 0 0 0 0 0 0 0 0 0 0 0 0 0 0 0 0 0 0 0 0 0 X WALL:
X X 7 X X X X X X X X X X X X X X X X X X X X X X X FILE: /var/log/syslog


Per File Statistics
File                    Tot     Dups    Nofwd   Errs
----                    ---     ----    -----   ----
/dev/console            0       0       0       0
/var/adm/messages       0       0       0       0
operator                0       0       0       0
root                    0       0       0       0
WALL                    0       0       0       0
/var/log/syslog         0       0       0       0

syslogd: restarted
off & running....
Logging to FILE /var/adm/messages
Logging to FILE /var/adm/messages
```

3. Wait for or cause events that will log to *syslog*.
   Example 1: The following command is run

   ```
   logger -p auth.notice "This is a test."
   ```

   and then *syslogd* in debug mode will display

   ```
   Logging to CONSOLE /dev/console
   ```

   and the following text will appear on the console window.

   ```
   May 15 16:21:31 alpha pete: This is a test.
   ```

   Example 2: the following command is run

   ```
   logger -p mail.crit "This is the next test."
   ```

   and then *syslogd* in debug mode will display

   ```
   Logging to FILE /var/adm/messages
   ```

   and the following entry will be written to */var/adm/messages*.

   ```
   May 15 16:21:49 alpha pete: This is the next test.
   ```

4. To stop testing *syslog*, press ^C in the window where *syslogd* is running
   in debug mode. *syslog* will display the following message:

   ```
   ^Csyslogd: going down on signal 2
   syslogd: going down on signal 2
   #
   ```

5. Restart *syslogd* in normal mode with the command */usr/sbin/syslogd* .

Note: *syslogd* should be run in debug mode only interactively. The system will hang if *syslogd* is run in debug mode in the system startup scripts (usually */etc/rc2.d/S74syslog*).

loginlog

Unsuccessful login attempts after five consecutive failures are logged in the file */var/adm/loginlog*, only if the file */var/adm/loginlog* exists and is owned by root, group sys, and has read and write permissions only for root. Follow this procedure to create and configure the file */var/adm/loginlog* for unsuccessful login attempt logging:

1. Log in (or *su*) as root.
2. Enter the command *touch /var/adm/loginlog*.
3. Enter the command *chown root /var/adm/loginlog*.
4. Enter the command *chgrp sys /var/adm/loginlog*.
5. Enter the command *chmod 600 /var/adm/loginlog*.

The following is an example entry written into */var/adm/loginlog*.

```
adm:/dev/pts/9:Tue May  5 21:07:49 1998
```

This entry indicates that a user attempted to log in as user *adm* on port */dev/pts/9* on May 5 at 9:07 P.M.

sulog

The *sulog* file, */var/adm/sulog*, is a log containing all attempts (whether successful or not) of the *su* command. An entry is added to the *sulog* file every time the *su* command is executed. An example of the *sulog* file follows:

```
SU 02/03 22:47 + tty root-daemon
SU 02/07 15:41 + pts/8 pete-root
SU 02/07 15:45 + console root-daemon
SU 02/13 21:43 + pts/5 pete-root
SU 02/13 22:18 + pts/5 pete-root
SU 02/15 20:03 + console root-daemon
SU 02/15 20:06 + pts/3 pete-root
SU 02/15 20:10 + tty root-daemon
SU 02/23 20:51 - pts/6 pete-root
SU 02/23 21:14 + console root-daemon
```

The fields in *sulog* are: date, time, successful (+) or unsuccessful (-), port, user executing the *su* command, and user being switched to. In the preceding example, all *su* attempts were successful, except for the attempt on 2/23 at 20:51, when user *pete* unsuccessfully attempted to *su* to user root.

Last Log

The *last* command displays login/logout and system boot information in time sequence order. *last* reads the binary file */var/adm/wtmpx*, which is written to every time a user logs in or out and when the system is rebooted. An example *last* command output is

```
pete        console      :0        Wed Apr  1 20:52    still logged in
pete        console      :0        Wed Apr  1 20:40 - 20:51  (00:10)
pete        console      :0        Mon Feb 23 21:31 - 20:39 (36+23:08)
reboot      system boot            Mon Feb 23 21:13
pete        console      :0        Sun Feb 15 20:03 - 21:11 (8+01:07)
reboot      system boot            Sun Feb 15 20:02
pete        console      :0        Sat Feb  7 16:05 - 20:00 (8+03:55)
reboot      system boot            Sat Feb  7 15:44
pete        console      :0        Tue Feb  3 22:50 - 15:42 (3+16:51)
root        console      :0        Tue Feb  3 21:04 - 22:50  (01:46)
pete        console      :0        Tue Feb  3 20:59 - 21:03  (00:04)
root        console      :0        Tue Feb  3 20:52 - 20:59  (00:06)
pete        console      :0        Tue Feb  3 20:38 - 20:52  (00:13)
```

```
root        console      :0              Tue Feb  3 20:35 - 20:38  (00:02)
pete        console      :0              Tue Feb  3 20:19 - 20:35  (00:15)
pete        console      :0              Tue Feb  3 20:18 - 20:19  (00:00)
pete        console      :0              Tue Feb  3 20:18 - 20:18  (00:00)
root        console      :0              Tue Feb  3 20:12 - 20:18  (00:05)
reboot      system boot                  Tue Feb  3 20:11
reboot      system boot                  Tue Feb  3 18:56
root        console      :0              Fri Jan 30 09:11 - 09:12  (00:00)
reboot      system boot                  Wed Jan 28 11:26
root        console      :0              Fri Jan 23 15:00 - 11:25 (4+20:25)
reboot      system boot                  Thu Jan 22 15:14

wtmp begins Thu Jan 22 15:14
```

Volume Manager Log

The volume manager log, */var/adm/vold.log*, is used by the Solaris Volume Manager (the software that manages the CD-ROM and diskette drives and automates the user-system interaction when using those drives).

Install Log

The system install log, found in */var/sadm/system/logs/install_log*, is generated when Solaris is installed on the system. The install log contains all of the character output generated throughout Solaris installation. The log contains information such as disk partitioning and formatting, software module installation status, and mount points.

sysidtool Log

The *sysidtool* log, found in */var/sadm/system/logs/sysidtool.log*, is generated by the *sysidtool* tool suite, itself run automatically at system installation time or when the system is unconfigured with *sys-unconfig*. This log can be useful for double-checking the configuration of a newly installed or reinstalled system to see what, if any, changes have occurred.

Tools to Help with Logging

Logcheck

Logcheck is a public-domain tool used to examine *syslog* and any other logfiles. When something suspicious is found, it sends an e-mail message alerting the UNIX administrator that something is up. Logcheck employs a filter file containing keywords; when a log entry containing a keyword is found, a message is sent. Logcheck utilizes the "report everything that is not explicitly ignored" feature—a nice feature, since it can be difficult to know in advance every possible type of message that could be logged. It is run from *cron* as often as needed (once per hour is the recommended minimum frequency).

This is a description of Logcheck configuration files.

- *logcheck.hacking*—File of known active hacking attack messages to look for. Only put messages in here if you are sure they won't cause false alarms. This is a rather generic way of checking for malicious activity and can be inaccurate unless you know what past hacking activity looks like. The default is to look for generic Internet security scan (ISS) probes and obvious *sendmail* attacks.

- *logcheck.violations*—File of security violation patterns to specifically look for. This file should contain keywords that administrators should probably be aware of. It may or may not cause false alarms sometimes. Generally, anything that is negative is put in this file. It may miss some items, but these will be caught by the next check. Move suspicious items into this file to have them reported regularly.

- *logcheck.violations.ignore*—File that contains more complete sentences that have keywords from the violations file. These keywords are normal and are not cause for concern but could cause a false alarm. An example of this is the word "refused" which is often reported by *sendmail* if a message cannot be delivered; it can also be a more serious security violation of a system attaching to illegal ports. Obviously, you would include the *sendmail* warning as part of this file. Use your judgment before putting words in here or you can miss really important events. The default is to leave this file with only a couple of entries. **Do not leave the file empty**. *grep* will assume that an **empty** file means a wildcard and will ignore everything! The basic configuration allows for the more frequent *sendmail* error. Again, be careful what you put in this file.

- *logcheck.ignore*—This is the name of a file that contains patterns that we should ignore if found in a logfile. If you have repeated false alarms or want specific errors ignored, you should put them in here. Once again, be as specific as possible, and go easy on the wildcards.

    Logcheck may be obtained from

    http://www.psionic.com/abacus/logcheck/

    ftp://coast.cs.purdue.edu/pub/tools/unix/logcheck/

Where to Go for Additional Information

Man Pages

- last(1)
- loginlog(4)
- login(1)
- logger(1)
- sulog(4)
- sysidtool(1M)
- syslog(3)
- syslogd(1)
- syslog.conf(4)
- sys-unconfig(1M)
- vold(1M)

Part Three

The Network-Connected System

Network communications have multiplied the usefulness of computers and information, but connecting any system to a network increases the risk of mishap. The amount of risk is proportional to the number of people who can access the system and to the number and type of services that are accessible by these people.

Topics covered include

- Chapter 9, "Network Interfaces and Services"
- Chapter 10, "Network/System Architecture"
- Chapter 11, "Electronic Mail"
- Chapter 12, "Printing"
- Chapter 13, "Network Access Control" (Authentication, Firewalls, Intrusion Detection, and Virtual Private Networks)
- Chapter 14, "Name Services" (DNS, NIS, NIS+)
- Chapter 15, "NFS and the Automounter"

9

NETWORK
INTERFACES AND
SERVICES

We'll talk about physical and logical network interfaces and network services in this chapter.

What's in this chapter

- About network interfaces
- How network interfaces are configured
- About network services
- How network services are configured
- How routing information is configured
- How to use *snoop* (Sun's network sniffer program)

Why this is important

UNIX system network interfaces and services are the facilities used to access a UNIX system over a network; UNIX system security is frequently compromised by improper knowledge and configuration of network interfaces and services.

Networks

A network is a specific collection of equipment and wiring set up to facilitate the communications between two or more computers (or other network devices such as printers, plotters, scanners, and modems). If you need more information on networks and how they work, refer to the list of publications at the end of this chapter.

Network Interfaces

A network interface is the physical part of a Sun computer used to communicate via a network to other computers. The interface consists of electronic circuitry plus one or more physical connectors used for attaching network cables to the computer. A network interface is configured with commands described later in this chapter.

Network Interface Characteristics

A network interface on a Sun system has a number of characteristics worth knowing about. These characteristics are

- **MAC address**. MAC is an acronym for Media Access Control, the name of the ISO communications layer 2, known as the data link layer.[1] Otherwise known as the *Ethernet address* or *physical address*, the MAC address is a generally unchangeable characteristic usually "burned" into each Ethernet network interface card in the computer. An example MAC address is 8:0:20:22:e3:e2. Ethernet standards assume that no two network interfaces (in the entire world) have the same MAC address.

  Note: In many cases (particularly in the newer architectures) the MAC addresses of network interface cards (NICs) *are* in fact changeable. Solaris does provide a way of changing a network interface's MAC address; this is disussed in the section on network interface configuration later in this chapter. However, except in rare circumstances (such as a server with multiple network interfaces connected to the same network), MAC addresses should be considered unchangeable and should not be modified. An example later in this chapter shows how to change the MAC address.

- **IP address**. This is the generally known network address assigned to the computer. An example IP address is 204.63.68.119. Unlike a MAC address (which is generally unchangeable), an IP address is defined and configured by the UNIX or network administrator according to a predetermined site addressing plan.

- **Subnet mask**. While not actually a characteristic of the network interface itself, the subnet mask is a characteristic used by the network drivers to determine whether outbound packets should be sent directly to their destinations or to the default router.

- **Promiscuous mode**. This characteristic, when turned on, determines that every packet seen on the network should be passed to the software drivers and buffered, presumably for use by a program running on the

---

1. For more information on TCP/IP concepts, please refer to the references listed at the end of this chapter.

system. Ordinarily, only those network packets actually intended for a particular computer are passed to the software drivers and buffered; the rest (those packets intended for *other* computers) are ignored. The *snoop* program places the network interface in promiscuous mode so that it can display all packets on the network. See the example *snoop* session at the end of this chapter.

Network Interface Configuration

Several commands are used to configure a network interface. Also, the static values in some configuration files determine initial network interface settings after system boot.

ifconfig

The *ifconfig* command is used to examine and change the following network interface characteristics.

- Status (up or down)
- IP address
- Subnet mask
- Broadcast address (the address used to send a packet to all computers on the same subnet)
- Maximum transmission unit (mtu)—the maximum packet size
- MAC address

For additional information see the ifconfig(1M) man page. The following are examples of *ifconfig*.

1. Show configuration settings for all interfaces, single physical interface.

```
# ifconfig -a
lo0: flags=849<UP,LOOPBACK,RUNNING,MULTICAST> mtu 8232
        inet 127.0.0.1 netmask ff000000
le0: flags=863<UP,BROADCAST,NOTRAILERS,RUNNING,MULTICAST> mtu 1500
        inet 207.127.1.83 netmask ffffff00 broadcast 207.127.1.255
#
```

The first interface listed is *lo0*, the loopback interface. Every system by definition has a loopback interface.

The second interface listed is *le0*, a 10MB Ethernet interface.

2. For interface *le0*, change the IP address to 207.127.1.88 and the netmask to 255.255.255.0.

```
# ifconfig le0 207.127.1.88 netmask 255.255.255.0
#
```

3. For interface *le0*, change the IP address to 207.127.1.88; the netmask is looked up in the file */etc/inet/netmasks,* in NIS or NIS+, depending upon the value for the *netmasks* entry in */etc/nsswitch.conf.*

```
# ifconfig le0 207.127.1.88 netmask +
#
```

4. Shut down interface *le0*.

```
# ifconfig le0 down
#
```

5. Change interface *le0* MAC address.

```
# ifconfig le0 ether aa:bb:cc:00:11:22
#
```

For more information refer to the ifconfig(1M) man page.

ndd

The *ndd* command is used to examine and change network device driver characteristics. Most of the settings that can be changed in the network drivers are not security related but are instead involved with network tuning. However, there are a few settings that the security-conscious administrator needs to know about. I describe them in the following sections.

Note: The *ndd* settings described here are related to packet routing on a network. These settings, some of which may alter the behavior of the network, should be coordinated with the LAN administrator.

Warning: Sun does not publish the */dev/ip* and */dev/tcp* tunable parameters; they may change at any time.

Configure IP Forwarding

IP forwarding is a characteristic of a Sun workstation acting as a *router*; in other words, a workstation having connections to two or more networks and forwarding network packets between them.

With inexpensive routers available today, a UNIX workstation seldom gets pressed into service as a router. However, it may still be common for a UNIX workstation to have connections to two or more networks—not for the purpose of being a router, but to give nodes on the two or more networks access to the service offered by the workstation. Figure 9.1 illustrates this distinction.

The Solaris network drivers give the workstation connected to two or more networks the ability to act as a router and forward packets. This is accomplished with the *ndd* command, shown in these examples.[2]

---

2. The usual underscoring in these examples is omitted because the underscores would hide the underscores in the commands themselves; i.e., : "ip_forwarding."

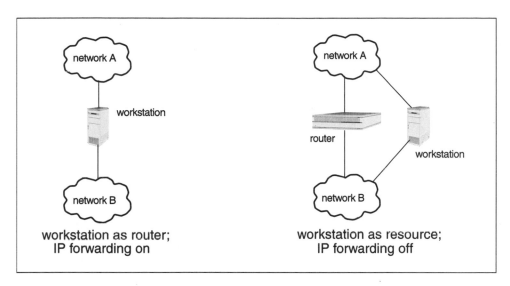

Figure 9.1   *Workstations with Multiple Network Connections*

1. Display the packet forwarding characteristic. In this example, IP forwarding is off (0). If IP forwarding is set or on, the result will be 1, as shown in example 2.

```
# ndd -get /dev/ip ip forwarding
0
#
```

2. Turn on packet forwarding.

```
# ndd -set /dev/ip ip_forwarding 1
#
```

Warning: Example 2 should be performed *only* in a situation where the system is deliberately being used as a router.

3. Turn off packet forwarding. I recommend that this entry be added to the end of */etc/init.d/inetinit*.

```
# ndd -set /dev/ip ip_forwarding 0
#
```

Ignore Redirects

A redirect packet is an Internet control message protocol (ICMP) message telling a system (or router) to change its routing table. This is potentially dangerous because an intruder, knowing that a Solaris system is acting as a router, can attempt to alter its routing table (for instance, as part of a denial-of-service attack) by sending it redirects.

Any Solaris system—even one configured as a router—should ignore redirects. To have the system do so, add the following entry to the end of */etc/init/inetinit*.

```
ndd -set /dev/ip ip_ignore_redirects 1
```

Send Redirects

Not only should Solaris systems ignore redirect packets, but they should also be configured to not send redirect packets. To accomplish this, add the following entry to the end of */etc/init/inetinit*.

```
ndd -set /dev/ip ip_send_redirects 0
```

Forward Directed Broadcasts

A directed broadcast packet is a packet whose destination IP address is the broadcast address of a network. For instance, the broadcast address for the class C network 10.31.6.0 is 10.31.6.255. Directed broadcasts are potentially dangerous because they permit a single packet to be sent to all systems on a network.

When a Solaris system is configured to be a router, it should *not* forward directed broadcasts. Add the following entry to the end of */etc/init/inetinit*.

```
ndd -set /dev/ip ip_forward_directed_broadcasts 0
```

Configure Source Routing

A source-routed packet is a packet wherein the sender specifies the path by which the packet will be taken to its destination, as opposed to letting the routers choose the best path. These are potentially dangerous because they may permit an intruder to launch an attack on a network.

I recommend that the Solaris system not forward source-routed packets. Add the following entry to the end of */etc/init/inetinit*.

```
ndd -set /dev/ip ip_forward_src_routed 0
```

Turn Off IP Forwarding with /etc/ notrouter

IP forwarding can also be disabled by creating the file */etc/notrouter* (Solaris 2.4 and newer) and then rebooting the system. This is not foolproof, however, as an intruder with root access can simply turn IP forwarding back on with the *ndd* command.

netstat

The *netstat* command is used to examine network device driver status, including the following:

- Routing tables
- Active sockets
- Streams statistics
- ARP tables
- Statistics by protocol

While I have listed some typical examples of *netstat* commands and their output below, it is beyond the scope of this book to exhaustively explain every permutation of what *netstat* output should look like. Rather, the security-conscious administrator should have a thorough understanding of her systems and how they relate to the surrounding network architecture. Only such an understanding will enable the systems administrator to recognize things that don't look right.

1. Display routing tables. A routing table is used by the system to determine how to send outgoing packets to ensure that they reach their destination.

```
# netstat -r

Routing Table:
Destination                Gateway              Flags  Ref  Use    Interface
--------------------       ------------------   -----  ----- ------ ---------
localhost                  localhost            UH     0    8      lo0
Subnet_0                   vulcan               U      3    2168   le0
BASE-ADDRESS.MCAST.NET     vulcan               U      3    0      le0
default                    router.vulcan.com    UG     0    4474
#
```

2. Display active sockets. A socket is an identifier associated with a specific network conversation between this system and another system. This display also shows the system's readiness to communicate with other systems via specific network services. Only part of the output is shown.

```
# netstat -a

UDP
    Local Address        Remote Address        State
-------------------- --------------------  -------
      *.route                              Idle
```

```
*.*                              Unbound
*.sunrpc                         Idle
*.*                              Unbound
*.32771                          Idle
*.name                           Idle
*.biff                           Idle
*.talk                           Idle
*.time                           Idle
*.echo                           Idle
*.discard                        Idle
*.daytime                        Idle
*.chargen                        Idle
*.32772                          Idle
*.32773                          Idle
*.32774                          Idle
*.32775                          Idle
*.32776                          Idle
*.32777                          Idle
*.32778                          Idle
*.32779                          Idle
*.lockd                          Idle
   .
   .
   .
```

3. Display network interfaces. This display shows the system's network interfaces and some basic statistics about each one.

```
# netstat -i
Name  Mtu  Net/Dest   Address     Ipkts     Ierrs Opkts     Oerrs Collis  Queue
lo0   8232 loopback   localhost   24939149  0     24939149  0     0       0
hme0  1500 Subnet_1   vulcan      221166262 0     220093434 0     0       0
hme2  1500 10.0.31.0  kaos31      3062352   0     6412005   0     0       0
#
```

4. Display the address resolution protocol (ARP) table. The ARP table is the translation between the MAC address and IP addresses.

```
# netstat -p
Net to Media Table
Device    IP Address               Mask           Flags  Phys Addr
------    --------------------     ---------------  -----  ---------------
hme2      spock                    255.255.255.255         08:00:20:8d:b6:c1
hme0      hermes                   255.255.255.255         00:10:ff:d0:78:a1
hme0      bones                    255.255.255.255         08:00:20:86:76:24
hme2      BASE-ADDRESS.MCAST.NET   240.0.0.0        SM     01:00:5e:00:00:00
hme0      BASE-ADDRESS.MCAST.NET   240.0.0.0        SM     01:00:5e:00:00:00
hme0      vulcan                   255.255.255.255  SP     08:00:20:7d:69:bd
#
```

For more information refer to the netstat(1M) man page.

Note: *netstat* is a powerful diagnostic tool. It is important for the UNIX administrator to be familiar with how *netstat* works and how to interpret its output. Those unfamiliar with UNIX network concepts

should consider one or more of the books mentioned at the end of this chapter.

/etc/inet/hosts

The /etc/inet/hosts file contains information used to configure system interfaces at boot time. The file /etc/hosts is a symbolic link to /etc/inet/hosts.[3] A typical /etc/inet/hosts file:

```
# Internet host table
#
127.0.0.1        localhost
207.127.1.7      loghost
207.127.1.83     dbserver
```

The *localhost* entry is found on all systems. The *loghost* entry is used by *syslog* (see chapter 8 for more information). The last entry, *dbserver*, is the name and IP address of *this* system.

The file /etc/inet/hosts is used to equate system names with their respective IP addresses. UNIX administrators and users tend to remember system names, whereas the systems themselves use IP addresses to communicate with one another. /etc/inet/hosts provides this name-to-address translation.

Each system must have its own copy of /etc/inet/hosts. In large networks, maintaining each system's /etc/inet/hosts file is impractical, so a centralized naming service is used instead (see chapter 14 for more information).

/etc/inet/netmasks

The /etc/inet/netmasks file is used to determine the range of IP addresses on the network(s) to which the system is connected. The file /etc/netmasks is a symbolic link to /etc/inet/netmasks. This information is needed so that the network drivers can determine whether packets to be sent out should be sent directly to the destination host(s) or instead to the default router.

```
207.127.1.0      255.255.255.0
96.0.0.0         255.255.0.0
```

Each entry in /etc/inet/netmasks contains two fields: a network number and its respective subnet mask.

---

3. Prior to Solaris 2.x (System V, Release 4), the files /etc/inet/hosts, /etc/inet/ netmasks, /etc/inet/services, /etc/inet/protocols, and /etc/inet/inetd.conf were known as /etc/hosts, /etc/netmasks, /etc/services, /etc/protocols, and /etc/ inetd.conf, respectively. The latter filenames are preserved for compatibility with earlier versions of Solaris and other UNIX OSs.

/etc/defaultrouter

The */etc/defaultrouter* file is a plain text file that contains the name or IP address of the default router. Packets destined for computers or devices not on the same subnet as the system sending them are sent instead to the default router, which presumably will forward them to the proper destination. For more information see the section on routing later in this chapter.

> **Note: If the name of the default router is used, there must be an entry for that name in the */etc/inet/hosts* file, since no directory service (i.e., DNS, NIS, or NIS+) is running on the system when the routing table is being set up.**

/etc/nodename

The */etc/nodename* file is a text file that contains only the name of the system. This name matches the name of the system defined in */etc/inet/ hosts*.

/etc/hostname.interface

The */etc/hostname.interface* file is a plain text file containing the host name of the "xxx" network adaptor. This file is used together with */etc/inet/hosts* to determine to which IP address the network adaptor should be assigned when the system is booted.

For example, consider a system with two network interfaces—*le0* and *le1*. Two *hostname.interface* files must be used—*/etc/hostname.le0* and */etc/ hostname.le1*. The next section describes how these files are used, together with */etc/inet/hosts* and */etc/inet/netmasks*, to configure a system's network interfaces.

How Adaptors Are Configured

Figure 9.2 illustrates the relationship between the configuration files, network adaptors, and their network addresses.

The system's network adaptors are configured at boot time as follows (refer to Figure 9.2).

1. The system inventories its network adaptors and then pairs them with the */etc/hostname.interface* files. This associates a hostname with each adaptor.

2. The hostnames are paired with IP addresses from the */etc/inet/hosts* file.

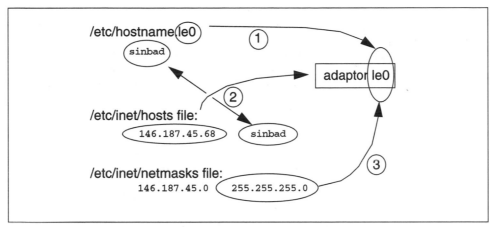

Figure 9.2 *Network Adaptor Configuration*

3. The subnet mask for each interface is derived from information in the */etc/inet/netmasks* file.

Promiscuous Mode

Promiscuous mode (defined earlier in this chapter) can be detected with the public-domain tool cpm (check promiscuous mode). cpm is available from ftp:// coast.cs.purdue.edu/pub/tools/unix/cpm/ .

Running cpm

The following examples demonstrate cpm detecting an interface in promiscuous mode.

1. Interface in promiscuous mode

```
# cpm
3 network interfaces found:
lo0: Normal
le0: *** IN PROMISCUOUS MODE ***
le1: Normal
1 of them is in promiscuous mode.
#
```

2. No interfaces in promiscuous mode

```
# cpm
3 network interfaces found:
lo0: Normal
le0: Normal
le1: Normal
0 of them is in promiscuous mode.
#
```

Network Services

A network service is a logical portion of the Solaris operating system used to communicate specific types of information among computers. A system with one or more services configured will consent to communicate with other computers requesting service.

Examples of network services include

- telnet—allows users on other systems to log in to this system and initiate a login shell from which UNIX commands may be entered
- ftp—allows users on other systems to initiate a file transfer session with this system in order to either pick up or drop off files
- sendmail—allows other systems to establish a connection in order to send and receive e-mail messages
- ntp—permits other systems to ask this system for the correct time of day, enabling the two systems to synchronize each other's clocks
- routed—facilitates the exchanging of routing information in situations where the workstation itself is a router, or where the workstation is on a complex network with multiple routers providing connectivity to other networks

Unnecessary Services

Solaris systems are shipped with a wide variety of network services, most of which are activated. It is in the best interests of each system (and its owner) to have all nonessential services deactivated. Refer to chapter 13 for information on disabling unnecessary network services.

Network Service Numbers

Network service numbers (also known as *port numbers*) are predefined in the Internet's *Request for Comments* (RFC) 1700. For more information on RFCs, refer to the appendix on suggested reading.

Network Service Configuration

Services are configured with two configuration files—*/etc/inet/services* and */etc/inet/inetd.conf*. These two files work together to determine which network services are activated and how they are configured.

/etc/inet/services

The */etc/inet/services* file equates each service name with a port number and port type. The file */etc/services* is a link to */etc/inet/services; /etc/services*

exists for system-level compatibility with older versions of UNIX. The fields in
/etc/inet/services are defined as

```
name  port/protocol  [aliases]
```

where *name* is the name for the service, *port* is the IP port number, *protocol* is
the protocol used (either transmission control protocol [TCP] or user data-
gram protocol [UDP]), and *aliases* is an optional list of alternate names for
the service.

A portion of an */etc/inet/services* file follows:

```
#ident "@(#)services 1.1697/05/12 SMI" /* SVr4.0 1.8 */
#
# Network services, Internet style
#
tcpmux    1/tcp
echo      7/tcp
echo      7/udp
discard   9/tcp      sink null
discard   9/udp      sink null
systat    11/tcp     users
daytime   13/tcp
daytime   13/udp
netstat   15/tcp
chargen   19/tcp     ttytst source
chargen   19/udp     ttytst source
ftp-data  20/tcp
ftp       21/tcp
telnet    13/tcp
smtp      25/tcp     mail
time      37/tcp     timserver
time      37/udp     timserver
name      42/udp     nameserver
whois     43/tcp     nicname # usually to sri-nic
...
```

/etc/inet/inetd.conf

The */etc/inet/inetd.conf* file equates each service (by its name) with network
services offered by the system. The file */etc/inet/inetd.conf* contains the configuration characteristics for each particular service needed to start that service properly.

The file */etc/inetd.conf* is a link to */etc/inet/inetd.conf*; */etc/inetd.conf*
exists for system-level compatibility with older versions of UNIX. The fields in
/etc/inet/inetd.conf are defined as follows:

```
name type protocol waitstatus userid path args
```

where *name* is the name for the service; *type* is one of these—stream, dgram,
raw, seqpacket, or tli; *protocol* is one of the protocol types listed in */etc/inet/
protocols*; *waitstatus* is either wait or nowait; *userid* specifies which account
will run the service; *path* is the full pathname of the service (the value *internal*

has a special purpose explained below); and *args* contains all program arguments (starting with *arg0*, usually the program name itself).

Here is a portion of an */etc/inet/inetd.conf* file.

```
#
#ident "@(#)inetd.conf  1.33  98/06/02 SMI" /* SVr4.0 1.5 */
#
#
# Configuration file for inetd(1M).  See inetd.conf(4).
#
# To re-configure the running inetd process, edit this file, then
# send the inetd process a SIGHUP.
#
# Syntax for socket-based Internet services:
# <service_name> <socket_type> <proto> <flags> <user> <path> <args>
#
# Syntax for TLI-based Internet services:
#
# <service_name> tli <proto> <flags> <user> <path> <args>
#
# Ftp and telnet are standard Internet services.
#
ftp    stream tcp nowait root /usr/sbin/in.ftpd     in.ftpd
telnet stream tcp nowait root /usr/sbin/in.telnetd in.telnetd
#
# Tnamed serves the obsolete IEN-116 name server protocol.
#
name   dgram  udp wait   root /usr/sbin/in.tnamed  in.tnamed
#
# Shell, login, exec, comsat and talk are BSD protocols.
#
shell  stream tcp nowait root /usr/sbin/in.rshd    in.rshd
login  stream tcp nowait root /usr/sbin/in.rlogind in.rlogind
exec   stream tcp nowait root /usr/sbin/in.rexecd  in.rexecd
comsat dgram  udp wait   root /usr/sbin/in.comsat  in.comsat
talk   dgram  udp wait   root /usr/sbin/in.talkd   in.talkd
...
```

How Network Services Are Started

The main Internet server process *inetd* is started when the system is booted. The startup script */etc/rc2.d/S72inetsvc* starts the *inetd* process. *inetd* reads the configuration files */etc/inet/services* and */etc/inet/inetd.conf* and then listens for connection requests from other computers over the network. The *inetd* process listens simultaneously on all ports defined in */etc/inet/services*.

If a connection request arrives on an *undefined* port (a port not defined in */etc/inet/services*), then no service is started. The requesting computer is sent a "connection refused" message.

When a connection request arrives on a *defined* port (one defined in */etc/inet/services* and */etc/inetd/inetd.conf*), then *inetd* will launch the service by starting the program listed in the *path* field in */etc/inetd/inetd.conf* (the program will be run as the userid specified in */etc/inetd/inetd.conf*). The new program will communicate over the network to the computer that originally requested the service connection.

Some services have the word *internal* in the *path* field in */etc/inetd/inetd.conf.* When a connection request arrives for these services, *inetd* does not start another process, but instead communicates over the network to the requesting computer *directly* (in other words, the network service functionality is built in to *inetd*). Only services that can be processed quickly are done using this method. Examples include *echo*, *chargen*, and *discard*.

Daemon Network Services Not Started with inetd

It is possible—in fact common—to start network services without *inetd*'s help. An example of one of these services is *sendmail*.

Sendmail, the network service used to send and receive electronic mail, is started independently of *inetd* by its own *rc* file, *S88sendmail*. The *sendmail* daemon listens on port 25 (as defined in */etc/inet/services*) and manages its own network communications. The *inetd* process is never involved in *sendmail*'s configuration or communications.

Here are other examples of network services that run independent of *inetd* and what starts them if they are used.

- DNS, started by *S72inetsvc*
- NIS, started by *S71rpc* or *S71yp*
- NIS+, started by *S71rpc*
- NFS, started by *S15nfs.server*
- in.routed, started by *S72inetsvc*

What does this all mean? The *inetd* process is used to manage commonly used network services, but not heavily used ones. Heavily used services listen on ports using dedicated daemon processes that are running all the time (the assumption with *inetd* is that the spawned process servicing the request exits after fulfilling the request).

This is really a matter of system efficiency. For those services not heavily used, *inetd* is a single process listening on a multitude of ports, so that a multitude of daemon processes don't have to. This saves space in the system's *process table*.

On the other hand, heavily used network services employ their own dedicated processes (daemons) that listen for and handle requests directly. This

improves response time for those network services. Were *inetd* to directly handle a heavily used network service such as *sendmail*, *inetd* would have to
launch the *sendmail* process *each time* a mail message arrived! This would
bring a heavily used mail relay system to a near standstill, since it would be
spending nearly all of its time starting (and starting, and starting...) *sendmail* processes.

Routing

For most UNIX systems, there is usually only one network router available to
route packets to other networks. There are cases, however, where a UNIX system has more than one router from which to choose when making a packet
delivery decision. Figure 9.3 illustrates this scenario.

The case of a single router leading to all networks is solved with the use of
/etc/defaultrouter. For example, if the IP address of the router is 10.12.17.2,
then */etc/defaultrouter* would appear as

```
10.12.17.2
```

The case of multiple routers leading to multiple networks is solved in one of
two ways: static routes and dynamic routes.

Figure 9.3   *Single and Multiple Routers and Networks*

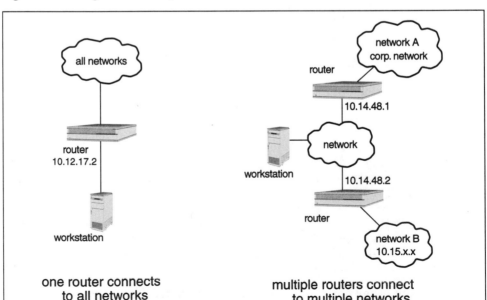

Adding Static Routes

Static routes are added manually to the workstation with the *route* command. The format of the *route* command is *route add net net-address subnet-mask router hops*, where *net-address* is the TCP/IP address for the entire network to be routed to; *subnet-mask* is the subnet mask for that network; *router* is the IP address of the router that routes to that network; and *hops* is the number of network hops to that network.

> **Note: UNIX and network administrators must work together when setting up routes on any workstation so that its routing configuration matches the actual network topology.**

Using the illustration in Figure 9.3 as an example, the UNIX workstation on the right-hand side of the illustration would be set up as follows:

- The file */etc/defaultrouter* would contain the IP address of one of the two routers—presumably the one leading to most other networks, in this case 10.14.48.1.
- To add a route to the second network, the following command line is added to the end of the startup file */etc/rc2.d/S72inetsvc*.

  ```
  route add net 10.15.0.0 255.255.0.0 10.14.48.2 1
  ```

  This effectively tells the UNIX workstation, "To reach IP network 10.15.x.x, send packets to router 10.14.48.2—and, by the way, network 10.15.x.x is one router hop away."

Adding Dynamic Routes

An alternative to adding static routes with the *route* command is to run *in.routed* or *in.rdisc*. Either of these routing daemons is started at boot time by adding the appropriate command line to */etc/rc2.d/S72inetsvc*. The advantage of using one of these routing daemons is that the UNIX system need only listen on the network for routing information packets and use the information in those packets to dynamically update the system's routing table. In a frequently changing network, this can be a boon to UNIX and network administrators because the UNIX system need not be reconfigured with new static routes each time the network topology changes; instead new routing information will reach the UNIX system automatically.

> **Warning: There is always a dark side to configurations and methods designed to save time and increase efficiency, and dynamic routing is no exception. An intruder can easily forge packets containing false routing information and send them to a UNIX system known to listen to routing information packets. This can be used to cause great harm to the organization that owns the system.**

This is a book on Solaris security, not general systems administration. Hence, discussions on how to set up dynamic routing will stop here. It should be enough for the UNIX administrator to know the pros and cons of static and dynamic routing and decide which is best for any particular environment. Further, the UNIX-network interactions can be so complex in the realm of network topology and routing that I could write several chapters on this topic alone. Please refer to "Where to Go for Additional Information" at the end of this chapter for references to books which discuss this topic.

Using *snoop*

snoop is a Solaris program used to listen to all packets on the network. It is important to know how to use *snoop* to diagnose a variety of network service problems. Here are several examples of ways to use *snoop*.

> Note: *snoop* is a useful diagnostic tool, but it is also potentially danger-ous. Only the root user can run *snoop*. Since *snoop* can be used to cap-ture session passwords and other sensitive data, (if for no other reason) the UNIX administrator must be careful about who has the root password on any UNIX system. One suggestion might be to remove *snoop* from a UNIX system whose user has the root password.

1. Show all packets passing to and from the machine *linus*.

   ```
   # snoop host linus
   ...
   ```

2. Show all packets on the network using the NTP protocol.

   ```
   # snoop port 123
   ...
   ```

3. Capture a *telnet* session, including the login password. In this example, the userid is *peterh*, and the password is *jeopardy*.

   ```
   # snoop -v host lucy port 23
   Using device /dev/hme (promiscuous mode)
       linus -> lucy      TELNET C port=42459
        lucy -> linus     TELNET R port=42459
       linus -> lucy      TELNET C port=42459
        lucy -> linus     TELNET R port=42459
       linus -> lucy      TELNET C port=42459
       linus -> lucy      TELNET C port=42459
        lucy -> linus     TELNET R port=42459
        lucy -> linus     TELNET R port=42459
       linus -> lucy      TELNET C port=42459
        lucy -> linus     TELNET R port=42459
       linus -> lucy      TELNET C port=42459
        lucy -> linus     TELNET R port=42459
       linus -> lucy      TELNET C port=42459
        lucy -> linus     TELNET R port=42459
        lucy -> linus     TELNET R port=42459 \r\n\r\nUNIX(r) System V
       linus -> lucy      TELNET C port=42459
        lucy -> linus     TELNET R port=42459
   ```

```
linus -> lucy      TELNET C port=42459
 lucy -> linus     TELNET R port=42459
linus -> lucy      TELNET C port=42459
 lucy -> linus     TELNET R port=42459 login:
linus -> lucy      TELNET C port=42459
linus -> lucy      TELNET C port=42459 p
 lucy -> linus     TELNET R port=42459 p
linus -> lucy      TELNET C port=42459
linus -> lucy      TELNET C port=42459 e
 lucy -> linus     TELNET R port=42459 e
linus -> lucy      TELNET C port=42459            <--- userid=peterh
linus -> lucy      TELNET C port=42459 t
 lucy -> linus     TELNET R port=42459 t
linus -> lucy      TELNET C port=42459
linus -> lucy      TELNET C port=42459 e
 lucy -> linus     TELNET R port=42459 e
linus -> lucy      TELNET C port=42459
linus -> lucy      TELNET C port=42459 r
 lucy -> linus     TELNET R port=42459 r
linus -> lucy      TELNET C port=42459
linus -> lucy      TELNET C port=42459 h
 lucy -> linus     TELNET R port=42459 h
linus -> lucy      TELNET C port=42459
linus -> lucy      TELNET C port=42459
 lucy -> linus     TELNET R port=42459
linus -> lucy      TELNET C port=42459
 lucy -> linus     TELNET R port=42459 Password:
linus -> lucy      TELNET C port=42459
linus -> lucy      TELNET C port=42459 j
 lucy -> linus     TELNET R port=42459
linus -> lucy      TELNET C port=42459 e
 lucy -> linus     TELNET R port=42459            <--- password=jeopardy
linus -> lucy      TELNET C port=42459 o
 lucy -> linus     TELNET R port=42459
linus -> lucy      TELNET C port=42459 p
 lucy -> linus     TELNET R port=42459
linus -> lucy      TELNET C port=42459 a
 lucy -> linus     TELNET R port=42459
linus -> lucy      TELNET C port=42459 r
 lucy -> linus     TELNET R port=42459
linus -> lucy      TELNET C port=42459 d
 lucy -> linus     TELNET R port=42459
linus -> lucy      TELNET C port=42459 y
 lucy -> linus     TELNET R port=42459
linus -> lucy      TELNET C port=42459
 lucy -> linus     TELNET R port=42459
linus -> lucy      TELNET C port=42459
 lucy -> linus     TELNET R port=42459 Last login: Tue Nov 20
linus -> lucy      TELNET C port=42459
 lucy -> linus     TELNET R port=42459 Sun Microsystems Inc
linus -> lucy      TELNET C port=42459
 lucy -> linus     TELNET R port=42459 You have mail.\r\n
linus -> lucy      TELNET C port=42459
 lucy -> linus     TELNET R port=42459 lucy%
linus -> lucy      TELNET C port=42459
^C
#
```

Where to Go for Additional Information

AnswerBook

- AnswerBook 2—System Administration Guide, TCP/IP and Data Communications Administration Guide

Man Pages

- defaultrouter(4)
- dmesg(1M)
- hosts(4)
- ifconfig(1M)
- in.rdisc(1M)
- in.routed(1M)
- inetd.conf(4)
- ndd(1M)
- netmasks(4)
- netstat(1M)
- route(1M)
- services(4)
- snoop(1M)
- uname(1)

Publications

- *Ethernet Interface FAQ/PSD*, SunSolve Infodoc 12306
- *Misc Networking Programs PSD/FAQ*, SunSolve Infodoc 12052
- Murhammer, Martin. *TCP/IP Tutorial and Technical Overview*, 6th ed. Upper Saddle River, NJ: Prentice Hall, 1998.
- Comer, Douglas. *Internetworking with TCP/IP, Vol. I: Principles, Protocols and Architecture,* 3d ed. Upper Saddle River, NJ: Prentice Hall, 1995.
- Comer, Douglas, and Stevens, David. *Internetworking with TCP/IP, Vol. II, ANSI C Version: Design, Implementation, and Internals,* 3d ed. Upper Saddle River, NJ: Prentice Hall, 1999.
- Stevens, W. Richard. *TCP/IP Illustrated*, Volume 1: The Protocols. Reading, MA: Addison-Wesley, 1994.
- Wright, Gary R., and Stevens, W. Richard. *TCP/IP Illustrated*, Volume 2: *The Implementation.* Reading, MA: Addison-Wesley, 1995.
- RFC1700, "Assigned Numbers" (official list of TCP/IP port number assignments), http://www.cis.ohio-state.edu/htbin/rfc/rfc1700.html

10

NETWORK/ SYSTEM ARCHITECTURE

The relationship between UNIX system (and systems') architecture to network architecture is discussed in this chapter.

UNIX and network architectures are symbiotic; when either is developed or modified, both need to be considered so that they will operate correctly and securely.

What's in this chapter

- Principles for overall system design and implementation that will lead to a more secure environment

Why this is important

The UNIX system administrator must have the ability to step back and consider the overall network and systems and applications architectures. UNIX systems in a network are rarely "islands," but instead usually have a complex web of relationships and dependencies. The stability and security of the individual systems and of the overall architecture depend upon choices made during the design and implementation of the systems.

What Is an Architecture?

Whether the scope is a system, many systems, a network, or all of these, an architecture is the collection of elements that work together to fulfill some intended objective. That objective could be

- A file-sharing system for a group of people
- A software development platform
- Electronic mail
- A network to facilitate communications among several users, each of whom uses a computer

Simple vs. Complex Architectures

Complex systems are inherently more difficult to administer than simple systems. A hacker, when given a choice, would probably choose to attack a complex system for the following reasons:

- A complex system inherently contains more components (whether hardware or software).
- The more components a system has, the greater the likelihood that there exists a poorly designed or misconfigured element.
- A poorly designed or misconfigured element can be an invitation to attack or exploitation.
- A system with many components may be more inviting to attack or exploitation simply because of the greater likelihood that an attack will go unnoticed.

For example, consider two e-mail architectures. The first architecture, which we'll call architecture A, consists of a central mail server and several mail clients. The second architecture, architecture B, consists of distributed mail servers and mail clients (perhaps in a distributed or load-balancing architecture). Assume that both architectures are applied to the same problem. Both of the architectures are illustrated in Figures 10.1 and 10.2.

Architecture A (the simpler architecture) has the *potential* to be more secure than architecture B. Why is this? First, architecture A has only one server to exploit, and architecture B has five. Further, the configuration in architecture B will be more complex than in architecture A; in architecture B, the servers are inherently more complex since they must be configured to communicate not only with clients, but presumably with other servers as well.

Architecture Principles

Security needs to be designed into IT architectures instead of being retrofitted into them. The following principles, when applied to the development of IT architectures, will result in systems that are simpler and, hence, more secure.

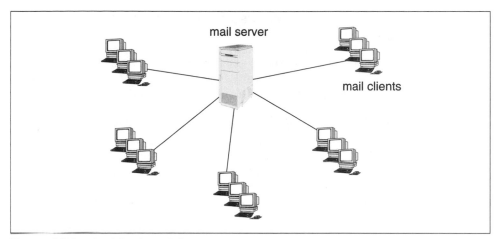

Figure 10.1 *Architecture A Example*

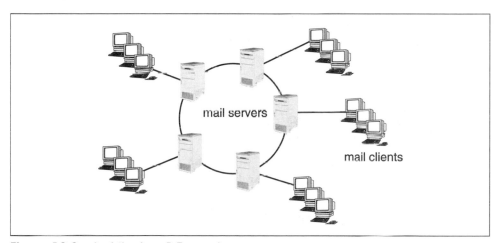

Figure 10.2 *Architecture B Example*

Principle 1: Minimize the Number of Failure Points (or Shorten the Critical Path)

A large number of failure points invites more opportunities for exploitation. Recall that architectures A and B accomplish roughly the same thing (although in different ways). Architecture B—with its greater number of components and higher complexity—will tend to be less secure.

Principle 2: Keep Services Close to Those Being Served

In some ways this is a restatement of principle 1. Imagine an e-mail client who must communicate to a server several network hops away, perhaps half-way around the world. Chances are that the e-mail connections pass through many network elements and travel over many networks. This is an example of a service (the mail server) that is topologically far away from the client being served. In this example, there may exist several weak points that could be exploited, such as improperly configured routers or e-mail gateways. When a weak point is exploited, information will be lost or stolen or service will be interrupted. Figure 10.3 illustrates these two architectures.

In this example, the client that is close to the server could be an e-mail or database server with its clients on the same LAN. The client distant from the server could be the same clients and servers, but connected via a worldwide satellite network.

One could also argue that principle 1 contradicts principle 2. In some scenarios this could be true. Maximum security is but one idealistic requirement that a complex system will have—the others are simplicity, low cost, and high performance. These competing requirements need to be considered in any proposed architecture, each on its own merit. No one said that balancing these needs would be easy!

Principle 3: Vertically Align Services with Their Applications

This is another restatement of principle 1. Consider the two architectures illustrated in Figure 10.4. The architecture on the left is more failure-prone

Figure 10.3   *Client Proximity to Server*

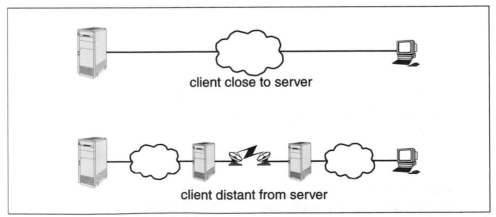

client close to server

client distant from server

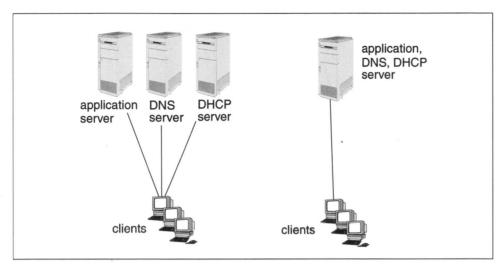

Figure 10.4 *Example of Vertical Service Alignment*

because it has more failure points—specifically (on the server side) three servers and three services (application, DNS, and dynamic host configuration protocol (DHCP)). The architecture on the right is less prone to failure because there are fewer physical components supporting the system.

Principle 4: Prepare for Increasing Network Partitioning

A trend is developing where companies are begining to deploy intranet firewalls, or firewalls *within* their company networks, in order to partition organizational and geographical networks from one another. The primary reason for this is to more effectively prevent and contain security incidents. Further, as IT organizations move toward greater standards-based models of business unit autonomy, intranet firewalls may be the means for company departments to protect themselves from other departments.

In environments with intranet firewalls, network architects will need to move network services closer to the clients being served. For example

- Each intranetwork should have its own e-mail gateway.
- Each intranetwork should have its own primary or secondary DNS and NIS/NIS+ servers (refer to chapter 14 for additional information).

See chapter 13 for additional information on firewalls.

Figure 10.5 illustrates a model of partitioned networks.

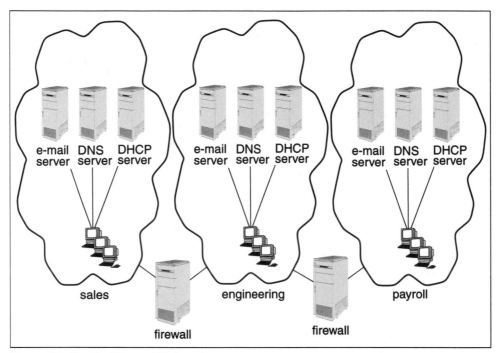

Figure 10.5   *Partitioned Networks*

11

ELECTRONIC MAIL

One of the most exploited network services is e-mail. Its complexity and ubiquity has led to the discovery of several security holes over the years. Configuration of e-mail is potentially complex and not easily understood; hence, a misconfigured system can have weaknesses that lead to bigger problems.

Most people think of e-mail as consisting only of the graphical user interface (GUI) or character interface used to read and send e-mail messages. Few consider the transport and delivery systems as part of the overall e-mail architecture.

What's in this chapter

- Basics of *sendmail* and mail agents
- A survey of e-mail-related security risks
- How to mitigate security risks

Why this is important

E-mail, used practically everywhere, presents the UNIX administrator with one of the most significant vulnerabilities that must be properly dealt with.

Overview of E-Mail

Solaris e-mail consists of three agents: transport agent, delivery agent, and user agent. Figure 11.1 illustrates these agents in end-to-end mail message delivery.

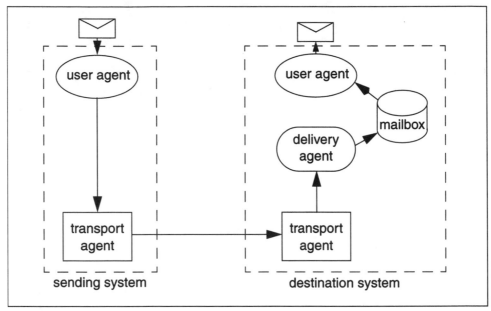

Figure 11.1   *Mail Agents*

Transport Agent

The transport agent for Solaris is *sendmail*. *Sendmail* receives new messages from users, makes mail delivery routing decisions by examining delivery addresses, and initiates the forwarding of mail messages by selecting and calling mail delivery agents.

Sendmail transports mail messages using the simple mail transport protocol (SMTP) message protocol. SMTP is a TCP protocol that uses port number 25.

Sendmail uses domain name service (DNS) in order to determine to which system to forward each mail message.

Delivery Agent

The delivery mechanism is used to deposit a mail message into a user's mailbox—that is, to actually perform the task of appending the message to the file */var/mail/<userid>*. The delivery agent used by Solaris is a program called *mail.local*.

User Agent

User agents are programs used by people to compose, read, and store e-mail messages. Solaris provides the following user agents:

- */usr/bin/mail* and */usr/bin/mailx*—character interface mail programs
- */usr/openwin/bin/mailtool*—the standard GUI mail program used with OpenWindows
- */usr/dt/bin/dtmail*—the standard GUI mail program used with CDE

User agents *read* mail messages stored in a user's mailbox, which is the file */var/mail/userid*, where *userid* is the user's account.

User agents *deliver* mail by establishing a network connection to the mail server's *sendmail* program via SMTP and then sending the contents of the mail message via the connection.

Other User Agents

It is worth mentioning that, in addition to the Solaris-supplied user agents, numerous others are in common use. They fall into two classes: graphical or character interface replacements for mail, mailx, mailtool, and dtmail; and POP clients.

Post office protocol (POP) is a network protocol used to deliver mail messages between a user's mailbox and a user agent GUI. A simple POP architecture is illustrated in Figure 11.2.

Types of E-Mail Security Weaknesses

E-mail has a number of features that for some people would be security weaknesses, while for others they would be an annoyance or perhaps inconsequential. I will describe a few of these features in the following sections.

Auth *(or* Identd*) Protocol*

When someone initiates a connection to an Internet site, that site may try to authenticate that user by querying the user's originating Internet site. The *auth* protocol is used in an attempt to verify the identity of the user.

Figure 11.2 *POP Client/Server Architecture*

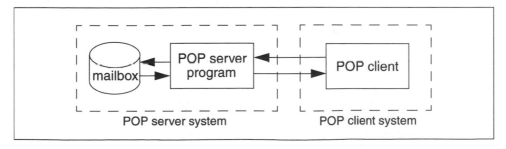

The *auth* protocol (sometimes known as *ident* or *identd*), described in the Internet's RFC's 1413, 1416, and 1700,[1] uses TCP port 113 when making an *auth* query. Any program can make an *auth* query; these queries are usually answered by the *sendmail* daemon on the site being queried.

Some sites choose to make *auth* information unavailable. This can generally be done without actually causing other services to fail—most services failing to get an *auth* protocol authentication will run anyway. It is recommended that *auth* be disabled at the firewall by blocking TCP and UDP port 113. Figure 11.3 illustrates how the *auth* protocol is used.

Message Brokering

A clever—but not exceedingly sophisticated—troublemaker can easily create an e-mail message that *appears* to be originating from almost anywhere. Moreover, this hacker can forge actual e-mail messages that *truly do originate* from almost anywhere. In this example, a hacker is forging an order cancellation memo.[2]

```
% telnet big-customer.com 25
Trying 146.52.76.3...
Connected to big-customer.com.
Escape character is '^]'.
220 big-customer.com. Sendmail SMI-8.6/SMI-SVR4 ready at Fri, 31 Jul 1998
    07:06:56 -0700
helo sinbad
250 alpha. Hello big-customer.com [203.8.21.4], pleased to meet you
Mail From: pres@big-customer.com
250 pres@big-customer.com... Sender ok
RCPT To: pres@big-mfg-co.com
250 pres@big-mfg-co.com... Recipient ok
DATA Subject: Cancel order
354 Enter mail, end with "." on a line by itself
```

Figure 11.3   auth *Protocol*

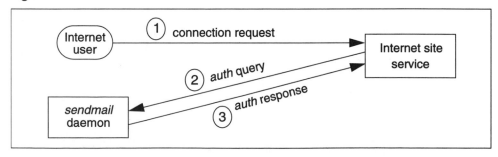

---

1. For more information on RFCs, refer to appendix D.

2. Hackers, accomplished and not so accomplished, know how to do this.

```
Tony,
Please cancel that $20 million order we placed yesterday.
Bill
.
250 HAA19816 Message accepted for delivery
quit
221 sinbad. closing connection
Connection closed by foreign host.
#
```

The resulting e-mail message in this example will actually originate at big-customer.com's e-mail server, travel over the Internet, and end up in the pres@big-mfg-co.com mailbox. Examination of e-mail headers will give few, if any, clues that the message is a forgery.

Sendmail has no direct defense against this kind of an attack. However, some firewalls are able to block connections originating on port 23 (*telnet*) and arriving on port 25; such a connection at blocked ports may certainly be an attempt at e-mail forgery.

Message Source Routing

An old trick in e-mail involves sending e-mail to a particular Internet site and forcing it there through another Internet site (illustrated in Figure 11.4). In the example in Figure 11.4, the ultimate destination of the message is user@nuts.com, but the message is first sent to bolts.com and then remailed to nuts.com.

Privacy

E-mail messages are still largely transported from server to server and from server to client "in the clear" (unencrypted). On a shared-media network, any-one with a network sniffer program can eavesdrop on others' e-mail messages.

Figure 11.4 *Message Source Routing*

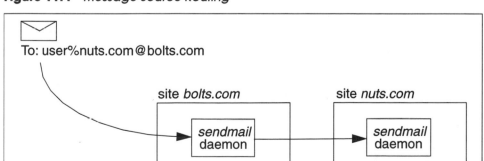

While Solaris—and standard UNIX—does not provide a prepackaged solution, public-domain solutions are available. The section on mitigating security weaknesses discusses possible solutions.

Authenticity

Authenticity is the measure of whether an e-mail message actually originated from the sender and whether or not the message is a forgery. Authentication mechanisms give message recipients confidence in the origination of a message by using digital signatures. The next section discusses ways to make sure messages are authentic.

Mitigating E-Mail Security Weaknesses

This section describes specific actions that can be taken to mitigate some or all of the risks associated with running e-mail.

Run Sendmail *Only on Mail Servers*

The bulk of the security risks associated with e-mail is directly associated with the *sendmail* program running as a daemon on a system. A commonly used architecture for a group of UNIX systems has *sendmail* running on every system. Figure 11.5 illustrates such an architecture.

Figure 11.5 *Less Secure Mail Architecture*

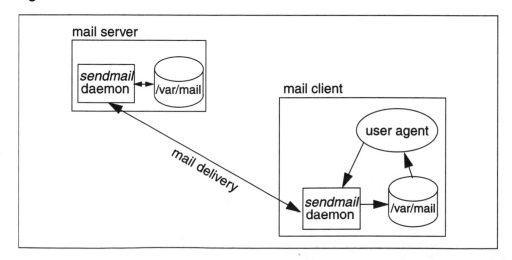

Table 11-1 Sendmail *Architecture Comparison*

Characteristic	Less Secure Architecture	More Secure Architecture
sendmail program	Runs as a daemon on every UNIX system	Runs as a daemon only on mail servers; runs at regular intervals on mail clients to process outbound mail
/var/mail	Separate copies present on every system	Master copy on mail server; NFS mounted by all mail clients
user aliases	Point to desktop client systems	Point to mail server
user agent	Runs on desktop client system	Runs on desktop client system (no change)

A more secure e-mail architecture is proposed that differs from the traditional, less secure architecture as shown in Table 11-1. The more secure e-mail architecture is illustrated in Figure 11.6, and its implementation details are discussed in the following sections.

Sendmail **Daemon**

Run *sendmail* as a daemon on each mail server. Refer to the Solaris *Mail Administration Guide* for details.

Figure 11.6 *More Secure Mail Architecture*

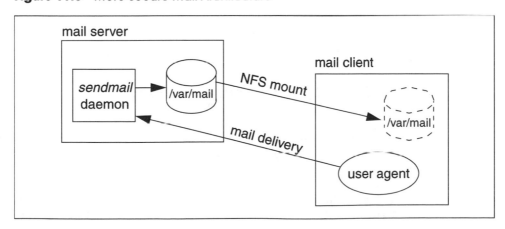

On each mail client, do not run *sendmail* as a daemon. Follow this procedure instead.

1. Comment the *sendmail* invocation (usually line 29) in */etc/rc2.d/ S88sendmail* as follows:

```
#              /usr/lib/sendmail -bd -q1h;
```

2. Adjust any aliases pointing to user accounts on the client system to instead point to accounts on the mail server. For example, in an environment where userid *jsmith* uses workstation *granite* (and where the mail server system name is *roundhouse*):

   Old alias entry: `jsmith: jsmith@granite`

   New alias entry: `jsmith: jsmith@roundhouse`

   Follow standard procedures for updating aliases in */etc/mail/ aliases*, NIS, or NIS+.

3. Each mail client will need to NFS mount the mailbox directory */var/ mail* from the mail server. Consider, for example, the mail server *roundhouse* and mail client *granite*.

   Mail server *roundhouse* entry in */etc/dfs/dfstab*:

   ```
   share -F nfs -o rw=mailclients -d "Mailboxes" /var/mail
   ```

   Mail client *granite* entry in */etc/vfstab*:

   ```
   roundhouse:/var/mail - /var/mail - no rw,hard,actimeo=0
   ```

Note: *actimeo=0* is required in order for mailbox locking to work properly.

   Then follow standard NFS procedures for exporting */var/mail* on the server and mounting it on the client system.

4. Add the following entry to root's *crontab* file:

   ```
   0 * * * * /usr/lib/sendmail -q > /var/adm/sendmail.log 2>&1
   ```

   This will cause any queued outbound mail on the client to be sent to the site's mail server each hour.

Disconnect Inside Mail Server(s) from the Internet

Many architectures employ an inside mail server to receive mail from the Internet. The weakness of this architecture is directly related to the fact that *sendmail* is running as a daemon on a system where literally anyone on the Internet is allowed to connect. A compromise to the mail server in this architecture means not only mail to and from the Internet is affected, but also all intraorganization mail as well. And the compromised system contains the organization's mail messages and, hence, potentially valuable information. This architecture is illustrated in Figure 11.7.

Instead, a mail relay server should be implemented. The mail relay permits the receipt of e-mail from the Internet while shielding the inside mail server from intrusion. This mail relay architecture is illustrated in Figure 11.8. In this architecture, the mail relay receives all mail on behalf of the mail server and then forwards it to the mail server. The mail relay has no specific knowledge of mail aliases and contains no local mailboxes. Likewise, outbound mail is forwarded from the mail server to the mail relay, which then forwards mail to the Internet.

If the mail relay is compromised due to a weakness in *sendmail*, there is a lower risk of losing inside company information because there are no mailboxes or aliases on the mail relay. If a compromise is detected, system administrators can temporarily take the mail relay out of service, but they could keep the mail server running. In this way, the impact of an intrusion is minimized since intraorganization mail delivery can continue.

To further protect the mail server, the firewall should prohibit direct access of any kind between the Internet and the mail server, allowing direct access only to the mail relay.

Figure 11.7   *Mail Server Connected to the Internet*

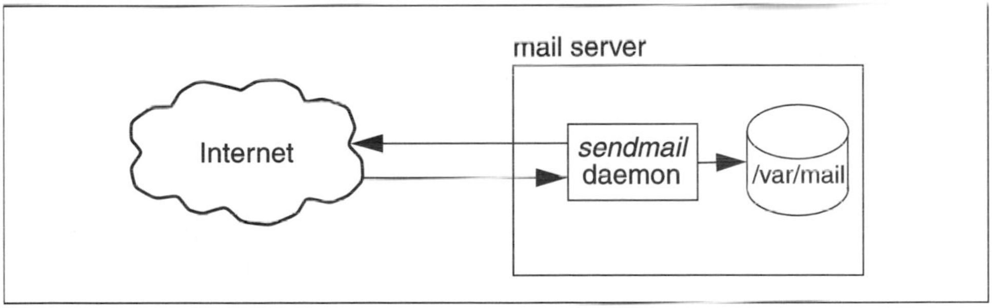

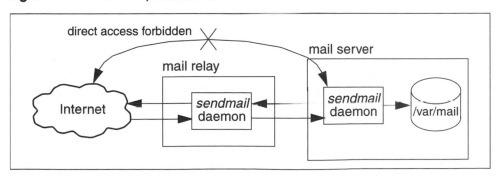

Figure 11.8   *Mail Relay Architecture*

This architecture also typically includes the use of interior and exterior DNS domains. See chapter 14 for complete information on Internet domain architectures. The Sun manual *Mail Administration Guide* also discusses this architecture in the section on setting up and administering mail services.

Prevent Message Source Routing

I explained message source routing earlier in this chapter. Now I will describe the process used to prevent message source routing for standard Sun *sendmail* configurations only.

For systems using a Main.cf configuration file, comment the following lines found in */etc/mail/sendmail.cf* (these entries are located throughout the file, not in one place).

```
R$+%$+                  $@$>3$1@$2                      user%host
R$*<@$%y.LOCAL>$*        $#ether $@$2 $:$1<@$2>$3        user@host.sun.com
R$*<@$%x.LOCAL>$*        $#ether $@$2 $:$1<@$2>$3        user@host.sun.com
R$*<@$%y>$*              $#ether $@$2 $:$1<@$2>$3        user@etherhost
R$*<@$%x>$*              $#ether $@$2 $:$1<@$2>$3        user@etherhost
R$+%$+                  $@$>30$1@$2                     turn % => @, retry
```

For systems using a Subsidiary.cf file, comment the following lines found in */etc/mail/sendmail.cf* (these entries are also located throughout the file).

```
R$+%$+                  $@$>3$1@$2                      user%host
R$*<@$%1>$*             $1<@$2.LOCAL>$3                 user@etherhost
R$*<@$%1.LOCAL>$*       $#ether $@$2 $:$1<@$2>$3        user@host.here
R$*<@$%x.LOCAL>$*       $#ether $@$2 $:$1<@$2>$3        user@host.here
R$+%$+                  $@$>30$1@$2                     turn % => @, retry
```

Note: *sendmail* configuration files can be difficult to work with and unforgiving. Use extreme caution when modifying */etc/mail/sendmail.cf*. I strongly recommend that *sendmail* changes be tested on test systems before being implemented on production systems. Refer to the references at the end of this chapter for more help with *sendmail*.

Implement Mail Encryption and Digital Signatures

Only the combined use of message encryption and digital signatures can assure that e-mail messages can be delivered without having been eavesdropped, altered, or forged.

Encryption is used to ensure the privacy of a message. Even if a message travels across public networks and even if it is snooped by a hacker, the hacker will have a very difficult time decrypting the message.

A digital signature is used to ensure that a message has actually originated from the claimed source and that it has not been altered in transit. Thus the recipient can have a high degree of confidence in the authenticity and integrity of the message.

The most popular encryption software available is Pretty Good Privacy (PGP); it is available in public-domain and commercial versions from http://web.mit.edu/network/pgp.html (only available to U.S. citizens in the United States or Canadian citizens in Canada) and at ftp://ftp.pgp.net/pub/pgp/ .

Replace Sendmail

The version of *sendmail* provided by Sun is liable to be a few revisions behind the latest version available on the Internet. While it is not a trivial task, *sendmail* can be replaced with one of several alternate mail transfer agents; I will discuss a few options here.

Note: Sun Microsystems will not support the replacement of the *sendmail* program supplied with Solaris. *Sendmail* should be replaced only by someone with thorough knowledge and experience with the mechanisms of e-mail transmission and delivery.

Public-Domain *Sendmail*

While the version of *sendmail* used by any current version of Solaris is quite recent, the best method for having the *very* latest *sendmail* is to acquire and maintain the latest version of public-domain *sendmail*.

Any site considering switching from Sun-supplied and -supported *sendmail* to unsupported public-domain *sendmail* needs to weigh the risks and benefits (see Note, above). Table 11-2 outlines the most basic risks and benefits of the two *sendmail*s.

Table 11-2 *Sun-Supplied* Sendmail *vs. Public-Domain* Sendmail: *Risks and Benefits*

sendmail Version	Risks	Benefits
Sun-supplied *sendmail*	Not the latest version; could be vulnerable to the latest security risks. The latest features will be delayed.	Supported by Sun.
public-domain *sendmail*	Not supported by Sun; site assumes a greater burden by having to support *sendmail* on its own.	The latest versions and features available without having to wait for Solaris to catch up.

Note: Exercise caution when applying patches on a system using public-domain *sendmail*. A patch may accidentally replace a public-domain *sendmail* file (including the *sendmail* program itself!) with Sun's *sendmail*.

You can obtain public-domain *sendmail* from one of the following sites:

- http://www.sendmail.org/
- http://www.sunfreeware.com/

Postfix (formerly Vmailer)

Postfix is a public-domain *sendmail* replacement that claims to be easier to administer than *sendmail*. Like other *sendmail* replacements, the UNIX administrator needs to thoroughly understand the implications of using an unsupported software package. But that said, the experienced administrator can use postfix to improve the security and administrative overhead in an enterprise environment.

The pros and cons of using postfix vs. *sendmail* are similar to the arguments of Sun-supported *sendmail* and public-domain *sendmail* in Table 11-2.

Postfix can be obtained from http://www.postfix.org/ or http://www.porcupine.org/ .

SMAP

Sendmail on a mail relay system can be replaced with Sendmail Wrapper (SMAP). SMAP is a simple mail acceptor and forwarder with none of the complexities (and, consequently, the vulnerabilities) of *sendmail*. SMAP listens for incoming mail on port 25 (the usual SMTP port), queues it to disk, and then forwards it to its destination using *sendmail* in bulk send mode (which is not a security risk like *sendmail* in daemon mode).

SMAP is available from ftp://ftp.tis.com/pub/firewalls/toolkit/ . Read the instructions in the *README* file to obtain the software. Be sure to also download the general and Solaris patches (which must be installed with the *patch* utility).

SMAP is part of the Firewall Toolkit package. There is a Firewall Toolkit mailing list; send mail to majordomo@ex.tis.com; in the body of the message, include the words "subscribe fwtk-users (*your-email-address*)."

Remove Unnecessary E-Mail Aliases

Unless the site is running UUCP (most aren't), the alias **decode** should be commented or removed. When properly commented, the */etc/mail/aliases* entry reads as follows:

```
# decode: "|/usr/bin/uudecode"
```

The permissions of the file */etc/mail/aliases* should be 644.

Implement Smrsh

If a nefarious user discovered that user *sue* had a world-writable *.forward* file, he could put something in it like this:

```
\sue, |"cp /bin/sh /home/sue/su-sh;chmod u+s /home/sue/sue-sh"
```

Then the troublemaker could send mail to user *sue*. *Sue*'s *.forward* file would execute the line *cp /bin/sh /home/sue/su-sh;chmod u+s /home/sue/sue-sh*, thereby creating a shell that runs as user *sue*. The troublemaker could then execute */home/sue/sue-sh* and effectively become *sue*, since */home/sue/sue-sh* is SetUID to user *sue*.

The public-domain program Smrsh prevents code like this example from running. When Smrsh runs a command (such as *cp* or *chmod* in this example), Smrsh looks for that program only in its own private *sm.bin* directory. If the command is not in *sm.bin*, the command fails and the e-mail message bounces back to the sender.

Smrsh is now bundled with public-domain *sendmail* (discussed earlier).

Sendmail.cf must be modified for Smrsh to take effect; the *prog mailer* entry is changed to run *smrsh* instead of *sh*.

```
Mprog, P=/usr/local/bin/smrsh, F= ...
```

Implement ForwardPath

In a NIS/Automounter environment where users' home directories are exported from desktop systems and mountable everywhere (a common architecture), a user can launch a denial-of-service attack on the mail server by turning off or disconnecting his workstation and then sending himself mail. The mail server will try to automount the user's home directory and could hang while doing so.

The ForwardPath option in *sendmail* version 8 (new in Solaris 7) permits the UNIX administrator to define a single directory on the mail server that will contain all the user's *.forward* files.

A sample ForwardPath entry in *sendmail.cf* would resemble

```
O ForwardPath=/usr/local/mailforwards/$u.forward:$z/.forward
```

This tells *sendmail* to first look for the file */usr/local/mailforwards/userid.forward*. If this file is found, then a user's *.forward* file in his home directory is ignored. If *sendmail* does not find a file */usr/local/mailforwards/userid.forward*, it will next look in the user's home directory for a *.forward* file.

Sites that wish to *never* permit *.forward* files in home directories can define ForwardPath as follows:

```
O ForwardPath=/usr/local/mailforwards/$u.forward
```

This tells *sendmail* to look only in */usr/local/mailforwards* for *userid.forward* files. This eliminates the need for *sendmail* to ever look in a user's home directory.

Where to Go for Additional Information

AnswerBook

- AnswerBook 2—Mail Administration Guide

Man Pages

- aliases(1)
- forward(1)
- mail.local (1M)
- sendmail(1M)

Publications

- *Sendmail PSD/FAQ* (Product Support Document), SunSolve Infodoc 12815
- Costales, Bryan, Allman, Eric, and Estabrook, Gigi. *Sendmail*. 2d ed. Sebastopol, CA: O'Reilly & Associates, Inc., 1997.
- Zimmerman, Philip R. *The Official PGP User's Guide*. Cambridge, MA: MIT Press, 1995.

Web Sites

- RFC1413, "Ident Protocol," http://www.cis.ohio-state.edu/htbin/rfc/rfc1413.html
- RFC1416, "Telnet Authentication Option," http://www.cis.ohio-state.edu/htbin/rfc/rfc1416.html
- RFC1700, "Assigned Numbers" (official list of TCP/IP port number assignments), http://www.cis.ohio-state.edu/htbin/rfc/rfc1700.html
- *Sun/Solaris-specific information at sendmail.org*, http://www.sendmail.org/sun-specific/

12

PRINTING

The printing subsystem can be another source of exploitation or attack. Like electronic mail, the printing mechanism is not well understood; configuration errors can lead to weaknesses and exploitation.

What's in this chapter

- Where printing information is stored and how it can be audited
- How to ensure that only the print spooler can access directly connected printers
- Access control for print devices

Why this is important

Valuable personal and/or company information is handled by the print subsystem in the form of the content of the information printed. Therefore, the print subsystem must be trustworthy and secure.

Printing Architectures

From a security perspective, printing is considered either as *local* printing or *network* printing. Local printing consists of a workstation sending print requests to a printer that is directly attached to that workstation. Network printing involves sending print requests over the network either to a print server or to a printer directly connected to the network. These architectures are shown in Figure 12.1.

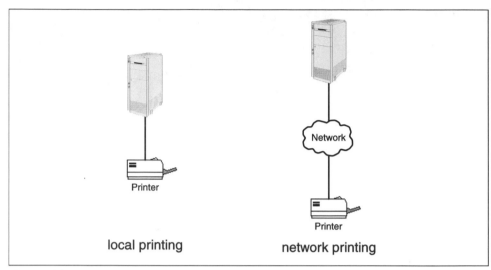

Figure 12.1 *Printing Architectures*

Print Subsystem Directories

The print subsystem maintains several log and temporary storage directories. The UNIX system administrator must make sure that as-delivered permissions in these files and directories are not altered in a way that would give access to people and processes that have no business snooping around there.

The top-level print subsystem directories are

- /var/lp
- /var/spool/lp

Auditing Print Subsystem Directories

The best way to keep tabs on the print subsystem's directories and files is through automated filesystem audits. ASET and Tripwire are recommended tools for these automated audits. Refer to chapter 4 for complete information on ASET and Tripwire.

Local Printing

Local printing involves a printer physically connected to a Sun parallel or serial port. The best measure of security specific to locally connected printers is to ensure that *only* the print service has write access to the print device.

Why? Suppose a sloppy UNIX administrator opened up permissions on a print device during testing or troubleshooting and forgot to change the permissions back to what they were supposed to be. No big deal? What if the printer was loaded with company letterheads, checks, or purchase orders? *Still* no big deal?

So perhaps it would be sloppiness on the part of the person responsible for POs or checks to make sure they don't leave those forms in an unattended printer. The principle of protecting in layers exists for this purpose. You should not rely on only one line of defense (locking up checks, for instance) as the only security measure. Keeping non-print-service users from being able to write to the print device should make everyone rest a *little* easier.

Local Print Devices

The two serial ports A and B are typically */dev/term/a* and */dev/term/b* . The parallel port is typically */dev/bpp0* .

These devices are usually logical links to actual files in the */devices* directory, but the details of the actual links are not important.

How to Determine Which Device a Specific Printer Uses

The *lpstat -v* command will list the device used for a printer.

```
# lpstat -v laser1
device for laser1: /dev/bpp0
# lpstat -v
device for laser1: /dev/bpp0
device for matrix: /dev/term/a
#
```

Print Device Permissions

A serial port or parallel port print device should be owned by root, group sys. The user root should have read and write permissions; no other permissions should be set. An example command to view these permission settings follows.

```
# ls -Ll /dev/bpp0
crw-------   1 root     sys       73,  0 Jan 22 1998 /dev/bpp0
#
```

Note: Solaris uses a mechanism of indirection to define its devices. */dev/term/a* and */dev/bpp0* are not the actual devices files, but are *symbolic links* to them. The L option is used with the *ls* command to show the ownership and permissions for the file pointed to by the logical

link */dev/bpp0* . **Permissions for the symbolic link itself are *lrwxr-wxrwx* and should not be changed.**

Auditing Print Device Permissions

The Tripwire program should be used to regularly check the permissions of all device files in */dev* and */devices* in order to detect ownership or permissions changes of the print devices. See chapter 4 for more information on using Tripwire.

Restricting Access to Printers and Print Servers

Each printer on a UNIX system can have user and system restrictions placed on it. This will allow the following types of access restrictions for each printer:

- Allow only certain users access to a printer.
- Deny certain users access to a printer.
- Allow all (or no) users from a certain system access to a printer.

In an environment with many users and printers, there can be several reasons why these restrictions would be put into place, such as:

- To restrict printing on expensive media (such as transparencies) to certain individuals
- To restrict printing on special media (such as letterhead, POs, and checks) to certain individuals
- To restrict printing on personal printers to their targeted users only

Restrictions are set up with the *lpadmin -u* command. Here are some examples.

1. Permit user *jroberts* to print to printer *checkprinter*.

   ```
   # lpadmin -p checkprinter -u allow:jroberts
   #
   ```

2. Permit all users on machine *vulcan* to print to printer *duplex2*.

   ```
   # lpadmin -p duplex2 -u allow:vulcan!all
   #
   ```

Both examples assume that the respective printers have already been set up and configured.

Refer to the lpadmin(1M) man page for complete information on allowing and denying access to printers.

Direct Access to Network Printers

A network printer is a printer connected directly to the LAN, not a UNIX workstation. Few, if any, network printers can be configured to allow access from only certain print servers. Rather, network printers usually accept print requests from any system on the network.

Depending upon your level of security concern, consider the following:

- A network and/or printer architecture that will permit *only* the designated UNIX print servers access to their respective printers. Possibilities include putting printers on a different subnet and restricting access using a firewall or router access control lists.

- Connect sensitive printers *directly* to print servers or end-user workstations.

Where to Go for Additional Information

AnswerBook

- AnswerBook 2—System Administration Guide, Managing Printing Services

Man Pages

- lpadmin(1M)
- lpstat(1M)
- ls(1M)

13

NETWORK
ACCESS CONTROL

Solaris is getting better about closing security holes, but in my opinion more can be done to introduce and tighten network access controls.

What's in this chapter

- Various network access methods
- How to deactivate network services to reduce security risks
- Which commonly used network services are potentially unsecure (and how to fix them)
- Intrusion detection
- Types of network authentication
- Virtual private networks

Why this is important

Network access represents the majority of a system's vulnerability. Knowledge of these services and how they are controlled is vital to the security of an entire organization.

Network Access Control Principles

This chapter is built around one underlying principle regarding network access: **disable what is *not* needed, and build access controls around what *is* needed**.

Unnecessary Network Access Points Are Security Risks

Consider the hypothetical network spelling service. You connect to a system's spelling service and type in a string of words; the service returns the same string but with misspellings corrected. Now suppose that a couple of unintentional bugs have been introduced into the spelling service, one or more of which permits someone clever to either penetrate, control, or disable the system.

At one time or another, one or more UNIX-based network services have suffered from this degree of weakness. And weaknesses such as this are still being discovered. For every network service that is turned off, potential security holes are eliminated. If, to continue our example, the spelling service is turned off, then any weaknesses in the spelling service are irrelevant. It is for this reason that all unnecessary services ought to be deactivated. Properly deactivated network services eliminate any current or future threat of system penetration, control, or disabling via that network service.

I'll describe the process of turning network services on and off after the next section.

Unguarded Network Access Points Are Security Risks

Not every network service *can* be turned off. Or, put another way, if every network service *were* turned off, then the system's network cable might as well be disconnected!

Usually, there are some network services that are necessary, but the good news is that most can have access controls applied. Later on I'll talk about the application of network access control for network services that must be turned on.

Necessary and Unnecessary Services

How can you determine if a network service is a necessary one? That is a difficult question to answer; this section will explain the services that are activated on a standard Sun Solaris 7 system, what they mean, what they are used for, and what happens if they are turned off. I'll also show you how to tell if a service is turned on or not, and how to create a simple service of your own.

A *necessary* service is defined as a service that is required for the system to carry out its required functions. Table 13-1 lists the services listed in the file */etc/inet/services* and configured by default on standard Sun Solaris 2.6 and Solaris 7 installations and under what conditions they are necessary.

Table 13-1 *Solaris Network Services*

Port #	Type	Name	Description
1	TCP	tcpmux	TCP port service multiplexer. Necessary.
7	TCP/UDP	echo	Echoes back any character sent to it. Used primarily for testing. Generally unnecessary.
9	TCP/UDP	discard	Swallows everything sent to it. Used primarily for testing. Generally unnecessary.
11	TCP	systat	Runs a *ps* command. Unnecessary and ill advised, because it gives system clues to someone with no permission to access the system.
13	TCP/UDP	daytime	Displays the date and time. Used primarily for testing. Generally unnecessary.
15	TCP	netstat	Runs a *netstat -f inet* command. Unnecessary and ill advised, because it gives system clues to someone with no permission to access the system.
19	TCP/UDP	chargen	Sends revolving pattern of ASCII characters. Used primarily for testing. This service can flood a network. Generally unnecessary.
20	TCP	ftp-data	One of two services used for ftp. This service is used during actual file transfers. Necessary only on an ftp server. See section on ftp.
21	TCP	ftp	One of two services used for ftp. This service is used for ftp commands. Necessary only on an ftp server. See section on ftp.
23	TCP	telnet	The *telnet* service. Necessary only if you want to be able to *telnet to* this system; otherwise unnecessary. See sections on TCP Wrappers and *telnet*'s lack of security.
25	TCP	smtp	E-mail is transported from system to system using this service. Only necessary if this system must *receive* mail from other systems. See chapter 11 for more information.

Table 13-1 *Solaris Network Services (Continued)*

Port #	Type	Name	Description
37	TCP/UDP	time	Outdated time service. Seldom used anymore. Generally unnecessary.
42	UDP	name	Obsolete IEN-116 name service. Seldom used anymore. Generally unnecessary.
43	TCP	whois	The *whois* service. Unnecessary unless the system is a *whois* server.
53	TCP/UDP	domain	The domain name service (DNS). Necessary only if system is a DNS primary or secondary server; unnecessary for DNS clients. See chapter 14 for more information.
67	UDP	bootps	The BOOTP service. Necessary only if this server is a BOOTP server.
68	UDP	bootpc	The BOOTP service. Necessary only if this server is a BOOTP client.
69	UDP	tftp	The trivial file transfer protocol service. Necessary only for tftp boot servers. Potentially dangerous and generally unnecessary. See tftp(1) and in.tftpd(1M) man pages for more information.
77	TCP	rje	The remote job entry service. Seldom used and generally unnecessary.
79	TCP	finger	The *finger* service. Potentially dangerous and generally unnecessary. See finger(1) and in.fingerd(1M) man pages for more information.
87	TCP	link	Private terminal link protocol. Seldom used and generally unnecessary.
95	TCP	supdup	The *telnet* SUPDUP protocol developed at MIT in the late 1970s (described in RFC734). Unnecessary.
101	TCP	hostnames	The hostnames service. Seldom used and generally unnecessary.

Table 13-1 *Solaris Network Services (Continued)*

Port #	Type	Name	Description
102	TCP	iso-tsap	Generally unnecessary.
103	TCP	x400	Used only for ISO X.400 e-mail. Generally unnecessary.
104	TCP	x400-snd	Used only for ISO X.400 e-mail. Generally unnecessary.
105	TCP	csnet-ns	Mailbox name nameserver protocol. Seldom used and generally unnecessary.
109	TCP	pop-2	The post office protocol, version 2. Seldom used and generally unnecessary.
111	TCP/UDP	sunrpc	The RPC suite of services. Necessary for servers only if one or more of the following services are run: NIS, NIS+, NFS, Kerberos, rquotad, rusersd, sadmind, wall. Unnecessary for clients of any of the above-mentioned services.
117	TCP	uucp-path	Used by UUCP over IP. Seldom used and generally unnecessary.
119	TCP	nntp	Network news transfer protocol. Necessary only if system is a Usenet News server.
123	TCP/UDP	ntp	Network time protocol. Necessary only if system is an NTP client or server.
144	TCP	NeWS	The old NeWS Window System protocol. Unnecessary unless the system is running NeWS.
512	TCP	exec	Used by the *rexec* command. Potentially dangerous—uses ~/.*rhosts* file for authentication; passwords and subsequent session transmitted in the clear, and, worst of all, *rexec* performs no logging. Necessary only if the system must receive inbound *rexec* requests. Workarounds possible. (See section on TCP Wrappers as well as the section on secure replacement for *telnet*, *rsh*, and *rlogin*.)

Table 13-1   *Solaris Network Services (Continued)*

Port #	Type	Name	Description
512	UDP	biff	Inbound mail notification ("bark if file found" is the unofficial but literal meaning). Seldom used and generally unnecessary.
513	TCP	login	Used by the *rlogin* command. Potentially dangerous—uses ~/.rhosts file for authentication; passwords and subsequent session transmitted in the clear. Necessary only if the system must receive inbound *rlogin* requests. Workarounds possible. (See section on TCP Wrappers as well as the section on secure replacement for *telnet, rsh,* and *rlogin.*)
513	UDP	who	Part of *rwho* subsystem. Generally unnecessary. See rwho(1) and in.rwhod(1M) man pages for more information.
514	TCP	shell	Used by the *rsh* command. Potentially dangerous—uses ~/.rhosts file for authentication; passwords and subsequent session transmitted in the clear, and, like *rexec*, it performs no logging. Necessary only if the system must receive inbound *rsh* requests. Workarounds possible. (See section on TCP Wrappers as well as the section on secure replacement for *telnet, rsh,* and *rlogin.*)
514	UDP	syslog	Used by *syslog* logging service. Necessary only if system is a *syslog* server. See chapter 8 for more information.
515	TCP	printer	Necessary only if system accepts print requests from other systems on the network.
517	UDP	talk	Used by the *talk* command. See talk(1) and in.talkd(1M) man pages for more information.
520	UDP	route	Used only if system is a network router (which is seldom the case anymore), or needs to receive routing protocol information across the network from one or more routers or workstations. See in.routed(1M) for more information. Generally unnecessary.

Table 13-1 *Solaris Network Services (Continued)*

Port #	Type	Name	Description
530	TCP	courier	An experimental RPC service. Unnecessary.
540	TCP	uucp	Used by UUCP over IP. Seldom used and generally unnecessary.
550	UDP	new-rwho	Part of new experimental *rwho* subsystem. Unnecessary.
560	UDP	rmonitor	Unnecessary.
561	UDP	monitor	Unnecessary.
600	TCP	pcserver	Sun IPC server. Unnecessary.
750	TCP/UDP	kerberos	Used only if system is a kerberos server or client.
1008	TCP/UDP	ufsd	Used by the Sun Online Disksuite product.
1103	TCP	xaudio	X-Windows audio server; used by CDE.
1524	TCP	ingreslock	Unnecessary.
2049	TCP/UDP	nfsd	Used only if system is an NFS server.
2766	TCP	listen	The System V listener; similar to *tcpmux*.
4045	TCP/UDP	lockd	NFS lock manager. Used only if system is an NFS server.
6112	TCP	dtspc	Used by CDE.
7100	TCP	fs	Font server. Used by CDE and OpenWindows.

Note: Unless otherwise specified in Table 13-1, the presence of each service permits the use of *inbound* service requests. For example, the presence of TCP service 23 (*telnet*) permits inbound *telnet* sessions. Removal of this service will not prevent *outbound telnet* sessions.

There are hundreds of officially assigned network services and hundreds more unassigned (but nevertheless used). You will find a complete list of officially assigned services in RFC1700 (see the references at the end of this chapter).

How to Disable Unnecessary Services

The following procedure is used to identify and disable a service determined to be unnecessary.

1. Use *vi* (or another editor) to comment the entry in the file */etc/inet/ services* by prepending it with a # character. It would also be useful to add a descriptive comment to the line above the commented line, explaining who is commenting it and why.

2. Use *vi* (or another editor) to locate any corresponding entry in */etc/inet/ inetd.conf* . A corresponding entry will begin with the name used as the first field in the */etc/inet/services* file. Comment the entry by prepending it with a # character. Add a descriptive comment as in step 1.

3. Locate the *inetd* process and send it a SIGHUP signal.

Figure 13.1 illustrates disabling the *telnet* service on a system.

Disable Service Not Defined in */etc/inet/services* and */etc/inet/inetd.conf*

Some services such as *sendmail* are not defined in */etc/inet/services* and */etc/ inet/inetd.conf*. Table 13-2 describes how to disable such services.

Strengthening Network Access Control

This section describes the steps used to apply and verify access control for common network services.

Figure 13.1 *Disabling a Network Service (Example)*

```
# disabled telnet on 7/8/98 (peter g.)
#) telnet        23/tcp
      commented line in /etc/inet/services

# disabled telnet on 7/8/98 (peter g.)
#) telnet   stream  tcp  nowait  root  /usr/sbin/in.telnetd  in.telnetd
      commented line in /etc/inet/inetd.conf

# ps -ef|grep inetd
    root   (136)     1  0   Feb 23 ?        0:02 /usr/sbin/inetd -s
    root  11035 10947  0 15:46:32 pts/9    0:00 grep inetd
# kill -1(136)
#                   restart inetd
```

Table 13-2 *Disable Other Network Services*

Service	How to Disable
sendmail	1. Rename (using the *mv* command) */etc/rc2.d/S88sendmail* to */etc/rc2.d/X88sendmail* . 2. Kill all *sendmail* processes.
DNS	1. Comment entry to start *in.named* in the file */etc/rc2.d/S72inetsvc* . 2. Kill *in.named* process and any *named.xfer* processes.
NFS server	1. Comment entries in */etc/dfs/dfstab*. 2. Rename (using the *mv* command) */etc/rc3.d/S15nfs.server* to */etc/rc3.d/X15nfs.server* . 3. Kill *nfsd* process(es).
NFS client	1. Comment *fstype=nfs* entries in */etc/vfstab* . 2. Unmount all NFS-mounted filesystems with *umount* command. 3. Rename (using the *mv* command) */etc/rc2.d/S73nfs.client* to */etc/rc2.d/X73nfs.client* .
Automounter	1. Rename (using the *mv* command) */etc/rc2.d/S74autofs* to */etc/rc2.d/X74autofs*, and/or 2. Remove */etc/auto* * .
ntp	1. Rename (using the *mv* command) */etc/rc2.d/S74xntpd* to */etc/rc2.d/X74xntpd* . 2. Kill *xntpd* process.
syslog	1. Rename (using the *mv* command) */etc/rc2.d/S74syslog* to */etc/rc2.d/X74syslog* . 2. Kill *syslogd* process.
print services	1. Rename (using the *mv* command) */etc/rc2.d/S80lp* to */etc/rc2.d/X80lp* . 2. Run *lpshut* command.

inetd *Connection Tracing*

inetd will attempt to trace all incoming TCP services if the *-t* (trace) option is used. In trace mode, *inetd* will log to *syslog*'s **daemon** facility at severity level **notice**. See chapter 8 for additional information on *syslog*.

Sample *syslog* output from *inetd* in trace mode follows:

```
Apr 11 05:37:14 alpha inetd[1771]: telnet[1773] from 199.8.20.11 3281
Apr 11 05:38:17 alpha inetd[1771]: ftp[1785] from 199.9.10.14 982
Apr 11 05:38:40 alpha inetd[1771]: login[1788] from 199.9.2.2 1023
```

By default these messages will appear in */var/adm/messages* .

Follow this procedure for turning on *inetd* tracing.

1. Edit the startup file */etc/init.d/inetsvc* . Add a *-t* to the *inetd* startup command line so that it looks like this

   ```
   /usr/sbin/inetd -s -t &
   ```

2. Stop and restart *inetd*. Here is a sample dialog.

   ```
   # ps -ef|grep inetd
       root  1880  1822  0 05:52:42 pts/4     0:00 grep inetd
       root  (114)    1  0 05:37:02 ?         0:00 /usr/sbin/inetd -s
   # kill (114)
   # /usr/sbin/inetd -s -t
   #
   ```

TCP Wrappers

TCP Wrappers is a public-domain tool used to control which systems (and, optionally, which users on those systems) can access network services. TCP Wrappers is used to restrict inbound network access only, and then only on certain services defined in the file */etc/inetd/inetd.conf* . TCP Wrappers can be found at ftp://ftp.porcupine.org/pub/security/ .

Converting a Service to TCP Wrappers

It is easy to convert most services to TCP Wrappers. The following example shows how inbound *telnet* is converted to TCP Wrappers. This example assumes that TCP Wrappers has already been built and installed.

Modify the file */etc/inetd/inetd.conf* . The original entry for *telnet* is

```
telnet stream tcp nowait root /usr/sbin/in.telnetd in.telnetd
```

The new entry for *telnet* is

```
telnet stream tcp nowait root /usr/sbin/in.tcpd /usr/sbin/in.telnetd
```

The fundamental difference is explained: responding to an inbound *telnet* request, instead of running *in.telnetd*, *inetd* runs *in.tcpd*, the TCP Wrappers program, which checks its access control lists before launching the real *in.telnet* program (and only if it should!).

Example: How to Restrict *Telnet* to Certain Systems

TCP Wrappers uses the two files */etc/hosts.allow* and */etc/hosts.deny* to determine which systems and users should have access to which services. An example */etc/hosts.allow* file follows.

```
# /etc/hosts.allow file
#
in.telnetd: .sun.com, 207.127.1.
in.rshd:    .sun.com, 207.127.1.
in.rlogind: .sun.com, 207.127.1.
in.ftpd:    .sun.com, 207.127.1.
```

A computer using this */etc/hosts.allow* file will permit inbound *telnet*, *rsh*, *rlogin*, and *ftp* from computers in the *sun.com* domain, as well as those on the 207.127.1 network. The */etc/hosts.deny* file uses the same syntax.

To be alerted when TCP Wrappers detects unauthorized connection attempts, add the following entry to the end of */etc/hosts.deny* (after all other entries):

```
ALL: ALL: /usr/bin/mailx -s "%d: unauthorized connection attempt from
    %c" sysadmin@domain.com
```

To log all TCP Wrappers connections (allowed and disallowed) to *syslog*, add the following entry to */etc/syslog.conf*:

```
auth.notice;auth.info<tab>/var/log/wrapperlog
```

Note that in this example, <tab> must be a literal *tab* character. Substitute another logfile for */var/log/wrapperlog* as appropriate for the site.

Please refer to TCP Wrappers documentation for complete installation and configuration information.

Public-Domain rpcbind

In situations where a system must be an NFS, NIS, or NIS+ server, a public-domain *rpcbind* is available that significantly enhances security over the original Solaris version of *rpcbind*. This is accomplished via a TCP-Wrappers-like mechanism whereby only systems on certain IP addresses or networks are allowed to access NIS/NIS+, NFS, and other RPC services.

This enhanced version of *rpcbind* requires *libwrap.a*, which is part of the TCP Wrappers tool described earlier. The TCP Wrappers files */etc/hosts.allow* and */etc/hosts.deny* are also used with *rpcbind*.

This *rpcbind* is available from ftp://ftp.porcupine.org/pub/security/rpcbind_2.1.tar.gz .

.rhosts File—Gateway to the r-Commands

The so-called r-commands consist of *rlogin*, *rsh, rcp,* and *rdist*. They are called r-commands because they all start with the letter *r*, which stands for remote. All have to do with running shells or commands on remote systems—

rlogin = remote login, *rsh* = remote shell, *rcp* = remote copy, *rdist* = remote distribution.

The *nice* thing—and the *bad* thing—about the r-commands is that, through the use of an *.rhosts* file, a user on one system can log in or execute commands on a remote system without having to supply a password.

> **Warning: The use of *.rhosts* to permit trusted r-commands across a network is not recommended, particularly by root. In all but the smallest environments, the implicit webs of trust set up through the overuse of *.rhosts* can quickly grow out of control and expose the site to unacceptable security risks.**

Similar to *telnet*, in the absence of an appropriate *.rhosts* entry, a user attempting to access a remote system via an r-command will be required to enter the account's password. This password is transmitted in the clear over the network.

The inherent weaknesses of the r-commands include

- Any password entered is done in the clear; anyone snooping the network will easily be able to see the password.
- The entire r-command session is in the clear. Every character of the session, including passwords, can easily be recorded.

See the section on secure replacement for *rsh* and *rlogin* below for information on a more secure alternative to *rsh* and *rlogin*.

/etc/hosts.equiv *File*

The */etc/hosts.equiv* file is similar to the *.rhosts* file, but opens a far wider security hole than does *.rhosts*.

> **Warning: *hosts.equiv* allows a user from a remote system to become *any* user on a local system. It can also permit *any* user on a remote system to become *any* user on a local system. For this reason the use of *hosts.equiv* is strongly discouraged.**

Auditing .rhosts *and* hosts.equiv *Files*

The *.rhosts* and *hosts.equiv* files should be audited periodically by the COPS and/or Tripwire tools.

The following COPS modules include checks for *.rhosts* and *hosts.equiv* security: *root.chk* and *root.pl*, *trust.pl*, *user.chk*, and *user.pl*.

Refer to chapter 4 for more information about obtaining and running COPS and Tripwire.

Secure Replacement for telnet, rsh, *and* rlogin

rsh and *rlogin* represent one of UNIX's biggest security holes. Unless equivalence is set up (which in itself can be dangerous) with *.rhosts* or */etc/ hosts.equiv*, the user will be prompted for a password that, if typed, is transmitted in the clear over the network. This means that anyone with a network sniffer, such as the Solaris *snoop* program, can easily see this password and save it for future mischief. Further, the entire *rsh/rlogin* session is transmitted in the clear.

ssh, or *secure sh*ell, is a nice drop-in replacement for UNIX's *rsh*, *rlogin*, and *telnet*. *ssh* functions the same way as *rsh*, but includes the following enhancements:

- Better authentication using RSA technology—this eliminates IP, host, and DNS spoofing weaknesses
- Full-session encryption, including passwords

Public domain *ssh* for Solaris is available at http://www.cs.hut.fi/ssh or ftp:// ftp.cs.hut.fi/pub/ssh/ . Commercially supported versions for Solaris (as well as Windows 3.x, 9x, and NT) are available at http://www.datafellows.com/ or http://www.ssh.fi/ .

ftp

ftp is a significant security risk. Like *telnet* and the r-commands, all *ftp* traffic is transmitted in the clear over the network. If *ftp* is a site necessity, then consider these recommendations:

- Avoid *anonymous ftp*. Instead, explicitly control and identify who will be accessing the site from the outside world and assign individual userids and passwords.
- Turn on *ftpd* logging and debugging. The *ftpd* entry in */etc/inet/ inetd.conf* should appear as follows:

```
ftp    stream   tcp   nowait   root   /usr/sbin/in.ftpd in.ftpd -dl
```

- Follow the recommendations in the ftpd(1M) man page.
- Never *ftp* as root (remember, the password is sent in the clear over the network); to enforce this, add root to */etc/ftpusers* (userids in this file are prohibited from connecting to the system using *ftp*).

Warning: If *anonymous ftp* is a site necessity, it is essential that the instructions in the ftpd(1M) man page regarding *anonymous ftp* be followed to the letter.

Sites requiring greater access control and/or logging capabilities should replace Sun's *ftpd* with Washington University's *ftp* package, known as *wu-ftp*. It is available at

- ftp://wuarchive.wustl.edu/packages/wuarchive-ftpd/[1]
- http://www.sunfreeware.com/ (look for *wu-ftpd*)
- ftp://ftp.cyber.com.au/pub/unix/wu-ftpd-2.4.tar.Z

tftp

Trivial file transfer program (*tftp*) is a host-to-host file transfer program similar to, but simpler than, *ftp*. *tftp* has no user or system authentication mechanism.

tftp is generally dangerous and, unless absolutely necessary, should be turned off. If *tftp* is a site necessity, limit its use to as few systems as possible (and never a system reachable from the Internet), and make sure it is restricted to use only a single directory with the *-s /tftpboot* option. Modify */etc/inet/inetd.conf* as follows:

```
tftp dgram udp wait root /usr/etc/in.tftp in.tftp -s /tftpboot
```

X-Windows Is Unsecure

Similar to the r-commands (*rlogin*, *rsh*, *rcp*) and *telnet*, all X-Windows traffic is transmitted in the clear over the network, and its authentication is weak (and easily disabled altogether).

ssh can be used to provide secure X-Windows sessions that are fully encrypted. An example X-Windows *ssh* session is described here (assuming *ssh* is installed on both systems).

1. With OpenWindows or CDE running, *ssh* from one system's console to a remote system with the command *ssh system-name*.
2. On the remote system, run any X-Windows program. *ssh* will cause that program's X-Windows output to be displayed back on the original system.

There is no need to run the *xhost* command on the original system, nor is it necessary to set the DISPLAY environment variable on the remote system. *ssh* takes care of both automatically.

See the earlier section on secure replacement for *telnet*, *rsh*, and *rlogin* in this chapter for information on obtaining *ssh*. For more information on X-Windows security, see chapter 5.

---

1. This site, recognized as the original source for wu-ftpd, was off the air at press time.

Firewalls

A firewall is a network device designed to allow the network administrator to determine which network protocols will be allowed to enter or leave a network, as well as which systems or networks those protocols will be allowed to pass. Firewalls accomplish this with a set of rules that define those network packets that are allowed through and those that are blocked. Some example firewall rules are[2]

- Deny all inbound *telnet* from the Internet to this site.
- Allow inbound and outbound SMTP mail between the local mail server *mail.mysite.com* and any site on the Internet.
- Allow *ftp* from the Internet to only the *ftp* server *ftp.mysite.com* .
- Allow www from the Internet only to the Web server *www.mysite.com* .
- Allow outbound *telnet* from this site to anywhere on the Internet.
- Allow outbound *ftp* from this site to anywhere on the Internet.
- Deny all other services except those listed above.

A firewall is typically placed in the network at the boundary between one organization and another and, most commonly, between an organization and the Internet.

Firewalls should not be considered *the* line of defense, but *a* line of defense—firewalls can be configured incorrectly, they can fail, and network paths can (accidentally and otherwise) be built around them.

In an organization where the UNIX administrator is not familiar with or responsible for the organization's firewall(s), it is imperative that firewalls be thoroughly understood so that the UNIX administrator can properly supplement access control policies on server and desktop systems.

Refer to appendix E for more information on Sun firewall products.

Testing System Accessibility

No UNIX administrator should trust his or her diligence and typing skills so much as to leave security configurations untested. But on the other hand, thoroughly testing a UNIX system for network access vulnerability can take hours, if not days. Some public-domain tools have been implemented that automate the work of uncovering vulnerabilities. I'll discuss a few of these in the following sections.

---

2. These rules are only examples and may not reflect security requirements for your site.

Satan

The Security Administrator's Tool for Analyzing Networks (Satan) is a tool used by UNIX and network administrators to discover weaknesses in system and network configurations.

Satan is a port scanner program that works by probing a system over the network—or all systems on a subnetwork—looking for known weaknesses (without actually exploiting them) and reporting to the user any weaknesses found. For each weakness found, Satan displays a tutorial explaining the problem and possible solutions.

Satan is available at the following sites:

*   http://www.fish.com/satan/
*   http://www.trouble.org/~zen/satan/satan.html

ISS

Internet Security Scan, or ISS, is a port scanning tool similar to Satan in that the tool scans systems or subnets looking for weaknesses that should be taken care of.

ISS is available from ftp://coast.cs.purdue.edu/pub/tools/unix/iss/ .

Note: The public-domain version of ISS has not been updated since 1995; its effectiveness has diminished since then. A commercial version with regular updates has replaced it; information is available at http://iss.net/.

Intrusion Detection

Upon reading the previous section, you might wonder whether an intruder could use these same tools to discover security weaknesses that could then be used to break into or otherwise disrupt a site. This is not only possible, but probable. Furthermore, hackers have tools far better than Satan and ISS for discovering a site's security weaknesses.

It used to be enough to simply disallow unauthorized data access, using devices such as firewalls and tools such as TCP Wrappers. Frequently, however, hacking attempts went unnoticed until it was too late. Intrusion detection, the practice of discovering, in real time, break-in attempts on a system or network, is a growing segment in the security tools arsenal and is maturing and getting the attention it deserves.

One or more suitable intrusion detection tools should be used in any site connected to the Internet. Certainly any system directly accessed from the Internet (inbound or outbound) should be outfitted with one or more of these tools, and perhaps some "interior" servers, such as DNS or e-mail, should be configured as well. The following sections cover a few public-domain intrusion detection tools.

Syn

Syn is a utility used to track port scanning activity generated by someone running Satan, ISS, or some other port scanning tool. It uses *tcpdump* to capture packets and logs suspicious events to *syslog*. Syn is written in perl; hence, perl is also required in order for syn to run.

Syn is available from ftp://ftp.pgci.ca/pub/syn/ .

Klaxon

Klaxon is a utility used to detect port scanning activity generated by tools such as Satan and ISS. Klaxon can also attempt to determine the identity (using the Ident protocol described in RFC931) of the remote user running the port scanner.

Klaxon is available from ftp://ftp.eng.auburn.edu/pub/doug/ .

Courtney

Courtney is a utility designed to detect incoming port scans from port scanners such as the Satan program. Courtney requires libpcap (available at ftp://ftp.ee.lbl.gov/libpcap-0.0.tar.Z), *tcpdump*, and perl version 5.

Courtney is available from http://ciac.llnl.gov/ciac/SecurityTools.html .

Tocsin

Tocsin is a promiscuous network monitor designed to detect SYN and RST attacks. These kinds of attacks are not detected by tools such as TCP Wrappers or Klaxon. For more information on SYN and RST attacks, see the glossary of attacks appendix.

Tocsin is available from ftp://ftp.eng.auburn.edu/pub/doug/ .

Gabriel

Gabriel is a port scanner detector used to detect Satan, ISS, and others. Unlike Syn and Courtney, Gabriel does not require perl or even a C compiler; Gabriel includes C-source code and ready-to-run binaries for Solaris 1 and Solaris 2.

Gabriel is available from http://www.lat.com/gabe.html .

Intrusion Detection: Staying Current

Intrusion detection is a developing technology. The security-conscious UNIX administrator would do well to stay current on the topic; Web sites with interesting information on intrusion detection include

- http://www.cs.purdue.edu/coast/projects/autonomous-agents.html
- http://www.cs.purdue.edu/coast/intrusion-detection

Authentication

Authentication refers to a process of identifying yourself to a system in order to access information. Solaris supports three authentication methods: System, DES (also known as Diffie-Hellman), and Kerberos. NIS and NIS+ support all three methods.

System Authentication

System authentication simply refers to the standard UNIX file/directory permissions and userid/groupid structure, nothing more. This is the default method used for authentication—there is nothing more to making this work than setting good file and directory ownership and permissions.

DES (Diffie-Hellman) Authentication

Data encryption standard (DES) is used to authenticate users and systems. DES uses the data encryption standard and public-key cryptography to safely encrypt authentication information over the network. Solaris systems include the complete DES authentication software needed to set up DES authentication, the procedure for which follows.

1. Ensure each computer participating in DES authentication is configured to be a member of the DNS, NIS, or NIS+ domain.
2. Set up public keys and secret keys with the *newkey* or *nisaddcred* commands for all users who will be accessing other systems (for example, using NFS), and have each user set up his or her Secure RPC password with the *chkey* command.
3. Verify that name service is running with the *nisping -u* command (for NIS+) or by checking if the *ypbind* process is running (for NIS) by typing *ps -ef | grep ypbind* .
4. Make sure the *keyserv* process is running (*ps -ef | grep keyserv*).

5. As root, decrypt and store the secret key with the *keylogin -r* command. This needs to be done only once, if the root secret key is changed, or if the file */etc/.rootkey* is lost.

6. Each user will need to decrypt and store the secret key with the *keylogin* command. This is necessary only if the login and network passwords differ (if the login and network passwords are the same, the user login will also perform the network login).

7. To convert an NFS mount to a secure NFS mount on the server, add the *-sec=dh* option to each *dfstab* entry in */etc/dfs/dfstab*. For example

```
share -F nfs (-o sec=dh) /export/home
```

8. For each NFS client, edit the corresponding */etc/vfstab* entries (or, when using automounter, the appropriate automount map entries). An example *vfstab* entry follows:

```
appserver:/d1/local - /usr/local NFS - yes ro,br (sec=dh)
```

Kerberos Authentication

Kerberos, like DES, is an authentication system that uses DES encryption to protect authentication information transmitted over the network.

Kerberos server software is not included with Solaris and must be obtained from a site such as http://web.mit.edu/kerberos/www/ . Solaris includes the client-side daemon kerbd as well as the routines used by a client to create, acquire, and verify Kerberos tickets.

Note: Considerable knowledge and effort are required to set up a Kerberos environment, and it may not be the appropriate authentication system for every site. See the references section for Kerberos references.

Note: MIT distributes Kerberos only to U.S. citizens located in the United States or to Canadian citizens located in Canada.

The following is the procedure for setting up a secure NFS mount using Kerberos authentication (assuming Kerberos is set up):

1. To convert an NFS mount to a secure NFS mount on the server, add the *-sec=krb4* option to each *dfstab* entry in */etc/dfs/dfstab* . For example

```
share -F nfs (-o sec=krb4) /export/home
```

2. For each NFS client, edit the corresponding */etc/vfstab* entries (or, when using automounter, the appropriate automount map entries). An example *vfstab* entry follows:

```
appserver:/d1/local - /usr/local NFS - yes ro,br (sec=krb4)
```

Virtual Private Networks

A virtual private network (VPN) is an encrypted network connection between two systems. A VPN allows two parties to connect via the Internet (or other public network) without fear of an eavesdropper recording and/or interfering with the connection. A system-to-system VPN is analogous to an encrypted telephone call—the parties on the call don't have to worry about the presence of a wiretap since their conversation will be encrypted and virtually uncrackable.

Frequently, VPNs are more cost effective than private, dedicated data circuits. This is because each party needs only to have a dedicated Internet connection through which they communicate. This becomes more cost effective as the number of parties using VPNs increases.

SKIP

Sun uses Simple Key-management for Internet Protocols (SKIP) encryption for its VPNs. SKIP client software is available for Sun workstations, servers, and PCs running Windows 9x.

SKIP is available on Sun's EFS, SPF, and Securenet products in a server configuration supporting multiple SKIP sessions between multiple sites.

A typical SKIP connection between a PC client and a Sun server is illustrated in Figure 13.2.

SKIP can also be used to encrypt all network traffic between two sites (see Figure 13.3).

IPsec

IP security protocol (IPsec), the public-domain VPN solution developed by the Internet Engineering Task Force (IETF) is growing in popularity. In a short

Figure 13.2 *SKIP Connection Between PC Client and Sun Server*

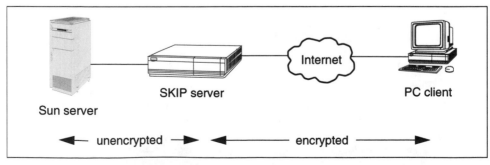

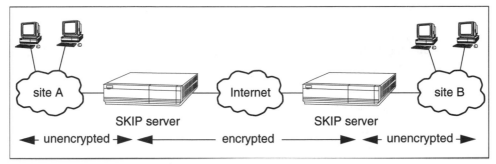

Figure 13.3 *SKIP Connection Between Two Sites*

time IPsec may eclipse or merge with SKIP as the Internet VPN standard. By the time this book goes to press, there should be one or more commercial versions of IPsec available for Solaris. Sun Microsystems itself has gone on record saying it will implement IPsec.[3]

A public-domain third-party VPN solution using the IPsec security standard is available. The National Institute of Standards and Technology (NIST) is the source for this standard—*The NIST IPsec Reference Implementation*, available to U.S. citizens within the United States and Canadian citizens within Canada only. This is a complete IPsec source, written for Slackware and patches for RedHat Linux. With minimal effort this will port to Solaris 2. All who wish to download this software must first register at this Web site: http://www.antd.nist.gov/itg/cerberus/ipsec-form.html .

Unlike many popular UNIX add-on tools, little public-domain IPsec client software is available for UNIX/Solaris. Instead, most IPsec products may be commercial. Some security tools vendors are indicating that IPsec products are in development.

Where to Go for Additional Information

AnswerBook

- AnswerBook 2—System Administration Guide, TCP/IP and Data Communications Administration Guide
- AnswerBook 2—System Administration Guide, NFS Administration Guide

Man Pages

- chkey(1)

---

3. Refer to http://www.sun.com/software/white-papers/wp-solaris7/.

- ftpd(1M)
- hosts.equiv(4)
- keylogin(1)
- mv(1)
- newkey(1M)
- nisaddcred(1M)
- nisping(1M)
- .rhosts(4)
- tftpd(1M)
- ypbind(1M)

Publications

- RFC1700, "Assigned Numbers" (official list of TCP/IP port number assignments), http://www.cis.ohio-state.edu/htbin/rfc/rfc1700.html
- *The Moron's Guide to Kerberos,* Brian Tung, http://gost.isi.edu/brian/security/kerberos.html
- *How to Kerberize Your Site,* Oak Ridge National Laboratory, http://www.ornl.gov/~jar/HowToKerb.html
- *Kerberos FAQ,* http://www.cis.ohio-state.edu/hypertext/faq/usenet/kerberos-faq/general/faq.html
- Cheswick, William R., and Bellovin, Steven M. *Firewalls and Internet Security: Repelling the Wily Hacker.* Reading, MA: Addison-Wesley, 1994.
- *Improving the Security of Your Site by Breaking into It,* Dan Farmer, ftp://ftp.porcupine.org/pub/security/admin-guide-to-cracking.101.Z
- *What Is a VPN?,* ftp://ftp.employees.org/ferguson/vpn.zip
- *CyLAN IPSec White Paper,* http://www.cylan.com/files/whpaper.htm
- RFC2411, "IPsec Document Roadmap," http://www.ietf.org/rfc/rfc2411.txt
- Scott, Charlie, Wolfe, Paul, and Erwin, Mike. *Virtual Private Networks,* 2d ed. Sebastopol, CA: O'Reilly & Associates, Inc., 1999.
- *How to Configure SKIP and a SunScreen SPF-200,* SunSolve InfoDoc 16282

Web Sites

- *MIT Kerberos site*—http://web.mit.edu/kerberos/www/
- *Sun firewalls*—http://www.sun.com/security/#products
- *USC/ISI Kerberos site*—http://gost.isi.edu/info/kerberos/
- *NIST Internetworking Technologies Group*—http://www.antd.nist.gov/antd/html/itg.html, http://www.antd.nist.gov/antd/
- *IETF's IPsec site*—http://www.ietf.org/html.charters/ipsec-charter.html

14

NAME SERVICES

Name services are often the least-understood facilities on a UNIX system; frequently they are cobbled together until they work, and then they aren't touched for fear they will break down again. All too often security holes exist that invite disaster should a UNIX administrator make a mistake or an intruder decide to make some trouble.

What's in this chapter

- Overview of DNS and ways to improve its security
- Architecture of split-horizon DNS and why it is useful
- NIS's security weaknesses
- Ensuring NIS+ security
- The name service switch
- Nscd and its role in name services

Why this is important

Name servers provide organization-wide information services which are only as reliable as the servers are secure.

Domain Name Service (DNS)

The unseen backbone of Internet navigation, DNS translates domain names into IP addresses and IP addresses into domain names.

Why is DNS needed? Computer software programs communicate with each other by referencing their respective IP addresses; however, because IP addresses are abstract, they can be easily forgotten. DNS was developed because people can remember names far easier than addresses. In every instance where a person types in a domain name (for example, in a Web browser), the software program must summon DNS in order to determine the IP address of the computer with that particular domain name.

DNS is a hierarchical directory service, with each server containing a list of node names and their respective IP addresses, as well as a possible list of sub-domains and the IP address(es) of server(s) that contain information about the subdomains.

Each name in Figure 14.1 is a DNS *domain*. Each DNS domain contains the following information:

- A list of computer names (and their IP addresses) that are registered domain servers for the domain.

- A list of computer names and their respective IP addresses that are part of the domain.

- A list of subdomains, and the computer names and IP addresses that are the domain servers for those subdomains. From Figure 14.1, the domain *sun* contains three subdomains—*corp*, *west*, and *east*—along with the names and IP addresses of the DNS servers for those respective domains. The process of naming a subdomain and assigning one or more servers for the subdomain is called *delegation*. This term will be used throughout the section on DNS.

Note: The top-most domains ".", "com," "org," "edu," "gov," "mil" (and, in fact, many others, principally the two-letter ISO country codes such as "us," "jp," and "ca") are controlled by the Internet Network Information Center (InterNIC), an organization that registers all top-level

Figure 14.1 *DNS Domain Hierarchy*

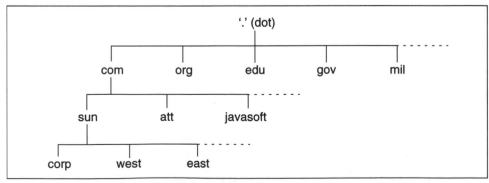

domain names. The domain names "sun," "att," and "javasoft" in the example above are registered and *delegated* from the InterNIC domain servers. Delegation and control of the domain names "corp," "west," and "east" in the example above are solely within the control of the organization responsible for the domain "sun."

Each domain has a *primary domain server*, which is the system containing the database of names and IP addresses. Each domain can also have one or more *secondary domain servers*; these servers are configured with the IP address(es) of only the primary domain servers they serve; the secondary servers then periodically request a *zone transfer*—a copy of the database from the primary server so that they, too, can answer queries for the domain.

All computers in a network with the need to perform DNS inquiries are called *resolvers*. Resolvers contain the software necessary to perform DNS inquiries, plus two configuration files, */etc/nsswitch.conf*, and */etc/resolv.conf*. Examples of these files appear below.

/etc/nsswitch.conf

The file */etc/nsswitch.conf* sets up directives for a variety of directory services. In the example below, the entry "files dns" tells the system, when looking up names or IP addresses, to first look in the file */etc/inet/hosts* and then to use DNS. Here is a typical */etc/nsswitch.conf* file. The "hosts" entry is underlined.

```
#
# /etc/nsswitch.files:
#
# An example file that could be copied over to /etc/nsswitch.conf; it
# does not use any naming service.
#
# "hosts:" and "services:" in this file are used only if the
# /etc/netconfig file has a "-" for nametoaddr_libs of "inet" transports.
passwd:      files
group:       files
hosts:       files dns
networks:    files
protocols:   files
rpc:         files
ethers:      files
netmasks:    files
bootparams:  files
publickey:   files
# At present there isn't a 'files' backend for netgroup;  the system will
# figure it out pretty quickly, and won't use netgroups at all.
netgroup:     files
automount:    files
aliases:      files
services:     files
sendmailvars: files
```

/etc/resolv.conf

The file */etc/resolv.conf* is used solely by DNS; it tells DNS which domain to use for lookups; it also lists one or more DNS server IP addresses to use for DNS lookups. A typical */etc/resolv.conf* file would appear as follows:

```
domain west.sun.com
nameserver 204.63.68.119
nameserver 204.63.67.7
```

In this example, the domain assumed is *west.sun.com*; the two DNS servers to be queried are at IP addresses 204.63.68.119 and 204.63.67.7.

The domain entry in */etc/resolv.conf* is used to help resolve *partially quali-fie*d domain names. For instance, a computer in the *west.sun.com* domain can query DNS for the IP address of the computer *mailserver.west.sun.com* by asking just for the name *mailserver*. DNS will assume that the computer wants the IP address for *mailserver.west.sun.com* .

DNS Security Weaknesses and Solutions

Too Much Information Visible to the Internet

Generally speaking, all of the machine names and their respective IP addresses in an organization can easily be queried by anyone on the Internet. Even if an effective, properly configured firewall is in place, the ability to view the names and IP addresses of servers and workstations is enough to make more than a few site administrators nervous. Consider, for example, DNS entries for machine names such as *billing*, *fin-server*, or *gl-master*. This would be like publishing the plans for a secret submarine base outside of the locked gates! Even with a firewall in place, publishing the names and addresses of important systems and devices poses a security threat because it defines named targets for intruders to try to attack. A DNS architecture called split-horizon DNS addresses this concern.

Split-Horizon DNS

A split-horizon DNS architecture is one in which publicly reachable systems and network elements are defined in the publicly reachable DNS domain, while the internal infrastructure of the same organization is defined in an iso-lated, unreachable DNS domain. Figure 14.2 illustrates this architecture.

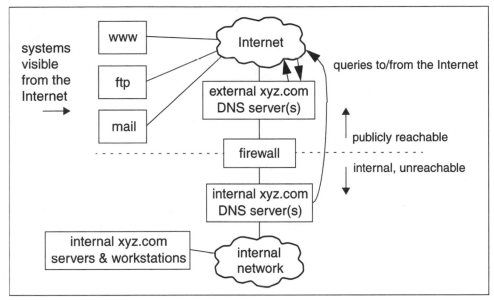

Figure 14.2 *Split-Horizon DNS Architecture*

Some important characteristics of this architecture include

- The public *xyz.com* DNS server, as well as the servers *www, ftp,* and *mail,* are the *only* systems defined in the public *xyz.com* DNS server database.

- Neither the internal DNS server(s) nor any internal servers or workstations are defined in the public *xyz.com* DNS database. From the perspective of the Internet, the internal DNS servers do not exist.

- *resolv.conf* entries on internal servers and workstations point to the internal *xyz.com* DNS server(s).

- The firewall allows the internal DNS server to query the Internet.

- The firewall blocks queries and zone transfer requests from the Internet from reaching the internal DNS server(s).

Follow this procedure for setting up a split-horizon DNS architecture.

1. Set up external DNS server. Follow the procedure described in Sun-Solve publication *DNS PSD/FAQ* (Infodoc 11975, version 2.5, February 19, 1997), section 3.7, "How to Set Up a Primary DNS Server." Include in the zone files only the publicly visible hosts that need to be accessed from the Internet.

2. Set up internal DNS server. Follow the procedure described in Sun-Solve publication *DNS PSD/FAQ* (Infodoc 11975, version 2.5, February 19, 1997), section 3.7, "How to Set Up a Primary DNS Server." Include in the zone files *all* internal and external hosts in the network.

3. Set up Internet firewall to block all TCP port 43 (DNS zone transfer) packets from the internal DNS server to and from the Internet. This will block all zone transfer attempts between the internal DNS server and the Internet.

4. Set up the Internet firewall to block all UDP port 43 (DNS query) packets to the internal DNS server from the Internet; the Internet firewall should permit UDP port 43 packets from the internal DNS server to the Internet. This will block all queries from the Internet to the internal DNS server, but will allow the internal DNS server to query the Internet.

Note: In an older variation of the split-horizon DNS architecture, the internal DNS servers would be set up with "forwarders" entries pointing to the exterior DNS servers. This forced the interior DNS servers to ask the exterior DNS servers for Internet DNS queries. This architecture has one primary weakness: if a hacker can take over the exterior DNS server (which is more vulnerable *because* it is an exterior server), she can modify the exterior DNS server so that some or all DNS queries originating from the inside DNS servers will return incorrect answers.

If the interior DNS servers query the Internet directly, the hacker wishing to corrupt Internet DNS queries must either break into the interior DNS server (which would presumably be more difficult since it can be better protected), or break into the DNS servers for the Internet domain(s) that the hacker wishes to corrupt.

Block Unwanted Queries with Allow-Query Function

Sites using BIND Version 8.1 or newer[1] can use a new security feature in the *named.conf* file called the allow-query function. This feature allows the UNIX administrator to specify which clients can query a nameserver. One practical use for this feature is to permit only *inside* systems to query a DNS server for *inside* DNS information. An example *named.boot* file fragment follows.

```
...
options {
        allow-query { 128.126.120/24; 128.126.130/24; };
};
...
```

In this example, the nameserver will accept queries only from systems on the 128.126.120.* and 128.126.130.* networks.

In BIND Version 8.1 and later, the allow-query function can also be enforced at the zone level. An example zone file fragment:

---

1. Refer to the section on how to know your BIND version later in this chapter for more information on determining which version of BIND is running.

```
zone "lab.sun.com" {
        type primary;
        file "db.lab.sun.com";
        allow-query { 124.30/16; };
};
```

In this example, only systems on the 124.30.*.* network may query this nameserver for information about the the domain *lab.sun.com*.

> **Note: Despite the protection that the allow-query function affords (by permitting domain queries only from certain networks), a firewall or filtering router should be used to prevent DNS queries from the Internet from reaching interior DNS servers. This is an example of protecting in layers (see chapter 2).**

Illicit Zone Transfers from DNS Servers

The *zone transfer* is the mechanism for replicating a DNS database from one server to another. Some UNIX/network administrators may not want just anyone to pull a zone transfer from their public DNS server (and certainly not from their private/internal DNS server!). Several means are available for preventing illicit zone transfers.

1. Set up the Internet firewall to block all TCP port 43 (DNS zone transfer) packets from the internal DNS server to and from the Internet. This will block all zone transfer attempts between the internal DNS server and the Internet. Open up holes in the firewall on that same port for registered and legitimate DNS secondary servers.

2. Obtain and apply the BIND 4.9.3 patches from Sun,[2] and then use the *xfernets* directive in the *named.boot* file.

3. Obtain and apply public-domain BIND (4.9.3 or newer) and use the *xfernets* directive in the *named.boot* file.

4. In BIND 8.1 and later,[3] use the *allow-transfer* option to specify which hosts or networks may pull a zone transfer from the domain.

Differences Between **nslookup** *and* *Actual DNS Queries*

I should note that it is possible for *nslookup* and an application program to arrive at different results when looking for a host or IP address. This is

---

2. Solaris 2.6 comes with BIND 4.9.4, so no patches are necessary. Patches are required for Solaris 2.5.1 and earlier releases. See the section on know your BIND version for more information.

3. Solaris 7 comes with BIND 8.1 or later. See the section on knowing your BIND version for more information.

because *nslookup* uses its own name lookup routines instead of the system-supplied standard *gethostbyname()* and *gethostbyaddr()* used by Solaris utilities and application programs. It is recommended that the DIG utility (discussed below) be obtained and used for DNS troubleshooting.

Public-Domain DNS (BIND)

The full source code and documentation for BIND are available for anyone requiring the latest BIND features or the source code itself for making site customizations. It is available at http://www.isc.org/ or http://www.dns.net/dnsrd/ .

> Note: Sun Microsystems will not support the replacement of the BIND programs supplied with Solaris. BIND should be replaced only by someone with thorough knowledge and experience with the DNS mechanism.

DIG Public-Domain Tool

The domain information groper (DIG), now included with public-domain BIND, is a DNS server and client diagnostic tool. DIG is a DNS debugging tool used to help diagnose DNS queries, both within an organization and over the Internet. DIG is available at http://www.isc.org/ .

Disable nscd Caching

Consider disabling *nscd*'s cache. *nscd* is known in certain circumstances to produce erratic behavior. See the section on disabling *nscd* caching later in this chapter.

Know Your BIND Version

The advanced and well-equipped UNIX administrator keeps up on the latest features in BIND, but if you use BIND from Solaris, how can you tell which version is being run?

The following example illustrates how the *what* command can be used to determine which version of BIND is running on a system.

```
# /usr/ccs/bin/what /usr/sbin/in.named
/usr/sbin/in.named:
     in.named (BIND 8.1.2) Tue Oct  6 00:50:47 PDT 1998 Generic-5.7-October 1998
     db_dump.c      4.33 (Berkeley) 3/3/91
     db_load.c      4.38 (Berkeley) 3/2/91
     db_lookup.c    4.18 (Berkeley) 3/21/91
     db_save.c      4.16 (Berkeley) 3/21/91
     db_update.c    4.28 (Berkeley) 3/21/91
```

```
db_glue.c       4.4   (Berkeley) 6/1/90
ns_forw.c       4.32  (Berkeley) 3/3/91
ns_init.c       4.38  (Berkeley) 3/21/91
ns_main.c       4.55  (Berkeley) 7/1/91
 Copyright (c) 1986, 1989, 1990 The Regents of the University of California.
ns_maint.c      4.39  (Berkeley) 3/2/91
ns_req.c        4.47  (Berkeley) 7/1/91
ns_resp.c       4.65  (Berkeley) 3/3/91
ns_stats.c      4.10  (Berkeley) 6/27/90
SunOS 5.7 Generic October 1998
#
```

In this example, BIND 8.1.2 is the version running on the system. Only the second line of input is useful. The other lines are versions of the various modules of *in.named*. The last line of the output (SunOS 5.7 Generic October 1998) is interesting, too, because it indicates which version of Solaris this version of BIND was intended for.

Once the UNIX administrator knows which version of BIND is on the system, it is possible to take advantage of security features associated with that version.

NIS

NIS was not part of the Solaris 2.x core OS until Solaris 2.6. For Solaris 2.5.1 and earlier, NISKIT (also known as NSKIT) is the add-on package that allows a site to continue using true NIS master and slave servers without having to maintain SunOS systems for that purpose.

> **Note: Because this book covers Solaris 2.x only (and not SunOS or Solaris 1.x), discussion in this section is limited to the use of native NIS or NISKIT 1.2 (or newer) for Solaris 2.x.**

NIS's purpose is the centralization of information found in the following files:

- Password information in */etc/passwd* and */etc/shadow*
- Group information in */etc/group*
- Hosts (names and IP addresses) information in */etc/inet/hosts*
- Various network configuration information in */etc/inet/networks*, */etc/inet/services*, */etc/inet/protocols*, */etc/rpc*, */etc/ethers*, */etc/inet/netmasks*, */etc/bootparams*, */etc/publickey*
- Network group definitions (for which there is no non-NIS implementation)
- Automount tables (*/etc/auto_master*)
- E-mail aliases and definitions in */etc/mail/aliases* and *sendmail* variables

Any or all of these settings can be centralized with NIS. Each client can be configured to read the NIS tables or its own flat files; this is controlled by the file */etc/nsswitch.conf* . Here is an example */etc/nsswitch.conf* file for a NIS client.

```
#
# /etc/nsswitch.nis:
#
# An example file that could be copied over to /etc/nsswitch.conf; it
# uses NIS (YP) in conjunction with files.
#
# "hosts:" and "services:" in this file are used only if the
# /etc/netconfig file has a "-" for nametoaddr_libs of "inet" transports.
# the following two lines obviate the "+" entry in /etc/passwd and /etc/group.
passwd:      files nis
group:       files nis
# consult /etc "files" only if nis is down.
hosts:       nis [NOTFOUND=return] files
networks:    nis [NOTFOUND=return] files
protocols:   nis [NOTFOUND=return] files
rpc:         nis [NOTFOUND=return] files
ethers:      nis [NOTFOUND=return] files
netmasks:    nis [NOTFOUND=return] files
bootparams:  nis [NOTFOUND=return] files
publickey:   nis [NOTFOUND=return] files
netgroup:    nis
automount:   files nis
aliases:     files nis
# for efficient getservbyname() avoid nis
services:    files nis
sendmailvars:   files
```

See the section on name service switch files later in this chapter for additional information.

While NIS is not particularly secure, I will discuss several steps that can be taken to strengthen NIS security in the section on NIS security weaknesses and solutions.

Obtaining and Installing NISKIT

The NISKIT (also frequently spelled NSKIT) package name in Solaris versions up to 2.5.1 is *SUNWnsktr, SUNWnsktu,* and *SUNWnskta* (AnswerBook). It is available on its own product CD, the Server Supplement, or the Solaris Migration Kit CDs.

NIS is included in Solaris 2.6; the package names are *SUNWypr* and *SUNWypru*.

Likewise, NIS is included in Solaris 7; the package names are *SUNWypu* and *SUNWypr*.

Obtain the SunSolve document *NSKIT PSD/FAQ* (Infodoc 11989) prior to installing NISKIT. This document contains information necessary to install the product properly.

NISKIT version 1.2 is far more stable and reliable than earlier versions.

NIS Security Weaknesses and Solutions

Move NIS Maps out of /etc Directory

By default, NIS will use the file */etc/passwd*, */etc/shadow*, */etc/inetd/netmasks*, etc. for its maps. Two problems arise from this: first, anyone with login access to the system will be able to read all of the NIS maps; second, with */etc/passwd* and */etc/shadow* as NIS map sources, root login will be possible only if NIS is running properly.

Protect NIS Maps Directory

Only root should be able to read (and write) the contents of */var/yp* . This directory should be part of a frequent filesystem audit performed by Tripwire and/or COPS. See chapter 4 for additional information on these tools.

Use a Hard-to-Guess NIS Domain Name

A user who does not know the name of the NIS domain cannot pull NIS maps. Hence, the name of the NIS domain name should not be intuitive—for instance, it should not be the same as the DNS domain name. This is a *security through obscurity* measure, and persistence will pay off for a lucky intruder (an intruder would resort to other means, such as sniffing the network, listening for NIS packets containing the domain name).

Implement /var/yp/securenets

NIS can be configured to make its maps available only to certain networks or systems. This is accomplished through the use of */var/yp/securenets* . Examples follow.

To restrict NIS map visibility to only the 128.116.71.0 and 126.116.73.0 networks, */var/yp/securenets* would contain the following:

```
255.255.255.0 128.116.71.0
255.255.255.0 128.116.73.0
```

To restrict NIS map visibility to hosts at IP addresses 128.116.71.3 and 128.116.71.5 and to the entire network 128.116.73.0, */var/yp/securenets* would contain the following:

```
255.255.255.255 128.116.71.3
255.255.255.255 128.116.71.5
255.255.255.0 128.116.73.0
```

Hide Shadow Fields

Anyone who can *ypcat* (the command used to dump a NIS table) a NIS password file containing shadow fields will have an easy time breaking into systems. Shadow fields are the encrypted passwords for all users in the NIS domain. A public-domain program like "crack" will use a large dictionary and some clever algorithms to guess the passwords for the accounts in the NIS database.

To hide the NIS shadow files, C2 security must be implemented. Refer to appendix F for more information.

There is an unsupported but purportedly effective alternative to C2 for hiding the NIS shadow files; refer to Doug's Tools Page at http://www.eng.auburn.edu/users/doug/nis.html for additional information. Note that the procedure described there applies to SunOS 4.x and not to Solaris 2.x.

Avoid Illicit NIS Servers

By default, NIS clients find servers at boot time by broadcasting an "are there any NIS servers out there?" message; the client will bind to the first NIS server to respond, legitimate or not. Measures to control this include

- Don't give root passwords to users of machines on your network. If some users must have root passwords, consider moving their machines to a lab subnet (the point here is to prevent someone from *creating* an unauthorized NIS server).
- Use Tripwire, COPS, and other tools to audit filesystems and detect changes such as NIS client or server configuration.
- Bind all NIS clients to specific known servers instead of having them broadcast to the entire subnet. This is done by running *ypinit -c* and specifying which NIS servers the system should bind to (in decreasing order of preference). *ypinit -c* must also be run when any new NIS servers are built or when old ones are decommissioned. Finally, any NIS server specified with *ypinit -c* must also be defined in */etc/inet/hosts* .
- Use *rpcinfo* commands to detect illicit NIS servers. An example dialogue follows.

```
# rpcinfo -b ypserv 1
128.116.71.18 dancer
# rpcinfo -b ypserv 2
128.116.71.18 dancer
128.116.71.20 vixen
128.116.71.76 prancer
128.116.71.217 bob
#
```

It is necessary to query for hosts running *ypserv* versions 1 and 2. In this example, the known NIS servers *dancer*, *vixen*, and *prancer* are listed (*dancer* is a SunOS server). Also present is the system *bob*, an end-user's workstation, not a known NIS server.

Note: The *rpcinfo* commands shown above must be run on each subnet at the site. This is because the *rpcinfo -b* queries (as well as any system's responses) generally will not cross subnet boundaries. The site's network administrator should be consulted for confirmation.

Keep Root and Other Administrative Accounts out of NIS

The root account should always be *local*; that is, the root account should not be in NIS. The two most important reasons for this are

- If the root password is discovered by an intruder, the intruder will have root access to all machines in the NIS domain.
- If NIS or the network malfunctions, it may not be possible to log in as root on any machine in the domain.

These can be at least partially mitigated by using a local root account in */etc/ passwd* and */etc/shadow* and by specifying "passwd: hosts nis" in */etc/ nsswitch.conf* to force logins to first consult the local passwd and shadow files. There is more information on */etc/nsswitch.conf* in the name service switch section of this chapter.

Disable nscd *Caching*

In certain circumstances *nscd* is known to produce erratic behavior. Consider disabling *nscd*'s cache. Refer to the *nscd* section at the end of this chapter.

Other NIS Weaknesses

Features absent in NIS include

- Quality password enforcement—NIS does not enforce the use of mixed-case and nonalphabetic characters in passwords; thus, user accounts in NIS will invariably contain easily guessed passwords. This makes the need to hide shadow fields much more urgent.
- Password aging—NIS does not support password aging.
- SecureRPC—ordinary UNIX permissions and nothing more govern which users have access to which directories and files.

NIS+

NIS+, introduced with Solaris 2.x, is an extensible version of NIS that includes the following additional features:

- More control over who can read the NIS maps.
- Users log into NIS+ with a network password (in addition to logging into their own machine).
- Scales for larger organizations.
- Delegation of maps to other administrators.

The following sections discuss NIS+ security weaknesses and solutions.

NIS+ Default Access Rights

NIS+ default access rights are the first line of defense, for they determine who can read the NIS+ maps. The *nisdefaults* command shows default NIS+ access rights for the domain (see Figure 14.3).

Figure 14.3   *NIS+ Principal Classes*

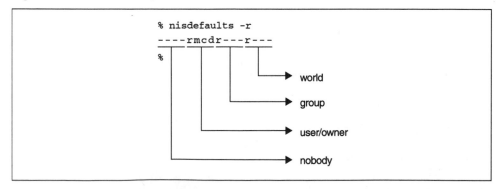

Within each principal class (nobody, user, group, world), the four symbols are **r** (read), **m** (modify), **c** (create), and **d** (destroy). Read permissions are all you need to read NIS+ tables. Modify, create, and destroy are needed only by domain owners, typically UNIX administrators.

The *niscat* command can show rights for an individual NIS+ table.

```
% niscat -o passwd
...
Access Rights : ----rmcdr---r---
%
```

In this example of rights for the passwd table, principal **nobody** has no rights, principal **owner** has full read, modify, create, destroy rights, and principals **group owner** and **world** have read-only rights. Any NIS+ table can be queried for current rights.

As long as there are no rights for **nobody**, the only principals who can read the NIS+ tables are those who have been given specific authorizations to NIS+.

Access Rights for Principal *nobody*

Access rights should be extended to principal **nobody** only if NIS+ tables need to be read by NIS clients (typically SunOS systems) or unauthenticated clients. Recognize, however, that this will have a significant impact on security: *anyone* will be able to read the tables with read access extended to **nobody**.

NIS+ Security Level

NIS+ should never be run at security level 0. To check the security level, run the *nisstat* command.

```
# /usr/lib/nis/nisstat
Statistics for domain west.sun.com. :
Statistics from server : coho.west.sun.com.
Stat 'root server' = 'ON'
Stat 'NIS compat mode' = 'ON'
Stat 'DNS forwarding in NIS mode' = 'OFF'
Stat 'security level' = '2'
Stat 'serves directories':
        west.sun.com.
        org_dir.west.sun.com.
        groups_dir.west.sun.com.
Stat 'Operation Statistics':
        2
        OP=LOOKUP:C=3300:E=0:T=424
        OP=LIST:C=5333:E=0:T=708
        OP=FINDDIR:C=3057:E=0:T=660
```

```
OP=STATUS:C=4:E=0:T=841
Stat 'directory cache' = 'C=8558:H=8556:M=2:HR=99%'
Stat 'group cache' = 'C=0:H=0:M=0:HR=100%'
Stat 'static storage' = '4284'
Stat 'dynamic storage' = '1966936'
Stat 'up since' = 'up 18D, 01:14:30'
#
```

The NIS+ security level is controlled by the *nisd -S* startup option found in the file */etc/rc2.d/S71rpc* . The default security level is 2. See the nisd(1) man page for additional details.

Administering NIS+

NIS+ should be administered with Admintool.

If Admintool cannot be used (for instance, if Xwindows is not available), then use the *nisaddent* command. For example, to change the netmasks file, perform the following steps:

```
# nisaddent -d -t netmasks > /tmp/netmasks
# vi /tmp/netmasks
...
# nisaddent -r -f /tmp/netmasks netmasks
```

In this example, *nisaddent* is first used to dump the *netmasks* table to a flat file; the flat file is edited, and *nisaddent* is used to reload the *netmasks* table from the modified flat file.

> **Note: When adding or removing entries from the *passwd* table, both the *passwd* and *shadow* tables must be dumped, edited, and restored. The proper sequence is**

```
# nisaddent -d -t passwd > /tmp/passwd
# nisaddent -d -t shadow > /tmp/shadow
# chmod 600 /tmp/shadow
# vi /tmp/passwd /tmp/shadow
...
# nisaddent -r -f /tmp/passwd passwd
# nisaddent -m -f /tmp/shadow -t passwd.org_dir shadow[4]
# rm /tmp/shadow
```

Back Up NIS+ Tables

All NIS+ tables must be backed up at least once per day to be safe. Prior to a tape backup, run the *nisbackup* command. *nisbackup* creates a snapshot of all NIS+ tables which can be handy during a data recovery operation.

---

4. This command is shown without underlines so that the underscore is visible.

Flush NIS+ Transactions

I recommend that the *nisping -C* command be executed periodically (at least once per day, but in a busy environment one or more times per hour) to checkpoint NIS+ and flush all transactions to disk.

Keep Root and Other Administrative Accounts Out of NIS+

The root account should always be local on each system; that is, the root account should not be in NIS+. Two important reasons for this follow:

- If the root password is discovered by an intruder, the intruder will have root access to all machines in the NIS+ domain.
- If NIS+ or the network malfunctions, it may not be possible to log in as root on any machine in the domain.

These can be at least partially mitigated by using a local root account in */etc/ passwd* and */etc/shadow* and by specifying "passwd: hosts nisplus" in */etc/ nsswitch.conf* to force logins to first consult the local passwd and shadow files. For more information on */etc/nsswitch.conf* see the name service switch section below.

Disable nscd *Caching*

In certain circumstances nscd is known to produce erratic behavior. Consider disabling *nscd*'s cache. Refer to the nscd section at the end of this chapter..

Name Service Switch

The file */etc/nsswitch.conf* found on each client system determines for that system which name services will be used for each type of information needed. A typical *nsswitch.conf* file for a system in a NIS+ environment appears as follows:

```
#
# /etc/nsswitch.nisplus:
#
# An example file that could be copied over to /etc/nsswitch.conf; it
# uses NIS+ (NIS Version 3) in conjunction with files.
#
# "hosts:" and "services:" in this file are used only if the
# /etc/netconfig file has a "-" for nametoaddr_libs of "inet" transports.
# the following two lines obviate the "+" entry in /etc/passwd and /etc/group.
passwd:     files nisplus
group:      files nisplus
```

```
# consult /etc "files" only if nisplus is down.
hosts: nisplus [NOTFOUND=return] files
services:    nisplus [NOTFOUND=return] files
networks:    nisplus [NOTFOUND=return] files
protocols:   nisplus [NOTFOUND=return] files
rpc:         nisplus [NOTFOUND=return] files
ethers:      nisplus [NOTFOUND=return] files
netmasks:    nisplus [NOTFOUND=return] files
bootparams: nisplus [NOTFOUND=return] files
publickey:   nisplus
netgroup:    nisplus
automount:   files nisplus
aliases:     files nisplus
sendmailvars:   files nisplus
```

The syntax for each entry is

database: directives

where *database* is the type of data to be looked up and *directives* is a list of one or more information sources and conditions under which they will be used.

For example, the entry **passwd: files nisplus** is interpreted as follows: for passwd entries, first look in the local system's file(s) (in this case, */etc/ passwd*) and, if the desired entry is not found, then consult NIS+.

The entry **services: nisplus [NOTFOUND=return] files** is interpreted: for services entries, first look in NIS+; if the entry is not found in NIS+, then return; if NIS+ is down, then look in local files.

There are many other status codes, including SUCCESS, UNAVAIL, NOT-FOUND, and TRYAGAIN. Consult the nsswitch.conf(4) man page for complete details on the use of *nsswitch.conf* .

Note: If */etc/nsswitch.conf* is changed on a running system, the *nscd* daemon must be restarted. Refer to the section on *nscd* below.

nscd

nscd, the name service cache daemon, caches name service requests for hosts, passwd, and group. It caches these services whether the system is using flat files (e.g., */etc/inet/hosts, /etc/group, /etc/passwd*), DNS, NIS, or NIS+.

nscd can be the cause of several problems, including

- Changes in */etc/nsswitch.conf* are not fully effective until nscd is restarted.
- Changes in *hosts, group,* or *passwd* in flat files or NIS+ may not immediately take effect; sometimes nscd caches the old information too long.

- Changes in NIS are ignored.[5] For example, a user changes his password on his NIS client with *yppasswd* and then logs out. The user cannot log in using the new password because *nscd* has cached the old password and will not query NIS for password (or other) changes until its cache has expired (the user can still log in with the old password).

- *nscd* performs negative caching. For example, a user tries to ping a host not yet defined in DNS. Minutes later, the host name is defined in DNS. However, the user is still unable to ping the server (by name) because *nscd* has cached the nonexistence of the host.

- *nscd* has been blamed for ping, arp, *sendmail*, *telnet*, and ftp problems.

- *nscd* has been known to peg the CPU and have memory leaks.

- *nscd*'s cache has been known to become corrupted.

Because it is integrated into the system mechanisms used to find host names (in */etc/hosts*, DNS, NIS, or NIS+), nscd cannot be disabled; some functions may not work.

nscd can be tamed somewhat by disabling its caching mechanism. To disable caching, the configuration file */etc/nscd.conf* needs to include the following three entries:

```
enable-cache   hosts    no
enable-cache   passwd   no
enable-cache   group    no
```

Once */etc/nscd.conf* has been changed, *nscd* needs to be stopped and restarted. The following dialogue illustrates this.

```
# /etc/init.d/nscd stop
# /etc/init.d/nscd start
#
```

To confirm that nscd's caching has been disabled, run the *nscd -g* command. An example dialogue follows.

```
$ /usr/sbin/nscd -g
nscd configuration:
        0   server debug level
"/dev/null"  is server log file
passwd cache:
       No   cache is enabled
        0   cache hits on positive entries
        0   cache hits on negative entries
        0   cache misses on positive entries
        0   cache misses on negative entries
       0%   cache hit rate
        0   queries deferred
```

---

5. *nscd* and NIS were never designed to coexist.

```
     0  total entries
   211  suggested size
   600  seconds time to live for positive entries
     5  seconds time to live for negative entries
    20  most active entries to be kept valid
   Yes  check /etc/{passwd,group,hosts} file for changes
    No  use possibly stale data rather than waiting for refresh
group cache:
    No  cache is enabled
     0  cache hits on positive entries
     0  cache hits on negative entries
     0  cache misses on positive entries
     0  cache misses on negative entries
    0% cache hit rate
     0  queries deferred
     0  total entries
   211  suggested size
  3600  seconds time to live for positive entries
     5  seconds time to live for negative entries
    20  most active entries to be kept valid
   Yes  check /etc/{passwd,group,hosts} file for changes
    No  use possibly stale data rather than waiting for refresh
hosts cache:
    No  cache is enabled
     0  cache hits on positive entries
     0  cache hits on negative entries
     0  cache misses on positive entries
     0  cache misses on negative entries
    0% cache hit rate
     0  queries deferred
     0  total entries
   211  suggested size
  3600  seconds time to live for positive entries
     5  seconds time to live for negative entries
    20  most active entries to be kept valid
   Yes  check /etc/{passwd,group,hosts} file for changes
    No  use possibly stale data rather than waiting for refresh
$
```

Where to Go for Additional Information

AnswerBooks

- AnswerBook 2—TCP/IP and Data Communications Administration Guide
- AnswerBook 2—Solaris Naming Setup and Configuration Guide
- AnswerBook 2—Solaris Naming Administration Guide
- AnswerBook 2—NIS+ Transition Guide

Man Pages

- defaultdomain(4)
- in.named(1M)
- nis+(1)
- nisaddent(1M)
- nisbackup(1M)
- niscat(1)
- nischmod(1)
- nisdefaults(1)
- nisping(1M)
- nisstat(1M)
- nscd(1M)
- nscd.conf(4)
- nslookup(1M)
- nsswitch.conf(4)
- resolv.conf(4)
- rpcinfo(1M)
- securenets(4)
- whut(1)
- ypcat(1)
- ypbind(1M)
- ypinit(1M)

Publications

- *DNS PSD/FAQ*, SunSolve Infodoc 11975
- *NSKit PSD/FAQ*, SunSolve Infodoc 11989
- *NIS+ PSD/FAQ*, SunSolve Infodoc 11988
- *NIS PSD/FAQ*, SunSolve Infodoc 12000
- *Misc Networking Programs PSD/FAQ*, SunSolve Infodoc 12052
- *How to Set Up NIS+ in Solaris 2.x*, SunSolve Infodoc 1014
- *How NIS Binding Works*, SunSolve Infodoc 3376
- *How to Tell What Version of BIND You Are Running*, SunSolve Infodoc 16255
- *Network Security PSD/FAQ*, SunSolve Infodoc 13335
- Albitz, Paul, and Liu, Cricket. *DNS and Bind*. Sebastopol, CA: O'Reilly & Associates, 1998.

- Stern, Hal. *Managing NFS and NIS*. Sebastopol, CA: O'Reilly & Associates, 1991.
- Ramsey, Rick. *All About Administering NIS+*. Upper Saddle River, NJ: Prentice Hall PTR, 1994.

Web Sites

- *InterNIC Domain registration services*—http://rs.internic.net/
- *InterNIC directory services*—http://ds.internic.net/
- *AlterNIC information*—http://www.alternic.net/
- *Hide NIS Shadow Field (and other NIS security information)*—http://www.eng.auburn.edu/users/doug/nis.html
- RFC1032, *Domain Administrators Guide*—http://www.cis.ohio-state.edu/htbin/rfc/rfc1032.html
- RFC1033, *Domain Administrators Operations Guide*—http://www.cis.ohio-state.edu/htbin/rfc/rfc1033.html
- RFC1034, *Domain Names—Concepts and Facilities*—http://www.cis.ohio-state.edu/htbin/rfc/rfc1034.html
- RFC1035, *Domain Names—Implementation and Specification*—http://www.cis.ohio-state.edu/htbin/rfc/rfc1035.html

15

NFS AND THE AUTOMOUNTER

The network file system (NFS) proves over and over to be the weak link in an enterprise's computing infrastructure. Often misunderstood, NFS security is frequently compromised in favor of enabling data access for business users. Given the nature of early NFS versions and its security features, it is no wonder that data security has been compromised in order to give people the access they need (or want).

In recent years, NFS security has improved markedly, and these features can be incorporated into the enterprise.

What's in this chapter

- Basic workings of NFS
- Improved NFS server and client security
- NFS authentication
- NFS and access control lists
- Automounter security

Why this is important

NFS and the automounter are network services; the network frequently proves to be the weak link in system security. System administrators need to know how to set up NFS and automounter so that they are secure.

NFS

NFS gives the appearance of the existence of specific directories and files on a computer, when in fact those specific directories and files reside on another computer. From the UNIX user's perspective, NFS is the invisible mechanism that makes one computer's specific directories and files appear to also exist on another, or several, computers.

All normal filesystem commands such as *ls*, *du*, *cat*, and *vi* work on files presented through NFS just as though those files were physically present on the system.

NFS Operations

The two principal operations carried out by machines participating in NFS are *share* and *mount*.

Share is an operation carried out by a system, making one or more of its physically resident directories available for access by other systems. This is the role of an *NFS server*. *Mount* is the complementary operation carried out by another system whereby the server's shared filesystem is made to appear to be resident on the mounting system, or *NFS client*. In Figure 15.1 the NFS server shares the directory */export/home*, which is mounted at the location */home* on the NFS client.

Improving Security with NFS Share

An NFS server's directories are shared with the *share* command. Security can be improved by restricting which systems may mount a server's NFS directory. Syntax of the *share* command follows.

```
share -F FStype -o options -d description path
```

Options consists of one (or more, separated by commas) of the following:

- ro—the directory is shared read-only to all clients.
- ro=*client* [, *client*...]—the directory is shared read-only to one or more clients or netgroups.
- rw—the directory is shared read/write to all clients (*not* recommended, because write access could be granted to a system/user who has no business having it).
- rw=*client* [, *client*...]—the directory is shared read/write to one or more clients, netgroups, DNS domains, or networks.
- sec=*mode*[:*mode*...]—security authentication mode. I'll discuss this in the section on NFS authentication.

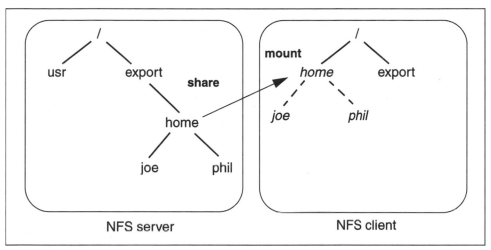

Figure 15.1   *NFS Architecture*

- nosuid—prevents the creation of SetUID programs on NFS-mounted directories; keeps NFS-SetUID mounted SetUID programs from running in SetUID mode.

See the share_nfs(1M) man page for a complete listing of share options.

Here is an example *share* command.

```
share -F NFS -o rw=homeusers -d "Home Directories" /export/home
```

In this example, the directory */export/home* is shared read/write to systems in the netgroup *homeusers*.

An NFS server's permanent collection of NFS shares is listed in the file */etc/dfs/dfstab* . An example */etc/dfs/dfstab* file is

```
share -F NFS -o rw=homeowners,ro -d "Home Dirs" /export/home
share -F NFS -o ro=allusers -d "Man Pages" /export/man
share -F NFS -o ro=allusers -d "AnswerBook" /export/ab
share -F NFS -o rw=.labs.sun.com -d "Mail" /var/spool/mail
```

In the first entry, the directory */export/home* is shared read/write to all systems in the netgroup *homeowners* and read-only to all other systems. The next two entries share man pages and answerbook in read-only mode to all systems in the netgroup *allusers*. The final entry shares */var/spool/mail* to all systems in the DNS domain *labs.sun.com* .

The most common weakness with NFS is that the NFS server shares its directory(ies) with too few restrictions.

- Directories are available to too many clients (possibly altogether unrestricted).

- Too many directories are shared.
- Directories are shared read/write when read-only would suffice.

Refer to the share(1M) and share_nfs(1M) man pages for complete information.

Improving Security with NFS Mount

An NFS client mounts directories shared by NFS servers with the *mount* command. Syntax of the *mount* command is

```
mount -F NFS -o [rw|ro] [bg|fg] [suid|nosuid] [soft|hard]
      [intr|nointr] [sec=option] server:/directory /localdirectory
```

Mount options are

- rw—directory is mounted read/write (settings on NFS server will prevail).
- ro—directory is mounted read-only.
- fg—if the first mount attempt fails, subsequent attempts will be made in the foreground (default).
- bg—if the first mount attempt fails, subsequent attempts will be made in the background.
- suid—SetUID execution is allowed (default).
- nosuid—SetUID execution is not allowed.
- hard—continue to retry the mount until the server responds (default).
- soft—return an error if the NFS server does not respond.
- intr—client can interrupt processes (with a keyboard interrupt) waiting on a mount (default).
- nointr—client cannot interrupt processes waiting on a mount.
- sec—secure RPC security setting (can be one of *none, sys, dh, kerb*).

Refer to the mount(1M) man page for a complete listing of options.

An example *mount* command is

```
mount -F NFS -o ro,bg,sec=dh appserver:/d1/local /usr/local
```

In this example, the client system wishes to mount the server *appserver* directory */d1/local* onto the local directory */usr/local*, in read-only mode, using DES authentication.

The file */etc/vfstab* is used to permanently set up NFS client mounts. The format of *vfstab* for NFS mounts is

```
server:/directory - /localdirectory NFS - yes options
```

Here is an example */etc/vfstab* entry.

```
appserver:/d1/local - /usr/local NFS - yes ro,bg,sec=dh
```

In this example, the */etc/vfstab* entry is corresponding to the preceding example *mount* command.

Improving Security by Setting NFS Portmon

Ordinarily NFS will respond to requests that originate from any UDP port. However, NFS can be configured to respond only to requests originating from privileged ports; that is, from ports originating from the root userid on another UNIX system.

When NFS *portmon* is set on a server, the server will ignore NFS mount and I/O requests coming from unprivileged ports. To set NFS portmon, add the following entry to */etc/system* (and then reboot the system):

```
* set portmon to deny unauthorized access
set nfssrv:nfs_portmon=1
```

NFS Authentication

The NFS *share* command provides four options for authenticating NFS mounts and subsequent accesses. They are

- sys—(Secure RPC *AUTH_SYS*) ordinary UNIX userid, groupid, and file/directory permission bits are passed over the network in the clear and not authenticated by the NFS server. This is the default.
- dh—(Secure RPC *AUTH_DES*) Diffie-Hellman/DES public key authentication.
- krb4—(Secure RPC *AUTH_KERB*) Kerberos Version 4 authentication.
- none—(Secure RPC *AUTH_NONE*) map all NFS client userid's to the userid *nobody* on the NFS server. Note: this mode is supported by *share*, but not by *mount* or the automounter.

This is an example NFS *share* command specifying authentication.

```
share -F NFS -o (sec=dh,)rw-homeusers -d "Home Dirs" /export/home
```

In this example, all NFS clients must use DES authentication in order to mount and access the shared */export/home* directory.

Both Diffie-Hellman and Kerberos options encrypt authentication information that is transmitted over the network. The other options, sys and none, do not use encryption.

The Diffie-Hellman and Kerberos options require Secure RPC. Refer to chapter 13 and the section on authentication for more information.

Servers as NFS Clients

NFS presents the UNIX administrator with opportunities to centralize information storage. However, these economies can be taken too far. Servers that depend on NFS servers for continued operation are jeopardizing their stability. Consider the architecture illustrated in Figure 15.2—the server *mailsvr* depends upon the integrity of the server *dbsvr* for its own integrity. The opportunities for system failure for the server *mailsvr* have been greatly increased with this NFS mount. If the server *dbsvr* crashes, or if the network connecting *mailsvr* and *dbsvr* fails, the system *mailsvr* is in trouble.

Possible remedies involve a change in the intersystem architecture so that the server *mailsvr* no longer depends upon the server *dbsvr* for its stability. Another remedy is to use a different mechanism such as *rdist* to make */usr/ local* visible on *mailsvr*.

Even more precarious examples of being held hostage by NFS include the following:

- A user logs onto a server, which in some environments causes the server to NFS-mount a user's home directory, which resides on his desktop system. The integrity of the server now depends upon the integrity of a desktop system. The desktop system could easily be turned off, thereby possibly hanging the server.
- In this case, your server depends on an NFS server *in a different organization*. The other organization, with goals and priorities of its own, may fail to perceive the importance of the stability of your server which depends on it (*your* emergency may not be *their* emergency).

These examples drive home the following point: **servers should not be NFS clients, particularly of NFS servers not in your *complete* control**.

NFS and Access Control Lists

ACLs, explained in chapter 4, were implemented in Solaris 2.5. NFS clients which support ACLs will use them. If an NFS server supporting ACLs encounters a client that does not support ACLs, the ACLs will be bypassed and normal UNIX userid/groupid permissions will be enforced. Likewise, if an

Figure 15.2   *Server-to-Server NFS Dependency*

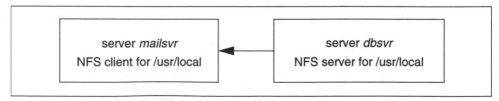

NFS client supporting ACLs mounts a filesystem from a server that does not support ACLs, then any ACL settings will be ignored.

NFS on the Network

Despite all of the remedies we have discussed, NFS traffic on the network is still in the clear—anyone with a sniffer in the right place can easily see and record all of the information being transmitted. This makes NFS over a public network (such as the Internet) especially perilous.

There are at least two ways to remedy this:

- Employ a SKIP tunnel[1] (or other tunneling protocol) between the NFS server and each NFS client.
- Employ encryption technology at the network level (for instance, between the routers connecting the server and client).

Disabling NFS

To disable NFS, refer to instructions in Table 13-2.

Automounter

The automounter is a client-side enhancement to NFS. Instead of mounting all NFS filesystems at system boot time, the automounter mounts NFS filesystems when they are needed and unmounts them when they are not needed. The automounter is configured with a set of maps that specify the mount point locations, the servers serving them, and any NFS mount options used.

The real power of the automounter lies in the ability to distribute the automounter maps via NIS or NIS+. Correspondingly, there is no mechanism for distributing /etc/vfstab (hard NFS mount) information via NIS or NIS+. Thus, the automounter is the only option able to leverage NIS or NIS+.

All of the NFS security principles and practices discussed thus far apply to the automounter. Attention to share options, authentication, and basic file/directory permissions apply equally to NFS and automounter. In addition to these, the following automounter features require attention.

1. Permissions of /etc/auto_master, /etc/auto_home, and any site-specific automounter map files. These should be owned by root, groupid

---

1. See the section on virtual private networks in chapter 13 for additional information on SKIP and IPsec.

bin, and permissions -rw-r--r--. Remove the read-only bit for *other* if you do not want users seeing what can be mounted.

2. By default, the automounter will query an NFS server only *once* when processing a new automounter mount. On a congested network, this can cause the automounter mount to fail. The *retry* setting should be set to 3. This setting is changed in *auto_master*; for example

```
/home auto_home -retry=3
```

Finally, most automounter problems are really underlying NFS problems. All filesystems that are mounted with the automounter should first be tried using NFS commands. If filesystems mount properly with NFS, then any problem experienced is probably with the automounter itself. Conversely, if filesystems *cannot* be mounted manually with NFS, then NFS is the source of any problem.

Indirect Automounter Maps

Indirect automounter maps are usually used for directories such as home directories or tools. Indirect maps include information about a parent directory, as well as its subdirectories. Here is an example of indirect automounter maps; the file */etc/auto_master* (or NIS/NIS+ *auto_master* map) would contain the following entry:

```
/home          auto_home
```

The NIS/NIS+ *auto_home* map referenced would contain the following entries:

```
bob            orcas:/export/home/bob
phil           cypress:/export/home/phil
susan          sanjuan:/export/home/susan
```

The *auto_master* and *auto_home* maps together define a collection of directories found under */home* (such as */home/bob*, */home/phil*, and */home/susan*). These directories are mounted only when referenced (such as with the *cd* or *ls* command) and are dismounted after a short period of not being used.

To continue this example, if the host *orcas* (which serves up bob's home directory */export/home/bob*) should fail or become unreachable, then any read or write attempts to */home/bob* will hang, but the automount client will continue running. If bob's home directory is not being accessed, the failure of the NFS server serving his home directory will not even be noticed by the automount client.

Direct Automounter Maps

Direct automounter maps are typically used for single directories such as */var/mail*, */usr/man*, or */usr/local*. This is an example of direct automounter maps.

```
/usr/man          beatle:/usr/share/man
/var/mail         mailsrv:/var/mail
```

Direct automount maps are decidedly less secure than indirect maps. If an NFS server crashes or becomes unreachable, all clients referencing that server via direct automount maps will hang until the NFS server is available again. This is true

- Regardless of client-side or server-side NFS mount options (such as *hard* or *soft*)
- Even if the automount client is not attempting I/O to the mounted file-system

For these reasons, direct maps should be changed to indirect maps; the procedure for doing is

1. Create a new *auto_master* entry called *indirect*.

   ```
   /indirect         auto_indirect
   ```

2. Move all direct map entries into the indirect map *auto_indirect*. For example, these direct map entries:

   ```
   /usr/man          beatle:/usr/share/man
   /var/mail         mailsrv:/var/mail
   ```

   become

   ```
   man       beatle:/usr/share/man
   mail      mailsrv:/var/mail
   ```

   These maps will cause host beatle's */usr/share/man* to appear as */indirect/man* on any automount client, and host mailsrv's */var/mail* to appear as */indirect/mail* on any automount client. Read on for the fix.

3. Create symbolic links on each automount client as follows:

   ```
   # ln -s /indirect/man  /usr/man
   # ln -s /indirect/mail /var/mail
   ```

   These symbolic links restore the desired existence of */usr/man* and */var/mail*.

Automomounter Browsing

Browsing (new in Solaris 2.6) is a feature wherein an automount client is able to view all of the entries in an indirect automount map without actually mounting them. Prior to Solaris 2.6, we would have had to examine the automount maps themselves to know what directories were available to be automounted under */home*, for example. But with browsing, all we need to do is *cd* to the automounted directory (in this case */home*); the *ls* command will list all mountable directories (before browsing was available, *ls /home* would list only mount*ed* directories, not mount*able* directories).

Browsability is disabled by default for /*home* and /*net* in Solaris 2.6 and later.

> **Warning: Be careful if you are considering activating automounter browsing for large indirect maps such as /*home* or /*net*. Besides the extra overhead involved, it might not be such a good idea to reveal to the curious (or malicious) user all of the mountable directories at a site.**

If browsing is not desired, consider disabling automounter browsing; we will discuss how in the following sections.

Disable All Automounter Browsing on an NFS Client

Follow this procedure to disable automounter browsing for all automount directories on a single NFS client.

1. Add the -*n* option to the automountd startup in the file /*etc*/*init.d*/ *autofs*. The automountd command line should look like this.

   ```
   /usr/lib/autofs/automountd -n < /dev/null > /dev/console 2>&1
   ```

2. Restart the autofs service as follows.

   ```
   # /etc/init.d/autofs stop
   # /etc/init.d/autofs start
   #
   ```

Disable Automounter Browsing for a Single Entry on an NFS Client

Follow this procedure to disable automounter browsing for a single automount directory on an NFS client. In this example, browsing capability will be disabled for /*net*. This procedure will work only if the client's automount maps are local and not in NIS or NIS+.

1. Edit /*etc*/*auto_master* and add the -*nobrowse* option to the /*net* entry as follows.

   ```
   # Master map for automounter
   #
   /net     -hosts    -nosuid, nobrowse
   /home    auto_home
   +auto_master
   ```

2. Run the *automount* command on the client to force the change.

Disable Automounter Browsing for All NFS Clients

Follow this procedure to disable automounter browsing for all NFS clients.

1. Edit the appropriate automounter maps (this may be on clients, or in NIS or NIS+) and add the *-nobrowse* option. An example */etc/ auto_master* entry follows.

   ```
   /home     auto_home     -nobrowse
   ```

2. Run the *automount* command on each client to force the change.

Automounter and the Name Service Switch

By specifying NIS or NIS+ as the only source for automounter information, the file */etc/auto_master* on any automount client is ignored and can even be removed. The *automount* entry in */etc/nsswitch.conf* would appear as follows on a NIS client.

```
automount:  nis
```

The file */etc/nsswitch.conf* entry for *automount* would appear as follows on a NIS+ client.

```
automount:  nisplus
```

Disabling Automounter

To disable the automounter, refer to instructions in Table 13-2.

Where to Go for Additional Information

AnswerBook

- AnswerBook 2—NFS Administration Guide
- AnswerBook 2—Solaris Naming Administration Guide

Man Pages

- automount(1M)
- df(1)
- dfstab(4)
- getfacl(1)
- ls(1)
- mount(1M)
- mount_nfs(1M)

- mountall(1M)
- nfssec(5)
- setfacl(1)
- share(1M)
- shareall(1M)
- share_nfs(1M)
- vfstab(4)

Publications

- *Automounter PSD/FAQ*, SunSolve Infodoc 11990
- *The NFS Distributed File Service*, SunSolve Whitepaper 1252
- *NFS PSD/FAQ*, SunSolve Infodoc 11987
- Stern, Hal. *Managing NFS & NIS*. Sebastopol, CA: O'Reilly & Associates, 1991.

Part Four

Disaster and Recovery

UNIX administrators pride themselves on the architectures, policies, and procedures they develop, and many a fine computing enterprise has been built based upon a good combination of technical knowledge, business acumen, and common sense. But, like life insurance, the effort required to prepare for recovery in the event of a disaster is a category of thought and action that many disregard. It is not human nature to be proactive about worst case scenarios.

Chapter 16 will expose the UNIX administrator to the thoughts and processes required to mitigate the effects of a man-made or natural disaster and restore system operations.

While one could argue that disaster recovery and security are unrelated topics that cannot be discussed together, it can also be argued that security can be defined as doing anything and everything to assure the continuation of business operations. The ideas presented in the following chapter are offered in light of the book's intended audience—UNIX administrators, security specialists, and their managers—and the ability they have to effect change in this area.

SYSTEM RECOVERY PREPARATION

The best-laid plans for success have little business value if there are no corresponding plans for what to do if and when the unthinkable occurs.

Disaster need not take the form of a disgruntled employee or a hacker. A flood, hurricane, tornado, extended power outage, and other events outside of our control have just as much potential for disrupting computer and business operations. While it may not be practical to prepare for these kinds of disasters by ensuring they will have zero impact on the business, it is exceedingly practical to prepare for how to pick up the pieces and continue on when a disaster does occur.

What's in this chapter

- What can go wrong with a system
- How to prepare in advance for an effective system recovery

Why this is important

Failures will occur, and recoveries will need to be done. Recovery preparedness is the single most important factor in recovery success!

What Can and Will Go Wrong

Natural Disaster

Earthquakes, tornadoes, hurricanes, floods, wind, ice storms, snow, and rain can literally spell disaster for a business by directly damaging company facilities and assets or by disrupting transportation, communications, or public utilities that enable the company to conduct business.

Man-Made Disaster

Sudden business failure of a key supplier, union strikes, terrorism, and war can threaten a company's survival by hindering its ability to continue business.

Inside Utility Failure

Electric power and air conditioning are the environmental utilities that support a data center or server room. Interruption of either of these inside utilities threatens the continued operation of company servers. An uninterruptible power supply (UPS) can—at a minimum—soften the impact of a power failure by giving UNIX system administrators an opportunity to cleanly shut down servers.

However, consider that, if a data center's computers are protected with a UPS, the air conditioning also needs to be on UPS (or a generator). Otherwise, the computers will continue running in a data center with no air conditioning, leading to more problems.

Hardware Failure

Hardware failures are probably the most familiar type of failure. These include failure of power supplies, system boards and adaptors, memory, disk storage, and especially cabling and cable connections.

UNIX Administrator Error

Nearly every experienced UNIX administrator has a tale to tell, such as having entered the command *rm -rf /tmp ** instead of *rm -rf /tmp/**, thereby removing all files from a system. UNIX administrators are human and capable of making honest, high-impact mistakes.

Documentation Error

Errors in procedural documentation can lead UNIX administrators, programmers, and users to do the wrong thing, sometimes without their knowing it until weeks or months later (if ever).

Programmer Error

Despite thorough testing (if and when one is fortunate enough to test thoroughly), software bugs creep to the surface and manifest themselves in the form of data corruption or destruction.

User Error

Through inadequate training, heavy workload, poor documentation, or lack of attention to detail, a user can corrupt or destroy information by making mistakes. Lack of (or inadequate) data access controls increases the exposure and impact to this type of error.

Sabotage

Whether from insiders or outsiders, the malicious corruption or destruction of information and information systems is probably the most sensational form of human-caused information destruction. Because it can be perpetrated by trusted insiders, it can be the most difficult to detect and prevent.

Preparing for Recovery

Recovery preparation begins when the building is designed, the data center location is chosen, hardware and software vendors are selected, and systems are designed. Recovery preparation, like security, is not a Band-Aid to be applied to an existing infrastructure, but part of a sound design methodology. Along every step of the way, consider what can go wrong and how the design can help to continue business.

With each advancing year, businesses depend more and more on computers and networks to help run the business; increasingly, computers and networks *are* the business. The popular notion 20 years ago was that every process performed by a computer system had its manual backup procedure with which everyone was familiar. If there was a system failure, data input screens filled in by mail-order clerks were replaced with hand-written forms. Draftsmen returned to their drafting tables. Marketers continued their marketing planning.

When the computer system fails, what will the Internet online bookstore do? When the computer fails, what will the banker (with online banking services) do? What will the online stock trader do? What will the ISP do? These businesses cannot fall back on manual procedures when their computers fail because they do not *have* manual procedures.

The answer lies in preparation. Business operations must continue as quickly as possible—long delays can cause a business to fail. Even short of outright failure, what does disruption of normal business operations cost and what is the organization willing to do to prevent that loss? And the finger-pointers will all look to the person responsible for the networks and computers. That person is probably you.

We'll take a closer look in the following sections at the aspects of system design and management, with a keen eye on recovery awareness, preparation, and ease of recovery.

Create an Incident Reponse Team

It is easy to do the wrong thing during a security incident. A UNIX adminis-trator not familiar with the concept of the chain of evidence might acciden-tally destroy evidence or render it unusable in a court of law. The UNIX administrator (or his boss) might not call the right people during an incident, costing the organization valuable time.

System Filesystem Design

How are the servers and desktop systems designed? Is there clean segrega-tion between OS partitions, home directories, and applications and tools? Are Solaris-furnished programs in */usr/bin* and */usr/sbin* modified or renamed? Are public-domain programs in */usr/bin* or */usr/sbin*?

Why does this matter? This is an important aspect of system recovery. To be effective, a system recovery must be executed quickly and accurately. A loosely managed system with locally written tools and data files sprinkled here and there (particularly in directories intended for other purposes, such as Solaris OS binaries and data files) will be difficult to recover.

Recommendation: In terms of the design and layout of individual desk-top and server systems, I urge the following:

- Maintain a high degree of segregation between OS partitions and parti-tions used for home directories and applications.

- Install all tools and applications on a centralized server and NFS-mount the server(s)' directories to local clients.

- Do not alter in any way the contents of */usr/bin* or */usr/sbin*; instead, put all local tools in a separate (preferably NFS-mounted) directory such as */usr/local/bin*.

- Similarly, where possible do not populate */etc* with local tools' configura-tion files; instead, use a separate (preferably NFS-mounted) directory such as */usr/local/etc*.

These recommendations lead to the following system *build* procedure:

1. Load OS from CD-ROM.
2. Localize the system, preferably using a canned shell script. This should include all settings peculiar to the site such as specifying DNS and NIS servers, print queues, NFS/automounter settings, patch updates, etc.

The same recommendations lead to the following system *recovery* procedure:

1. Load OS from CD-ROM.
2. Localize the system, preferably using a canned shell script. This should include all settings peculiar to the site such as specifying DNS and NIS servers, print queues, NFS/automounter settings, patch updates, etc.
3. Recover home and application(s) directory(ies) from latest backup.

These build and recovery procedures appear to be ridiculously simple, as well they should be. They are the product of strict segregation of the OS from home and application directories and of a discipline to "leave the OS alone" when and where possible.

Filesystem Geometry

A filesystem's *geometry* is defined as the settings used by *mkfs* (make filesystem) to create the filesystem on a disk partition. *mkfs* generally does a decent job of setting up the right number of *inodes* and *superblocks* on a filesystem, but a skilled UNIX administrator can customize *mkfs*'s settings in order to squeeze more space or performance out of a filesystem.

The downside of *mkfs* customizing is that the emergency repair of a filesystem using *fsck* (filesystem check) can make recovery of a filesystem difficult, if not impossible. The reason for this is that *fsck* assumes default locations for the filesystem's superblocks; if the filesystem was built with custom *mkfs* settings, the superblock locations will not be where *fsck* expects to find them. If the UNIX administrator did not record the superblock locations when *building* the filesystem, then she will not be able to tell *fsck* where they are; without that information, a corrupted filesystem is potentially an unrecoverable filesystem.

Recommendation: When building filesystems with custom geometry, use the *-v* option with *mkfs* and make a hardcopy of the *mkfs* session. It just might be needed someday.

Tape Backups

Sooner or later, backups are the life blood of an organization. At some point, hardware or software will fail; a UNIX administrator, operator, database administrator (DBA), or user will make a mistake; and data will need to be recovered from a tape backup. *Next to making systems, tools, and data available to users, the next most important activity is making sure that backups are working.*

Recommendations:

- Examine backup run logs daily to ensure backups are working properly.
- Have another UNIX administrator audit the backup system configuration to make sure that all systems are being backed up and that all filesystems are being backed up.
- Randomly examine backup media to ensure that restore software can actually copy the contents to a system. The ability to merely *read* a tape's contents are insufficient.
- *Utilize off-site storage of backup media.* Fires, floods, and sabotage will surely destroy a server along with the backup tapes, which are usually right next to it.

System Recovery Testing

Without system recovery experience, a UNIX administrator can find the prospect of a ground-up system recovery frightening. This is a healthy but needless fear. There is only one way to overcome this.

Recommendation: Conduct a full server recovery test every three months. Use the following procedure:

1. When possible, clone the server and practice recoveries on the clone; this will enable the UNIX administrator to practice full recoveries during working hours without disrupting production system availability.
2. Backup the production server *twice*; make sure both backup sets are readable.
3. Rebuild the clone from scratch (typically: boot and load the OS from CD, install backup recovery software, recover the rest of the system from backup tapes).
4. Perform regression testing on the functions of the server clone to ensure that it is providing services.

Release Media

A vital part of a system recovery is having release media and knowing where it is.

Recommendation: Have two or more sets of release media for each Solaris version supported on the site. Have one set of release media for each supported version stored with off-site backup tapes.

System Event Logbooks

Without adequate recordkeeping, during a system recovery it may be difficult to determine

- Disk partitioning
- Filesystem customizations
- OS version and install options
- SCSI device addresses
- Patches

Recommendation: Maintain a meticulous journal of every detail of a system's construction, wiring, device addresses, out-of-the-ordinary configurations, and other changes made along the way.

Solaris and Tool Patches

During a real recovery, it might be difficult to retrieve Solaris patches; for instance, the Internet connection (if patches are obtained over the Internet) may be down.

Recommendation: Maintain a local archive of all patches used at the site.

CD-ROM Drives

Chapter 3 recommends that servers not have CD-ROM drives directly attached. Otherwise, an intruder with Solaris release media who has gained physical access to a system will have too easy a time breaking into the system if a CD-ROM drive is attached.

Recommendation: Have one or more internal or external CD-ROM drives available. Make sure that the SCSI address for CD-ROM drives is free (the SCSI address is 6 by default).

Hardware and Software Service Agreements

A full spectrum of hardware service agreements is available from Sun to match the business's needs for each desktop and server system. Options range from carry-in and cross-ship service to on-site repair and replacement. *Carry-in* service means the failed system must be taken to a service depot. In *cross-ship* service, the vendor will ship a replacement system to the customer before receiving the failed system from the customer.

Recommendation: Match business continuation needs for each server and desktop system to an appropriate hardware service plan.

Keep Hardware Spares

Even with the best hardware service plan, sooner or later it may take an unacceptably long period of time to get a special part to repair a desktop or, worse yet, a server system.

The most convenient way to keep spare parts is to have a spare *system*. This spare system can be in the form of a development server, a test server, or (!) a test recovery server. It need not sit idle—in fact, it is better if it does *not* sit idle; an idle system has a way of not working when it is needed.

The spare system does not necessarily need to have the entire CPU or memory complement that its production counterpart has; this can make the spare system unnecessarily costly. Instead, equip it with the minimum necessary to run the most important functions or applications. After all, this is an emergency spare system, and the real production system will (hopefully) be fixed and online quickly.

Recommendation 1: Have a spare system available that can run critical applications or be cannibalized for parts in the event of a hardware failure.

Recommendation 2: Employ as few hardware system types as possible; this will minimize the number of spares needed.

Copies of Critical Server PROMs

Many business tools have licensing agreements that prohibit moving the software from one server to another. The recommendation in the preceding section of having a spare system is easily defeated if any of the server software packages are tied to the server's hostid.

One possible remedy is to have a spare PROM for each server. This will permit the UNIX administrator to temporarily move software packages tied to specific hostid's from one server to another.

Recommendation: Obtain a spare PROM for each server that serves hostid-specific software. Contact your nearest Sun branch office for information.

Note: Systems with the same hostid should not be running concurrently. Any spare PROM should be used only if the other system with the same hostid is not running. Software vendors whose licensing schemes are tied to hostid may object unless they are well informed. Ethical behavior is the responsibility of the UNIX administrator and others involved with having and using spare PROMs.

Disk Space to Spare

One possible solution in the event of a server failure is to temporarily recover all or part of its contents to one or more *other* servers until the failed server can be recovered.

For this alternative to be possible, servers must be running well below their disk capacity. Flexibility is sacrificed if servers are run at close to 100% disk utilization.

Recommendation: Have enough spare online disk capacity to accommodate at least some configurations of having data temporarily served by other servers. Use of NIS+ (or NIS) and the automounter make these transitions easier to accomplish.

Recovery Documentation

Without adequate documentation, a UNIX administrator may find it difficult to properly recover a server.

Recommendation: Maintain up-to-date documentation on server architecture, backup and recovery procedures, off-site storage media recovery, and operational procedures. Make sure that a hard-copy list of passwords is available (and well protected!). Keeping only online copies is fruitless if the system they are stored on is down. And make sure that everyone who has to use it has the most current version and knows where it is. Destroy old copies!

Contacts and Cross-Training

Disasters always seems to happen after hours or on three-day weekends when key personnel are out of town. During natural disasters, key people may be unable to return to work premises to assist with recovery operations. This signals the need for contact lists, pagers, cell phones, and cross-training so that everyone on the UNIX team knows how to recover systems. It is also important to make sure that enough people on the team have authority to make emergency purchases, authorize return of off-site storage media, initiate contingency plans, and so on.

Recommendation: Ensure that key people are reachable after hours by utilizing contact lists, pagers, and cell phones. Cross-train technical staff to maximize likelihood of successful recoveries. Delegate authority to enough personnel so that the few who can assist with a recovery are empowered to do what's needed to continue recovery operations. Have a backup communications plan in the event that power failure or phone service problems make ordinary communications procedures unavailable.

Partner with Inside Suppliers

Next to the company's network engineers, the UNIX team's most important ally is the facilities group—the team who delivers electric power and air conditioning.

Large-scale UPS systems or on-site generators are expensive, but may be easily justifiable if they assure continuing business operations. Likewise, redundant heating, ventilation, and air conditioning (HVAC) systems, portable rental AC systems, and a few powerful electric fans can reduce the impact of an HVAC failure by buying time for repairs or for a clean shutdown.

Recommendation: Coordinate disaster recovery plans with the team that provides electric power and air conditioning; without these facilities, you might as well stay home.

Partner with Outside Suppliers

Frequently, computer equipment will become damaged beyond repair during natural or man-made disasters. Community or regional disasters exacerbate the matter by disrupting the transportation systems needed to facilitate the shipment of replacement computers and supplies.

Recommendation: Partner, formally or informally, with key hardware suppliers to ensure the rapid availability of replacement systems and supplies so that recovery operations can begin as soon as possible.

Where to Go for Additional Information

Publications

- Butler, Janet G., and Badura, Poul. *Contingency Planning and Disaster Recovery: Protecting Your Organization's Resources.* Computer Technology Research Corp., 1997.
- *Contingency Planning & Management*, http://www.contingencyplanning.com/

Web Sites

- *Disaster Recovery Planning*—http://www.utoronto.ca/security/drp.htm
- *Disaster Recovery Journal*—http://www.drj.com/
- *Institute for Crisis Management*—http://www.crisisexperts.com/

Part Five

Appendices

The following topics are covered in the appendices:

- Appendix A: Online Sources for Security Information—security Web sites, hacker Web sites, and security mailing lists
- Appendix B: Online Sources for Public-Domain Security Tools—TCP/IP, access control, intrusion detection, filesystem security, e-mail security, DNS, other tools, security tools sites, and hacker tool sites
- Appendix C: Obtaining and Applying Solaris Patches
- Appendix D: Suggested Reading—books, publications available online, and SunSolve publications, periodicals, and RFCs
- Appendix E: Sun/Solaris Commercial Security Products
- Appendix F: Implementing C2 Security
- Appendix G: Verifying the Integrity of Public-Domain Software
- Appendix H: Glossary of Attacks
- Appendix I: Secure System Checklist

A

ONLINE SOURCES FOR SECURITY INFORMATION

Web site URLs can become quickly outdated. Please refer to the section about Websites in the book's preface for more information.

Security Web Sites

AntiOnline: http://www.antionline.com/ (a commercial security site)

CERIAS (Center for Education and Research in Information Assurance and Security): http://www.cerias.purdue.edu/

CERT (Computer Emergency Response Team, at Carnegie Mellon University): http://www.cert.org/ (security bulletins, tools, etc.)

CIAC (Computer Incident Advisory Capability): http://ciac.llnl.gov/ (security bulletins, tools, etc.)

COAST (Computer Operations, Audit, and Security Technology) sites

   The COAST project page: http://www.cs.purdue.edu/coast/coast.html

   COAST index to security sites: http://www.cs.purdue.edu/coast/hotlist/

Computer Security Institute: http://www.gocsi.com/ (membership organization offering training to information security professionals)

Disaster Recovery Planning: http://www.utoronto.ca/security/drp.htm

Encryption Privacy and Security Resource: http://www.crypto.com/

HERT (Hacker Emergency Response Team): http://www.hert.org/ (security bulletins)

IETF's IPsec site: http://www.ietf.org/html.charters/ipsec-charter.html (discussion of IPsec protocol)

Infowar: http://www.infowar.com/ (a commercial security site)

Institute for Crisis Management: http://www.crisisexperts.com/ (commercial crisis management site)

International Computer Security Association: http://www.icsa.net/ (a commercial Internet security site)

LIST (Laboratory for Information Security Technology): http://www.list.gmu.edu/ (general information security site)

National Institutes of Health Computer Security Information: http://www.alw.nih.gov/Security/security.html (general information security site)

SANS Institute: http://www.sans.org/ (a cooperative research and education association for system administrators, security professionals, and network administrators)

Sun OnLine Documentation: http://docs.sun.com/ (Sun's AnswerBook, Man Pages, whitepapers, and more, on the Internet)

Sun Security Bulletin: http://sunsolve.sun.com/pub-cgi/secbul.pl (Sun Solaris security alerts)

SunSolve: http://sunsolve.sun.com/ (an information service made available to Sun customers on maintenance or support contracts; SunSolve is periodically distributed to customers on CD-ROM and is also available online at this site; a userid and password are required to access the site)

University of Toronto Computer Security Administration: http://www.utoronto.ca/security/ (general information security site)

UNIX Guru Universe: http://www.ugu.com/ (tools, news, and other information for UNIX system administrators)

Hacker Web Sites

2600: http://www.2600.com/ (one of the originals; started as a bulletin board system [BBS]; the early issues provide interesting reading)

Deter: http://www.deter.com/unix/ (UNIX security information and tools)

Hacker's Club: http://hackersclub.com/

Hacker's Lair: http://hackerzlair.org/

Hack Net: http://hack-net.com/

Hack Palace: http://www.hackpalace.com/

Nomad Mobile Research Center: http://www.nmrc.org/

Phrack: http://www.phrack.com/ (a popular hackers' online magazine)

Security Mailing Lists

Bugtraq: http://www.netspace.org/lsv-archive/bugtraq.html
or http://www. geek-girl.com/bugtraq/

CERT: http://www.cert.org/contact_cert/certmaillist.html

CIAC: http://ciac.llnl.gov/ciac/CIACMailingLists.html

Firewall Toolkit: majordomo@ex.tis.com ("subscribe fwtk-users" in message body)

HERT: http://www.hert.org/ or alert@hert.org

SANS Network Security Digest: digest@sans.org

Sun Patch Club Report: SunSolve-EarlyNotifier@Sun.com

Sun Security Bulletin: security-alert@sun.com

SunSolve Early Notifier Alerts: SunSolve-EarlyNotifier@Sun.com

Patches

Refer to appendix C for a list of Solaris patch sources.

B

ONLINE SOURCES FOR PUBLIC-DOMAIN SECURITY TOOLS

This appendix contains a complete list of all of the security tools mentioned in this book, as well as a collection of good security tools and information sites.

Web site URLs can become quickly outdated. Please refer to the section about Web sites in the book's preface for more information.

TCP/IP Security Tools

ISS (Internet security scan)

ftp://coast.cs.purdue.edu/pub/tools/unix/iss/

Note: This public-domain security tool has not been updated since 1995; its effectiveness has diminished since then. A commercial version with regular updates has replaced it; information is available at http://iss.net/ . This is not an endorsement of this commercial product.

Satan (Security Administrator's Tool for Analyzing Networks)

http://www.fish.com/satan/

http://www.fish.com/~zen/satan/satan.html

ftp://ftp.porcupine.org/pub/security/satan-1.1.1.tar.Z

cpm (check promiscuous mode)

ftp://coast.cs.purdue.edu/pub/tools/unix/cpm/

tcpdump (network monitoring and data acquisition)

ftp://ftp.ee.lbl.gov/

Access Control Security Tools

TCP Wrappers

ftp://ftp.porcupine.org/pub/security/tcp_wrappers_7.6.tar.gz

rpcbind

ftp://ftp.porcupine.org/pub/security/rpcbind_2.1.tar.gz
(requires *libwrap.a*, a part of TCP Wrappers—see above entry)

Ssh (secure shell)

ftp://ftp.cs.hut.fi/pub/ssh/
(commercially supported version at http://www. ssh.fi/)

Kerberos

(Kerberos is available only to U.S. citizens located in the United States or to Canadian citizens located in Canada.)

http://web.mit.edu/kerberos/www/ (about Kerberos)

http://web.mit.edu/network/kerberos-form.html (form for U.S. citizens)

http://web.mit.edu/network/kerberos-form-canada.html/ (form for Canadian citizens)

crack (password cracker)

ftp://coast.cs.purdue.edu/pub/tools/unix/crack/

fwtk (firewall toolkit)

ftp://ftp.tis.com/pub/firewalls/toolkit/README
(it is necessary to register for this public-domain package)

S/Key

ftp://ftp.coast.cs.purdue.edu/pub/tools/unix/skey/
(30-day trial version for Windows 3.X, Windows 9x, and NT available at
http://www.bellcore.com/SECURITY/skey.html)

> **Note: At press time, Bellcore had announced an end to Windows S/Key availability and support. It may take some sleuthing to find another source for S/Key for Windows.**

Intrusion Detection Tools

Klaxon

ftp://ftp.eng.auburn.edu/pub/doug/

Courtney

http://ciac.llnl.gov/ciac/SecurityTools.html
(requires libpcap [available at ftp://ftp.ee.lbl.gov/libpcap.tar.Z], tcpdump [see
"TCP/IP Security Tools" in this appendix], and perl v.5 [see "Other Tools and
Sources" in this appendix])

Tocsin

ftp://ftp.eng.auburn.edu/pub/doug/

Gabriel

http://www.lat.com/gabe.html

syn

ftp://ftp.pgci.ca/pub/syn/
(requires perl [see "Other Tools and Sources" in this appendix] and tcpdump
[see "TCP/IP Security Tools" in this appendix])

Filesystem Security Tools

Tiger

ftp://coast.cs.purdue.edu/pub/tools/unix/tiger/TAMU/

Tripwire

ftp://coast.cs.purdue.edu/pub/tools/unix/Tripwire/

> **Note: This public-domain security tool has not been updated since 1994. A commercial version with regular updates has replaced it; information is available at http://www.tripwiresecurity.com/ . This is not intended to be an endorsement of this commercial product.**

COPS

ftp://coast.cs.purdue.edu/pub/tools/unix/cops/

Encryption Tools

PGP

http://web.mit.edu/network/pgp.html (only for U.S. citizens in the United States or Canadian citizens in Canada)

ftp://ftp.pgp.net/pub/pgp/

MD5

ftp://coast.cs.purdue.edu/pub/tools/unix/md5/

E-Mail Security Tools

SMAP (sendmail *wrapper*)

ftp://ftp.tis.com/pub/firewalls/toolkit/README

sendmail *V8 (public-domain* sendmail*)*

http://www.sendmail.org/

http://www.sunfreeware.com/

Postfix (formerly Vmailer)

http://www.postfix.org/

smrsh

smrsh is included with public-domain *sendmail*. See the *sendmail* reference above.

DNS Tools

Public-Domain BIND

http://www.dns.net/dnsrd/

http://www.isc.org/

Dig

Now a part of public-domain BIND. See previous entry.

Other DNS Tools

ftp://ftp.is.co.za/networking/ip/dns/

Other Tools and Sources

logcheck

http://www.psionic.com/abacus/logcheck/

ftp://coast.cs.purdue.edu/pub/tools/unix/logcheck/

lsof (list open files)

http://sunfreeware.com/

ftp://vic.cc.purdue.edu/pub/tools/unix/lsof/ (this site also has *lsof* binaries available in the event no C compiler is available)

Patchdiag

http://sunsolve.sun.com/sunsolve/patchdiag/, or on a SunSolve CD (available only to Sun customers on current maintenance or support contracts)

fix-modes

ftp://ftp.fwi.uva.nl/pub/solaris/fix-modes.tar.gz

perl

Perl is required by several public-domain security tools.

http://www.perl.com/

ftp://ftp.uu.net/systems/gnu/

http://www.sunfreeware.com/

Washington University ftpd

ftp://wuarchive.wustl.edu/packages/wuarchive-ftpd/[1]

ftp://ftp.cyber.com.au/pub/unix/wu-ftpd-2.4.tar.Z

http://www.sunfreeware.com/ (look for *wu-ftpd*)

Security Tools Sites

CERT Tools

ftp://ftp.cert.org/pub/tools/

CIAC Tools

http://ciac.llnl.gov/ciac/SecurityTools.html

COAST Tools

ftp://coast.cs.purdue.edu/pub/tools/unix/

---

1. This site, recognized as the original source for *wu-ftpd*, was off the air at press time.

Doug's Tools

ftp://ftp.eng.auburn.edu/pub/doug/

LIST (Laboratory for Information Security Technology) Security Tools

http://www.list.gmu.edu/software.htm

Sun Freeware Site

http://www.sunfreeware.com/

Wietse Venema's UNIX Security Tools Collection

ftp://ftp.porcupine.org/pub/security/

Hacker Tools Sites

This section contains UNIX hacking sites and tools. Use the information you find here responsibly!

1. http://www.vc3.com/~caldwm/security/rootkits/
2. http://agape.kuntrynet.com/hack/trojan/misc/
3. http://www.tekniq.net/archive/security/hack/
4. http://hack-net.com/html/exploits/1998/10/index.shtml
5. http://www.nswc.navy.mil/ISSEC/Docs/how.to.hack.unix.html
6. http://hackerzlair.org/members/pROcon/information.html
7. http://www.hackpalace.com/hacking/unix/rootkits/
8. http://www.deter.com/unix/
9. http://www.hoobie.net/security/exploits/
10. http://www.rootshell.com/
11. http://www.enslaver.com/files/rootkits/

Obtaining and Applying Solaris Patches

Patches are used to repair software bugs and security holes. A patch is a group of files including a newer version of one or more operating system modules, device drivers, system programs or utilities, or configuration files. The newer version of the program, driver, or file contains a fix or repair of some kind intended to correct a vulnerability or malfunction.

A system lacking the latest security patches is vulnerable to the latest hacking techniques.

Sources for Patch Information

SunSolve: http://www.sunsolve.com/ (web site for registered Sun maintenance customers, containing whitepapers and patches; also, periodically mailed CDs containing same)

Sun Patch Club Report (weekly e-mail reports on new Solaris patches): SunSolve-EarlyNotifier@Sun.com

Sun Security Bulletin: security-alert@sun.com (periodic e-mail reports on Solaris security bugs and recommended fixes)

CERT (Computer Emergency Response Team, at Carnegie Mellon University): http://www.cert.org/

CIAC (Computer Incident Advisory Capability): http://ciac.llnl.gov/

Understanding Solaris Patches

Solaris patches are uniquely identified with a six-digit patch number and a two-digit patch version number. For example, patch *106242-03* is the third version of the patch *106242*. Sun uses one serial numbering system for all versions of Solaris.

Solaris patches are typically distributed as compressed *tar* archives. Example Solaris patch filenames are *106242-03.tar.Z, 106242-03.tar.gz*, or *106242-03.tar.zip*.

Note: The following procedure does not need to be performed routinely. It is included only for those who wish to understand Solaris's patch architecture.

To unwrap a patch: create a new directory, copy the patch file to it, and run one of the following commands. Using our example Solaris patch filenames *106242-03.tar.Z, 106242-03.tar.gz*, and *106240-03.tar.zip*:

- For a patch filename ending in *.Z*, enter *zcat file | tar xvf -*, where *file* is the name of the patch file.
- For a patch filename ending in *.gz*, enter *gzcat file | tar xvf -*, where *file* is the name of the patch file.
- For a patch filename ending in *.zip*, enter *unzip file | tar xvf-*, where *file* is the name of the patch file.

Unwrapping the patch causes a directory to be created; the name of the directory is the same as the name of the patch, example *106242-03*. The patch directory contains the following files and directories:

- *Install.info*—a text file containing generic patch installation instructions.
- *README.patch* (for example, *README.106242-03*)—a text file containing specific information about this patch.
- One or more Sun package directories, for example *SUNWaccr*. This directory contains updated Solaris files to be replaced.
- *installpatch*—the patch install script (obsolete in Solaris 2.6).
- *backoutpatch*—the patch backout script (obsolete in Solaris 2.6).

Patch history and backout information resides in */var/sadm/patch* . This is the directory that grows as patches are installed (particularly if older versions of patches are not backed out).

Understanding Solaris Patch Clusters

Solaris patch clusters are collections of Solaris patches that are packaged together for some common purpose. Examples of patch clusters include

- Solaris 2.x or Solaris 7 recommended patches
- Solaris 2.x or Solaris 7 patches containing security fixes (Sun includes security patches in its list of recommended patches)
- Solaris 2.x or Solaris 7 Year-2000 patches

Note: The Solaris recommended patches are the most important patches and fix critical system and security holes. While generally the set of recommended patches are interoperable and should not cause undesirable system behavior, the experienced and wary UNIX administrator should err on the side of caution and proceed slowly and carefully when installing even recommended patches.

Sources for Patches

Sun service customers can access Sun's complete patch archive at the Sun-Solve Web site at http://sunsolve.sun.com/ . Users will be asked for a userid and password (this gets assigned for site contacts once a Sun service contract is in force) when accessing this site. Sun service customers also periodically receive SunSolve CDs, which include patches for current and some prior releases of Solaris.

Sun users who are not on maintenance can access Sun's publicly available patch archive at

- http://sunsolve.sun.com/sunsolve/pubpatches/patches.html
- ftp://ftp.uu.net/systems/sun/sun-dist

Patch Installation Strategies

Patches consume disk space—sometimes *lots* of disk space—on Solaris systems. When installed as recommended, patch installation includes *backout* data, which is used to back out the patch in case problems are encountered with the patched version of any software.

Before Installing Patches

Before you install patches, you should

1. Consider installing the patch on a test system to ensure that no unexpected behavior occurs.
2. Find and study all related *README* files. On a SunSolve Patch CD, they can be found:

- As the file *README.FIRST* file at the topmost directory on the Sun-Solve Patch CD
- As the file *<VER>_<PKG>_README* (example: *2.3_MCAD_GFX.README*) for specific package or product patches; in the subdirectory files on the SunSolve Patch CD;
- As the file *<VER>_Recommended.README* (example: *2.6_Recommended.README*)
- As the file *<PATCH>.README* (example: *106242-01.README*) in an individual patch

3. Do a full backup of every system being patched.

4. Back out earlier versions of the same patch. For example, if patch *106242-06* is being installed on a system that contains patch *106242-05* (or any prior version), then patch *106242-05* (or any prior version) should first be backed out.

5. Reboot the system and stay in single-user mode. Be sure */usr* and */var* are mounted (in case the system does not mount them in single-user mode).

6. Be sure that no applications, database servers, etc. are running.

Which Patches to Install

Every Solaris system should contain the recommended patches.

Sun's position on other patches (those not included in the Solaris patch clusters) is that patches should be installed only to counteract actual observed problems that the patch is designed to address. In other words, Solaris patches should not be installed *because they are there*. Reasons *not* to install patches not on the recommended list include

- The problem that the patch was designed to solve may not be occurring on your system.
- A patch can introduce new problems or anomalies.
- Patches consume disk space.

Testing Patches

Don't assume that systems will behave normally after the installation of a patch. Patches should first be installed on a small number of systems, and then the systems should be tested to ensure that the patch installation does not cause any undesired behavior.

For Patches Requiring System Reboot

Read the *<PATCH>.README* in each patch to determine if any special procedures are required, such as a system reboot. In cases where a reboot is required, the reboot should be performed as soon as possible after the installation of *each* patch.

The patchdiag *Program*

The *patchdiag* command examines a local system to determine whether it needs additional patches or patch updates. A system's complement of patches is compared to a data file of current patches that can be downloaded from SunSolve. *patchdiag* is included on the SunSolve CD starting with Version 3.0.12 and is also available online at SunSolve (available only to Sun customers on current maintenance or support contracts).

Patch Installation Procedure, Solaris 2.x—2.5.1

The *installpatch* and *backoutpatch* scripts, included with every patch, are used to install and remove patches. The *showrev -p* command is used to list the patches installed on the system.

> **Note: Do not use the *installpatch -d* option when installing patches. This option does not save backout information needed to remove the patch later. The penalty for backing out a patch installed without the backout option is a complete OS install.**

Patch Installation

To install a single patch on a system, use the following procedure.

1. Enter the command *mkdir /tmp/patch* .
2. Copy the patch file to the directory */tmp/patch* .
3. Uncompress the patch file with *uncompress* (if the patch filename ends with *.Z*) or *gunzip* (if the patch filename ends with *.gz*).
4. Unwrap the patch file with the *tar* command. For example, if the patch filename is *106545-03.tar*, the command would be *tar xvf 106545-03.tar* .
5. Install the patch with the *installpatch* command found in the patch archive. For example, enter the command */tmp/patch/106545-03/installpatch /tmp/patch/106545-03* .
6. Examine the patch installation log. To continue this example, the log file is */var/sadm/patch/106545-03/log* .

Bulk Patch Installation

To apply many patches at once on a system, use the following procedure.

1. Enter the command *mkdir /tmp/patch* .
2. Copy all patch archives to the directory */tmp/patch* .
3. Run the following script to install all patches unattended.

```
#!/bin/sh
#
cd /tmp/patch
uncompress *Z
for patch in *
do
    tar xvf $patch
    installpatch /tmp/patch/$patch
done
rm -rf /tmp/patch
```

To apply many patches at once on several systems, first use *rdist* (or similar tool) to distribute patches and the above wrapper script to all of the systems; then use *rsh* or *Ssh* to execute the wrapper script above.

Although it may be potentially time consuming to do so, you should examine the logs for all patch installs on all systems for errors.

Patch Installation Procedures for Solaris 2.6 and Solaris 7

The *patchadd* and *patchrm* commands were introduced with Solaris 2.6. Instead of being shipped with each patch (as are *installpatch* and *backoutpatch*), *patchadd* and *patchrm* are part of Solaris.

patchadd provides a means for the bulk installation of patches, including installation of patches to client systems over the network. Thus, on Solaris 2.6 and later, there is no need for bulk installation wrappers such as the example in the preceding section.

Note: Do not use the *patchadd -d* option when installing patches. This option does not save backout information needed to remove the patch at a later time.

Patch Installation

To install a single patch on a system, use the following procedure.

1. Enter the command *mkdir /tmp/patch* .
2. Copy the patch file to the directory */tmp/patch* .

3. Uncompress the patch file with *uncompress* (if the patch filename ends with *.Z*), *gunzip* (if the patch filename ends with *.gz*), or *unzip* (if the patch filename ends with *.zip*).

4. Unwrap the patch file with the *tar* command. For example, if the patch filename is *106545-03.tar*, the command would be *tar xvf 106545-03.tar* .

5. Install the patch with the *patchadd* command. For example, enter the command *patchadd /tmp/patch/106545-03* .

6. Examine the patch installation log. To continue this example, the log file is */var/sadm/patch/106545-03/log* .

Bulk Patch Installation

To apply many patches at once on a system, use the following procedure.

1. Enter the command *mkdir /tmp/patch* .

2. Copy all patch archives to the directory */tmp/patch* .

3. Uncompress the patch file with *uncompress* (if the patch filename ends with *.Z*), *gunzip* (if the patch filename ends with *.gz*), or *unzip* (if the patch filename ends with *.zip*).

4. Unwrap the patch file with the *tar* command. For example, if the patch filename is *106545-03.tar*, the command would be *tar xvf 106545-03.tar*.

5. Install the patches with the *patchadd* command. For example, enter the command *patchadd -M /tmp/patch/106545-03 /tmp/patch/ 107436-01 /tmp/patch/108974-02* .

6. Examine the patch installation logs.

To apply many patches at once on several systems, first use *rdist* (or similar tool) to distribute patches to all of the systems; then use *rsh* or *Ssh* to execute *patchadd*.

Although it may be potentially time consuming to do so, you should examine the logs for all patch installs on all systems for errors.

Solaris OS Upgrades

Because patches are specific to a particular version of Solaris, an OS upgrade removes the patch history by removing */var/sadm/patch*. Thus, when upgrading Solaris, you are starting with a clean system in regard to patches. Although you might be thinking about all the disk space that was recovered by the upgrade removing those old OS patches, keep in mind that patches on the new version may consume that much space over time.

When installing or upgrading to a new version of Solaris, you should immediately install any patches or maintenance updates on the release CD. Also, you should acquire the latest recommended patches for the new Solaris release from SunSolve and install them.

Where to Go for Additional Information

AnswerBook

- AnswerBook 2—System Administration Guide, Volume 1: Managing Software
- AnswerBook 2—Solaris Advanced Installation Guide

Man Pages

- patchadd(1M)
- patchrm(1M)
- pkgparam(1)
- showrev(1M)
- unzip(1)

Publications

- *How to Patch Autoclient and Diskless Systems*, SunSolve Infodoc 15677
- *Removing Saved Patch Data to Free Up Disk Space*, SunSolve Infodoc 16110
- *How to Install Patch When Booted Off CD-ROM*, SunSolve Infodoc 16790
- *Patch Install Quick Troubleshooting Steps*, SunSolve Infodoc 17914
- *Practical Overview of Troubleshooting Patches and Patch Installation*, SunSolve Infodoc 17973

Web Sites

- SunSolve—Solaris patches and information (for Sun customers on maintenance contracts only)—http://sunsolve.sun.com/ or ftp://sunsolve1.sun.com/
- Solaris publicly available patches—http://sunsite.unc.edu/ or ftp://sunsite.unc.edu/

D

SUGGESTED READING

Books

1. Ramsey, Rick. *All About Administering NIS+*. Upper Saddle River, NJ: Prentice Hall PTR, 1994.

2. Butler, Janet, and Badura, Paul. *Contingency Planning and Disaster Recovery: Protecting Your Organization's Resources*. Computer Technology Research Corp., 1997.

3. Albitz, Paul, and Liu, Cricket. *DNS and Bind*. Sebastopol, CA: O'Reilly & Associates, 1998.

4. Cheswick, William, and Bellovin, Steve. *Firewalls and Internet Security: Repelling the Wily Hacker*. Reading, MA: Addison-Wesley, 1994.

5. Pipkin, Donald. *Halting the Hacker: A Practical Guide to Computer Security*. Upper Saddle River, NJ: Prentice Hall PTR, 1997.

6. Meinel, Carolyn. *The Happy Hacker: A Guide to Mostly Harmless Hacking*. Show Low, AZ: American Eagle Publications, 1998.

7. Comer, Douglas E. *Internetworking with TCP/IP: Principles, Protocols, and Architecture*. Upper Saddle River, NJ: Prentice Hall PTR, 1995.

8. Comer, Douglas E., and Stevens, David L. *Internetworking with TCP/IP: Design, Implementation, and Internals*. Upper Saddle River, NJ: Prentice Hall PTR, 1998.

9. Stern, Hal. *Managing NFS & NIS*. Sebastopol, CA: O'Reilly & Associates, 1991.

10. Anonymous. *Maximum Security: A Hacker's Guide to Protecting Your Internet Site and Network*. Indianapolis, IN: Sams Publishing, 1998.

11. Scott, Charlie, Wolfe, Paul, and Erwin, Mike. *Virtual Private Networks*. Sebastopol, CA: O'Reilly & Associates, 1999.

12. Zimmerman, Phillip R. *The Official PGP User's Guide*. Cambridge, MA: MIT Press, 1995.

13. Costales, Bryan, and Allman, Eric. *Sendmail*. Sebastopol, CA: O'Reilly & Associates, 1997.

14. Murhammer, Martin. *TCP/IP Tutorial and Technical Overview*. Upper Saddle River, NJ: Prentice Hall PTR, 1998.

15. Stevens, W. Richard. *TCP/IP Illustrated, Volume 1: The Protocols*. Reading, MA: Addison-Wesley, 1994.

16. Stevens, W. Richard, and Wright, Gary R. *TCP/IP Illustrated, Volume 2: The Implementation*. Reading, MA: Addison-Wesley, 1995.

17. Stevens, W. Richard. *TCP/IP Illustrated, Volume 3: TCP for Transactions, Http, Nntp, and the UNIX Domain Protocols*. Reading, MA: Addison-Wesley, 1996.

18. Meinel, Carolyn. "How Hackers Break In." New York, NY: *Scientific American*, October 1998.

Publications and Articles Available Online

1. *Best Current Practices RFCs*
   http://www.faqs.org/rfcs/bcp/bcp-index.html
   http://www.garlic.com/~lynn/rfcdoc.htm#BCPdoc

2. *Disaster Recovery Journal*
   http://www.drj.com/

3. Spafford, Eugene H. *The Internet Worm Incident*
   ftp://coast.cs.purdue.edu/pub/doc/morris_worm/spaf-IWorm-paper-ESEC.ps.Z

4. Spafford, Eugene H. *The Internet Worm Program: An Analysis*
   ftp://coast.cs.purdue.edu/pub/doc/morris_worm/spaf-IWorm-paper-CCR.ps.Z

5. *CyLAN IPSec White Paper*
   http://www.cylan.com/files/whpaper.htm

6. *Trusted Computer System Evaluation Criteria* (also known as *The DOD Orange Book*)—contains the official C2 specification
   http://www-library.itsi.disa.mil/org/dod_std/dod_std_5200_28.html
   (how to order a hardcopy)
   http://ftp.za.kernel.org/pub/linux/libs/security/Orange-Linux/refs/Orange.html (softcopy)

7. Farmer, Dan. *Improving the Security of Your Site by Breaking into It*
   ftp://ftp.porcupine.org/pub/security/admin-guide-to-cracking.101.Z

8. *What is a VPN?*
   ftp://ftp.employees.org/ferguson/vpn.zip

9. Tung, Brian. *The Moron's Guide to Kerberos*
   http://gost.isi.edu/brian/security/kerberos.html

10. *How to Kerberize Your Site*, Oak Ridge National Laboratory
    http://www.ornl.gov/~jar/HowToKerb.html

11. *Kerberos FAQ*
    http://www.cis.ohio-state.edu/hypertext/faq/usenet/kerberos-faq/
    general/faq.html

12. *Sun / Solaris-specific information at sendmail.org*
    http://www.sendmail.org/sun-specific/

SunSolve Publications

Note: SunSolve publications are available to Sun customers who are
on current maintenance or support contracts. SunSolve is periodically
distributed to customers on CD-ROM and is also available online at
http://sunsolve.sun.com/. A userid and password are required to use
this site.

1. *A Practical Guide to Solaris Security*, Whitepaper 1164

2. *Introduction to Sun System Security*, Infodoc 2143

3. *Mastering Security on the Internet for Competitive Advantage*, Whitepaper 1353

4. *Internet Service Provider Configuration Guidelines*, Whitepaper 1342

5. *Security in the Solaris Environment*, Whitepaper 1272

6. *Sun System Security*, Whitepaper 913

7. *Managing Your Mission-Critical, Open Enterprise,* Whitepaper 1288

8. *Solaris—Networked Computing for the Global Enterprise*, Whitepaper 1290

9. *Brief Description of NIS+ Security for Solaris SPARC*, FAQ 1926

10. *C2 Security Frequently Asked Questions*, Infodoc 14313

11. *Network Security PSD / FAQ*, Infodoc 13335

12. *Security in Practice*, Whitepaper 1390

13. *What to Do if Root Password Is Lost*, Infodoc 16786

14. *How to Set Up Quotas on a File System*, SRDB 4652

15. *How to Enable User Storage Space Quotas for Solaris*, FAQ 1946

16. *How to Find What Software Package a File Belongs To*, Infodoc 18393
17. *How to Modify ACLs*, Infodoc 12718
18. *How to Set ACL Entries on a File*, Infodoc 12714
19. *How to Delete ACL Entries on a File or Directory*, Infodoc 12728
20. *Boot and Run Levels*, Technical Bulletin 1077
21. *Administration and Usage of Crontab*, Whitepaper 918
22. *Crontab Administration and Usage*, Infodoc 3959
23. *Ethernet Interface FAQ/PSD*, Infodoc 12306
24. *Misc Networking Programs PSD/FAQ*, Infodoc 12052
25. *Sendmail PSD/FAQ*, Infodoc 12815
26. *DNS PSD/FAQ*, Infodoc 11975
27. *How to Tell What Version of BIND You Are Running*, Infodoc 16255
28. *NSKit PSD/FAQ*, Infodoc 11989
29. *NIS+ PSD/FAQ*, Infodoc 11988
30. *NIS PSD/FAQ*, Infodoc 12000
31. *How to Set Up NIS+ in Solaris 2.x*, Infodoc 1014
32. *How to Implement Secure RPC Without NIS or NIS+*, Infodoc 18021
33. *How to Rebuild a NIS+ Rootmaster*, Infodoc 16402
34. *Network Security PSD/FAQ*, Infodoc 13335
35. *Why Do All My Ethernet Addresses Have the Same Ether MAC Address?*, Infodoc 16733
36. *Automounter PSD/FAQ*, Infodoc 11990
37. *The NFS Distributed File Service*, Whitepaper 1252
38. *NFS PSD/FAQ*, Infodoc 11987
39. *How to Patch Autoclient and Diskless Systems*, Infodoc 15677
40. *Removing Saved Patch Data to Free Up Disk Space*, Infodoc 16110
41. *How to Install Patch When Booted Off CD-ROM*, Infodoc 16790
42. *Patch Install Quick Troubleshooting Steps*, Infodoc 17914
43. *Practical Overview of Troubleshooting Patches and Patch Installation*, Infodoc 17973

Periodicals Online

1. *Contingency Planning & Management*, http://www.contingencyplanning.com/
2. *First Strike*, e-mail newsletter from Sun, (e-mail) FSsubscribe@emailch.com
3. *Inside Solaris*, http://www.cobb.com/sun/

4. *Internet Security Advisor*, http://www.advisor.com/

5. *SC Magazine, Infosecurity News*, http://www.infosecnews.com/

6. *SKIP Newsletter*, http://skip.incog.com/newsletter2.html

7. *SKIP Website*, http://skip.incog.com/

8. *Server/Workstation Expert* (formerly *Sun Expert*), http://sun.expert.com/

9. *SunHELP*, http://www.sunhelp.com/

10. *SunServer*, http://www.pcinews.com/sun/

11. *SunWorld*, e-mail newsletter from Sun, http://www.sunworld.com/, (e-mail) swunsub@emailch.com

12. *Sys Admin*, http://www.samag.com/

13. *UNIX Review/Performance Computing*, http://www.performancecomputing.com/

Internet RFCs

Request for Comments, or RFCs, are the official published collection of technical protocols and policies used on the Internet. They are available from several sources; a few are listed here.

- http://www.ietf.org/rfc.html
- http://www.cis.ohio-state.edu/hypertext/information/rfc.html
- http://www.ietf.org/rfc.html
- http://www.faqs.org/rfcs/
- http://www.pmg.lcs.mit.edu/rfc.html
- http://info.internet.isi.edu/in-notes/rfc/files
- http://www.rfc-editor.org/rfc.html

1. RFC1032, Domain Administrators Guide, http://www.ietf.org/rfc/rfc1032.txt

2. RFC1033, Domain Administrators Operations Guide, http://www.ietf.org/rfc/rfc1033.txt

3. RFC1034, Domain Names—Concepts and Facilities, http://www.ietf.org/rfc/rfc1034.txt

4. RFC1035, Domain Names—Implementation and Specification, http://www.ietf.org/rfc/rfc1035.txt

5. RFC 1281, Guidelines for the Secure Operation of the Internet, http://www.ietf.org/rfc/rfc1281.txt

6. RFC1413, Ident Protocol, http://www.ietf.org/rfc/rfc1413.txt

7. RFC1416, Telnet Authentication Option,
   http://www.ietf.org/rfc/rfc1416.txt

8. RFC1700, Assigned Numbers (official list of TCP/IP port number assignments)
   http://www.ietf.org/rfc/rfc1700.txt

9. RFC 2196, The Site Security Handbook,
   http://www.ietf.org/rfc/rfc2196.txt

10. RFC2401, Security Architecture for the Internet Protocol,
    http://www.ietf.org/rfc/rfc2401.txt

11. RFC2411, IPsec Document Roadmap,
    http://www.ietf.org/rfc/rfc2411.txt

12. RFC2504, Users' Security Handbook,
    http://www.ietf.org/rfc/rfc2504.txt

E

SOLARIS SECURITY PRODUCTS

This appendix contains a description of Sun's security products for firewalls, virtual private networks, and the highly secure Trusted Solaris operating system.

SunScreen EFS

SunScreen EFS is a firewall software product that runs on Sun workstations and servers. EFS contains a packet filtering engine that allows the administrator to specify which network services can pass through the firewall as well as those systems and networks to and from which these network services may pass.

EFS also contains a SKIP module in order that secure virtual private networks can be established from site to site over the Internet.

More information is available at http://www.sun.com/security/efs.html .

SunScreen SPF

SPF is a *standalone* firewall software product that runs on Sun servers. Unlike EFS, SPF is a "stealth" firewall: having no MAC or IP address, it is virtually invisible on the network and difficult to attack.

Like EFS, SPF also contains a SKIP module in order that secure virtual private networks can be set up from site to site over the Internet.

More information is available at http://www.sun.com/security/spf200-efs.html .

SunScreen SKIP

SunScreen SKIP is a product that is used for key management and virtual private networks. As a server (as part of EFS or SPF), SKIP facilitates multiple virtual private network connections from SKIP clients running on Solaris or Windows operating systems.

A SKIP client can communicate directly to other SKIP clients. Or a SKIP client can communicate through a SKIP server (as part of EFS or SPF) to servers or clients *behind* the SKIP server.

More information is available at http://www.sun.com/security/skip/index.html . See the section on virtual private networks in chapter 13 for more information on using SKIP.

Sun Security Manager

Sun Security Manager is a security-enhancement package for servers and desktop systems. It provides access control, administration segmentation, password management, system file-integrity checking, and auditing. More information is available at http://www.sun.com/security/ .

SunScreen SecureNet

SecureNet is a bundled security product consisting of SunScreen EFS; SKIP clients for Solaris, Windows 95, and Windows NT; and Sun Security Manager. Refer to the previous descriptions of SunScreen EFS, SunScreen SKIP, and Sun Security Manager for additional information.

Trusted Solaris

Trusted Solaris is a highly secure version of Solaris, designed and certified for trusted computer system evaluation criteria (TCSEC) compartmented mode workstation (CMW), otherwise known as security level B1.

Two versions of Trusted Solaris are available.

- Trusted Solaris 1.2—based on SunOS 4.1.3_U1
- Trusted Solaris 2.5.1—based on Solaris 2.5.1 11/97

Trusted Solaris is designed for an environment where the utmost in information security is required. Extensions to the filesystem, kernel, system administration utilities, user interfaces, and networking effectively restrict the flow of sensitive information so that individuals lacking proper security clearances cannot get access to it.

Trusted Solaris was designed so that most third-party products can run without modification or recompilation.

Refer to the *Trusted Solaris 2.5 Technical White Paper* for more information. This document is available from

> Sun Microsystems Federal Inc.
> 2550 Garcia Avenue
> Mountain View, CA 94043 USA
> 415-969-9131

A FAQ document on Trusted Solaris is available at http://www.sun.com/products-n-solutions/government/ts_faq.html .

Where to Go for Additional Information

Web Sites

- SKIP Web site—http://skip.incog.com/
- SKIP Newsletter—http://skip.incog.com/newsletter2.html

F

IMPLEMENTING C2 SECURITY

The Basic Security Module (BSM) package is Sun Microsystems' implementation of C2 security. This appendix describes the steps used to install, activate, and manage C2 security on a Solaris system.

Why run C2 security? Primarily, C2 security enables the tracing of all system events back to specific users through the use of extensive audit trails.

This appendix is an overview of C2 security. For complete information, consult the texts listed in the references at the end of this appendix.

What Is C2 Security?

C2 security enhances system security and offers several benefits, including

- Traceability of all system events back to specific users
- Inability to abort the system using Stop-A (if a user's stopping the system is truly a concern, then the system should also be in a locked room, since there is little that C2 security can do to prevent a user from simply turning the system off and on)

Implications of C2 Security

C2 security has several side effects (some people would call these detriments), including

- The audit trail logs can consume a considerable amount of disk space (as much as tens or hundreds of MB).
- The system will run slower by 5–10% due to the overhead of capturing and writing to the audit trail logs; a system "on the edge" from a performance perspective will appear to run *much* slower.
- Volume manager is unavailable. This means that diskettes and CD-ROM discs are not automatically mounted when inserted into their drives. Instead, they must be mounted manually with the *mount* command.

Enabling C2 Security

This section assumes the installation of the following packages from the Solaris OS media (these packages are installed by default *unless specifically excluded* during an install or upgrade):

- SUNWcar—Solaris core architecture
- SUNWcsr—core SPARC
- SUNWcsu—core SPARC
- SUNWhea—header files
- SUNWman—man pages

Follow this procedure to enable C2 security.

1. Bring the system to single-user mode with the *init 1* command.
2. Change to the BSM directory with the *cd /etc/security* command.
3. Execute the *bsmconv* script with the *./bsmconv* command. Sample dialogue follows.

```
# ./bsmconv
This script is used to enable the Basic Security Module (BSM).
Shall we continue with the conversion now? [y/n] y
bsmconv: INFO: checking startup file.
bsmconv: INFO: move aside /etc/rc2.d/S92volmgt.
bsmconv: INFO: turning on audit module.
bsmconv: INFO: initializing device allocation files.

The Basic Security Module is ready.
If there were any errors, please fix them now.
Configure BSM by editing files located in /etc/security.
Reboot this system now to come up with BSM enabled.
#
```

4. Bring the system back to multiuser mode with the *init 6* command.

Disabling C2 Security

Follow this procedure to disable C2 security.

1. Bring the system to single-user mode with the *init 1* command.
2. Change to the BSM directory with the *cd /etc/security* command.
3. Execute the *bsmunconv* script with the *./bsmunconv* command. Sample dialogue follows.

```
# ./bsmunconv
This script is used to disable the Basic Security Module (BSM).
Shall we continue the reversion to a non-BSM system now? [y/n] y
bsmunconv: INFO: moving aside /etc/security/audit_startup.
bsmunconv: INFO: restore /etc/rc2.d/S92volmgt.
bsmunconv: INFO: removing c2audit:audit_load from /etc/system.

The Basic Security Module has been disabled.
Reboot this system now to come up without BSM.
#
```

4. Bring the system back to multiuser mode with the *init 6* command.

Managing C2 Security

Sites that have implemented C2 security have done so for a variety of reasons, but the common theme is the ability to account for all system changes. Regardless of this, the essential issues with C2 security are

- Configuration of C2 audit capture
- Management of C2 logs
- Management of system performance with C2 security turned on
- Audit events
- Audit trail analysis
- Management of removable media
- Device allocation

Each of these is discussed in the following sections.

Configuration of C2 Audit Capture

The configuration files */etc/security/audit_class*, */etc/security/audit_event*, and */etc/security/audit_control*, along with the *auditconfig* command, determine what events are recorded and in which directory they are stored.

Management of C2 Logs

This is primarily a matter of managing the *space* that C2 logs consume. Every site's auditing needs and C2 log disk space consumption rates are different. Depending upon the logging granularity needed—as well as the storage capacity of the system itself—finding space for and managing the C2 logs will be insignificant, nightmarish, or somewhere in between.

Management of Performance

C2 may break the back of a system that is already near the edge with regard to performance. The extra I/O related to writing out C2 logs may turn a sluggish system into an excruciatingly slow system. This matter requires expertise in system performance and tuning in order to determine the cause of any performance problems exacerbated by C2 logging.

Audit Events

On a system with C2 auditing turned on, certain events require immediate attention. The audit system will launch the *audit_warn* script when disk space runs low or other malfunctions occur. *Audit_warn* sends e-mail to the alias *audit_warn*, and it also writes a message to the system console.

Audit Trail Analysis

The *auditreduce* and *praudit* tools form the core of audit trail analysis. *auditreduce* is used to extract and filter audit trail records for specific reports, and *praudit* makes the records that are somewhat human readable. The Basic Security Module Guide includes several examples of shell scripts used to further process *auditreduce* and *praudit* output.

Removable Media Management

When C2 is turned on, Volume Manager is disabled; hence, diskettes and CD-ROM discs are *not* automatically mounted. This can be a problem on a system where frequent diskette and/or CD-ROM access is needed by an end user. But then again, the functions requiring C2 security should probably reside on a separate system from that of an end user needing to mount and dismount CDs and diskettes.

If a mounted CD or diskette is required on a C2 system, consider these alternatives:

- Permanently mount the device at boot time and allocate the device to a specific user (see the next section on device allocation).
- Copy the contents of the diskette or CD to a fixed hard disk.
- Redesign the application requiring both C2 and mountable diskettes or CDs.

Device Allocation

UNIX ordinarily permits all users read and write access to read/write cartridge devices such as tape drives and diskettes. This openness is unacceptable in a C2 environment where strict and verifiable control over file access is required.

Consider, for example, a UNIX administrator who needs to archive some files to a tape. He will put the tape in the drive, walk back to his desk, perform the backup commands, and then walk back to the server to retrieve the tape. During his trek back to the data center to retrieve the tape, another user could have copied all or part of the contents of the tape to her own home directory, or even altered the contents of the tape.

The *allocate*, *deallocate*, *dminfo*, and *list_devices* commands are used to control and monitor these kinds of accesses by allowing access to tape and other devices to one user at a time.

Recommendations

1. When starting out with C2, experiment first on a testing or development platform, *not* on the production server(s) for which it is ultimately intended.
2. Read and learn the *SunSHIELD Basic Security Module Guide*.
3. Experiment with *audit_class*, *audit_control*, *audit_event*, and *auditconfig* settings in order to ensure the correct level of audit trail capture.
4. Set up the *audit_warn* e-mail alias to point to one or more UNIX admin accounts.
5. Experiment with the *auditreduce* and *praudit* tools.

Where to Go for Additional Information

AnswerBook

- AnswerBook 2—SunShield Basic Security Module Guide

Man Pages

- allocate(1M)
- auditconfig(1)
- auditreduce(1)
- audit_class(4)

- audit_control(4)
- audit_event(4)
- bsmconv(1M)
- bsmunconv(1M)
- deallocate(1M)
- dminfo(1M)
- list_devices(1M)
- praudit(1M)

Publications

- *C2 Security (BSM) Frequently Asked Questions,* SunSolve Infodoc 14313
- *Trusted Computer System Evaluation Criteria* (also known as *The DOD Orange Book*), contains the official C2 specification; available at
  - http://www-library.itsi.disa.mil/org/dod_std/dod_std_5200_28.html (how to order a hardcopy)
  - http://ftp.za.kernel.org/pub/linux/libs/security/Orange-Linux/refs/Orange.html (softcopy)
  - http://www.geocities.com/Baja/Canyon/2983/orange.html (softcopy)

G

Verifying the Integrity of Public-Domain Software

The days of blindly trusting the integrity of public-domain software—even on well-known sites—are over. A popular public-domain security package (used throughout this book) was compromised by a hacker and subsequently downloaded by unsuspecting UNIX administrators before its back door was discovered and the package repaired. This appendix provides information needed to raise your confidence in your ability to verify the integrity of public-domain software.

Note: This procedure verifies only the archive site's software package integrity—that it has not been tampered with since its last official release. It does not ensure anything about its *behavior* while running on a system. In other words, if the software obtained is the genuine article with regard to its digital signature, that does not mean that the software will *work* properly.

Verification Using PGP

PGP is a frequently used tool for the verification of digital signatures and, hence, the integrity of software packages. PGP is available from

- http://web.mit.edu/network/pgp.html (only for U.S. citizens in the United States or Canadian citizens in Canada)
- ftp://ftp.pgp.net/pub/pgp/

The process of verifying the integrity of a package is shown here by way of example: we obtain the software package rpcbind from ftp.porcupine.org and copy two files from the site:

- rpcbind_2.1.tar.gz—the software package archive
- rpcbind_2.1.tar.gz.sig—the software package archive digital signature

While the site manager's public key is on the FTP or Web site (in the file *wietse.pgp*), it is important to obtain the public key by some other means. In this example, the site manager's key is available from CERT advisory *CA-99-01 Trojan TCP Wrappers* (see the URL at the end of this appendix), or from MIT's public PGP key server at http://pgp5.ai.mit.edu/pks-commands.html# extract, or from his personal Web site at http://www.porcupine.org/wietse/ .

> **Note: Obtaining and trusting a PGP public key obtained from the same site as a software package is ill-advised. This is because an intruder who compromises a site will also be able to create a phony public key that will "validate" any compromised software.**
>
> **Instead, any public key associated with a site should be obtained independently or verified by other means, such as a direct phone call to the owner of the public key.**

The following example assumes that PGP has been obtained and installed on the system.

1. Import originator's PGP key to your keyring.

```
% pgp -ka wietse.pgp
ViaCrypt PGP 2.7.1 - Pretty Good Privacy for everyone.

U. S. Patent Nos. 4,200,770, 4,218,582, 4,405,829 and 4,424,414
    licensed exclusively by Public Key Partners.
U. S. Patent No. 5,214,703 licensed by Ascom Tech AG.
Zip compression by Mark Adler and Jean-loup Gailly, used with permission.
(c) 1990-1994 Philip Zimmerman
    (except for DigiSig+ Cryptographic Engine and IDEA Cipher).
(c) 1993-1995 DigiSig+ Cryptographic Engine by ViaCrypt,
    a division of Lemcom Systems, Inc,  24 Feb 95  B
ViaCrypt PGP is export restricted.  Refer to ViaCrypt PGP software license.
Current time: 1999/03/28/ 07:24 GMT

Looking for new keys...
pub  1022/D5327CB9 1992/09/25  wietse venema <wietse@wzv.win.tue.nl>

Checking signatures...
pub  1022/D5327CB9 1992/09/25  wietse venema <wietse@wzv.win.tue.nl>
sig!       D5327CB9 1995/04/01  wietse venema <wietse@wzv.win.tue.nl>
sig!       D5327CB9 1998/02/05  wietse venema <wietse@wzv.win.tue.nl>

Keyfile contains:
   1 new key(s)

One or more of the new keys are not fully certified.
Do you want to certify any of these keys yourself <y/N>? Y
```

```
Key for user ID: wietse venema (Wietse@wzv.win.tue.nl>
1022-bit key, Key ID D5327CB9, created 1992/09/25
Key fingerprint =   78 96 4A 4D F0 F0 D1 3C  45 E9 03 FC 17 67 DC D8
This key/userID association is not certified.
  Questionable certification from:
  (KeyID: 7E0AB281)
  .
  .
  .

  Questionable certification from:
  (KeyID: EF27E771)

Also known as: wietse venema <wietse@porcupine.org>
This key/userID association is not certified.
  Questionable certification from:
  wietse venema <wietse@wzv.win.tue.nl>

Do you want to certify this key yourself <y/N)? y
%
```

2. Verify the signature of the archive file.

```
% pgp rpcbind_2.1.tar.gz.sig
ViaCrypt PGP 2.7.1 - Pretty Good Privacy for everyone.

U. S. Patent Nos. 4.200,770, 4,218,582, 4,405,829 and 4,424,414
    licensed exclusively by Public Key Partners.
U. S. Patent No. 5,214,703 licensed by Ascom Tech AG.
Zip compression by Mark Adler and Jean-loup Gailly, used with permission.
(c) 1990-1994 Philip Zimmerman
    (except for DigiSig+ Cryptographic Engine and IDEA Cipher).
(c) 1993-1995 DigiSig+ Cryptographic Engine by ViaCrypt,
    a division of Lemcom Systems, Inc, 24 Feb 95  B
ViaCrypt PGP is export restricted.  Refer to ViaCrypt PGP software license.
Current time: 1999/03/28/ 07:29 GMT

File has signature.  Public key is required to check signature.
File 'rpcbind_2.1.tar.gz.sig' has signature, but with no text.
Text is assumed to be in file 'rpcbind_2.1.tar.gz'.
  .
Good signature from user "wietse venema <wietse@wzv.win.tue.nl>".
Signature made 1998/04/11 00:12 GMT

WARNING:  Because this public key is not certified with a trusted
signature, it is not known with high confidence that this public key
actually belongs to: "wietse venema <wietse@wzv.win.tue.nl>".

Signature and text are separate.  No output file produced.
%
```

An example of a bad file-signature match follows.

```
% pgp rpcbind_2.1.tar.gz.sig
ViaCrypt PGP 2.7.1 - Pretty Good Privacy for everyone.

U. S. Patent Nos. 4.200,770, 4,218,582, 4,405,829 and 4,424,414
    licensed exclusively by Public Key Partners.
U. S. Patent No. 5,214,703 licensed by Ascom Tech AG.
```

```
Zip compression by Mark Adler and Jean-loup Gailly, used with permission.
(c) 1990-1994 Philip Zimmerman
    (except for DigiSig+ Cryptographic Engine and IDEA Cipher).
(c) 1993-1995 DigiSig+ Cryptographic Engine by ViaCrypt,
    a division of Lemcom Systems, Inc,  24 Feb 95  B
ViaCrypt PGP is export restricted.  Refer to ViaCrypt PGP software license.
Current time: 1999/03/28/ 07:29 GMT

File has signature.  Public key is required to check signature.
File 'rpcbind_2.1.tar.gz.sig' has signature, but with no text.
Text is assumed to be in file 'rpcbind_2.1.tar.gz'.
.
```
(WARNING: Bad signature, doesn't match file contents!)
```
Bad signature from user "wietse venema <wietse@wzv.win.tue.nl>".
Signature made 1998/04/11 00:12 GMT

WARNING:  Because this public key is not certified with a trusted
signature, it is not known with high confidence that this public key
actually belongs to: "wietse venema <wietse@wzv.win.tue.nl>".

Signature and text are separate.  No output file produced.
%
```

Note: Different sites use different methods for storing digital signature files. As shown in the example above, some sites put the signature file in the same directory as the archive file. Other sites package the signature file differently. Look for *README* files to see if a particular site has adopted digital signatures for its content.

Verification Using MD5

Some sites post MD5 checksums of software source code as an alternative—and equally reliable—to PGP. MD5 is available from ftp://coast.cs.purdue.edu/pub/tools/unix/md5/ .

The process of verifying the integrity of a package is shown here by way of example: obtain the software package *TCP Wrappers* from ftp.porcupine.org and copy the file *tcp_wrappers_7.6.tar.gz* from the site. This *tar.gz* file is verified against the MD5 checksum posted in the CERT advisory http://www.cert.org/advisories/CA-99-01-Trojan-TCP-Wrappers.html . An example session follows.

```
# md5 tcp_wrappers_7.6.tar.gz
MD5 (tcp_wrappers_7.6.tar.gz) = (e6fa25f71226d090f34de3f6b122fb5a )
#
```

The circled checksum above is compared to the checksum shown on the CERT Web page. If the checksums compare, then the TCP Wrappers archive file *tcp_wrappers_7.6.tar.gz* can be considered to be intact.

Where to Go for Additional Information

Publications

- Zimmerman, Phillip R. *The Official PGP User's Guide*. Cambridge, MA: MIT Press, 1995.

Web Sites

- *CERT Advisory CA-99-01 Trojan TCP Wrappers*—http://www.cert.org/advisories/CA-99-01-Trojan-TCP-Wrappers.html (site containing a press release describing the TCP Wrappers break-in; also contains Wietse Venema's public PGP key)

GLOSSARY OF ATTACKS

This glossary contains a collection of the various types of attacks that can be launched upon a network, system, or organization. Examples follow many of the definitions.

Note: Hackers have proven themselves to be among the world's most creative people. Hence, the following list will probably be obsolete by the time this book goes to press. The best way to stay on top of new forms of attack is to subscribe to CERT and other security alert mailing lists, as well as to periodically visit security Web sites. Refer to appendix A for a list of mailing lists and Web sites.

back door

Computer code written into an application that permits the application developer (or anyone else with the necessary knowledge) to gain access to information or application features without having to supply authentication information.

Most applications' back doors are placed intentionally for use during application development and debugging; generally speaking, back doors are present in production versions of programs because the application developer forgot to remove them.

Back doors are also the result of break-ins; left behind by hackers, they are the means for subsequent unauthorized returns to a system in order to facilitate further illegal behavior.

denial of service

An action or event that prevents a system from providing its usual services. Examples include

- Sending hundreds or thousands of e-mail messages to a site in an attempt to fill a mail server's queue or to cause it to crash

- Consuming space in filesystems in order to prevent legitimate disk space uses

- Sending phony routing information protocol (RIP) packets to a router in order to alter its routing tables and prevent it from functioning correctly (this would cause a loss of network connectivity)

- Sending thousands of TCP SYN packets to a system in order to prevent it from being able to accept legitimate TCP connections

- Shutting off a building's electric power

All of these examples rely on a common theme: consume one or more resources in order to prevent or disrupt the functioning of legitimate processes also needing those resources.

dictionary attack

An attempt to break into a user account by guessing passwords from a dictionary. See also *password cracking* and *password guessing*.

DNS cache attack (also known as a poison cache attack)

An attack on a DNS server whereby phony DNS responses (to queries that were never sent) are sent to a DNS server in order to alter the DNS server's cache. Since the DNS server answers frequently hit queries from its cache, responses to queries after the attack will be incorrect..

The most common reason for a DNS cache attack is to cause the DNS server to change its responses. For example

> A hacker constructs phony DNS response packets and sends them to sun.com's DNS server. The hacker has built a phony Sun Microsystems Web server and is trying to corrupt Sun's DNS server so that Internet queries to www.sun.com will point to the hacker's Web server instead of Sun's Web server.

DNS rogue server

Not really a direct attack, but a case of someone running a phony DNS server, presumably hoping that systems will query it and get phony answers back. This can cause clients to use the wrong servers for higher-level services such as the World Wide Web, e-mail, or news.

dumpster diving

Going through a company's trash (or recycle) bins in order to retrieve documents (or equipment) yielding clues about the company's computing and network infrastructure. The worst possible discovery would be a printout (or sticky note) containing a password.

e-mail message source routing

Sending e-mail to a site address that forces the site to forward the message to its destination. For example

A troublemaker sends e-mail to joe%mycompany.com@yourcompany.com.

The message is first sent to *yourcompany.com*, then is forwarded to *mycompany.com*, and delivered to *joe*.

.forward attack, form 1

Hacking a user's world-writable *.forward* file in order to fool *sendmail* into executing any command on behalf of the user. For example

A hacker changes the user *sue*'s *.forward* file to contain the following:

```
\user
|"cp /bin/sh /home/sue/su-sh;chmod u+s /home/sue/sue-sh"
```

and then sends mail to *sue*. The command sequence above is then executed. The command creates a version of *sh* that runs as user *sue*.

.forward attack, form 2

A special form of a *denial of service* attack; for example

A mail server NFS-mounts home directories from end-user workstations in order to read users' *.forward* files. A clever user can simply turn off his workstation; the next time someone sends mail to that user, the mail server may hang while trying to mount the user's home directory (the user's home directory cannot be mounted because his machine has been turned off). See "Implement ForwardPath" in chapter 11 for information on how to prevent this type of attack.

In a variant of this attack, a user turns off his workstation and then causes hundreds or thousands of e-mail messages to be sent to his system. This causes the process table (or virtual memory) on the mail server to completely fill up, effectively hanging the system. This is because the *sendmail* processes (one for each mail message generated) cannot open his *.forward* file, and so the *sendmail* processes sit and wait. This is an especially troublesome attack since, upon reboot, *sendmail* again attempts to process the huge mail queue and potentially fills the process table again.

IP address spoofing

Configuring a system so that its stated IP address is that of another system. This is done in an attempt to break into a system in cases where it is suspected of trusting another. For example

A server named *pumpkin* at IP address 11.40.34.16 trusts (via an
.rhosts file) another server, named *melon*, at address 11.40.36.18.
An intruder, suspecting this trust relationship, configures her system so that the "from" IP address field in packets it sends to
pumpkin is really that of *melon*. The intruder could, for instance,
construct a phony *rsh* packet in an attempt to fool *pumpkin* into
thinking that her phony packets were being sent from *melon*; if
successful, the intruder's phony commands might get carried out
on *pumpkin*.

LD_LIBRARY_PATH attack

Some programs use *shared libraries* (those files with names ending in *.so*,
found in the */usr/lib, /usr/openwin/lib,* or */usr/dt/lib* directories); the
LD_LIBRARY_PATH variable is used by these programs to figure out which
shared library routines to use and in what order. The *LD_LIBRARY_PATH*
attack is a special kind of a Trojan horse attack, similar in fact to one where
the *PATH* statement is set up incorrectly (see *Trojan horse* and its example in
this section). It works by taking advantage of an error (usually by a UNIX system administrator) in the *LD_LIBRARY_PATH* environment variable, so that
Trojan horse library routines are used instead of the intended library routines.

logic bomb

An otherwise legitimate program is contaminated with a section of code
designed to do something nasty when a specific condition is met. (See also *time
bomb*.) For instance

A shell script launched by *cron* detects the presence of the file
/tmp/halt and halts the system.

MAC address spoofing

Configuring a system so that its MAC address is the same as that of another
system on the network. This would disrupt any attempts to communicate with
the correct system, particularly if the masquerading system is faster than the
real one.

NIS/NIS+ server spoofing

In an environment where NIS/NIS+ clients bind to servers by sending NIS
broadcast packets, a devious person could create a phony NIS/NIS+ server in
order to prevent NIS/NIS+ clients from connecting with legitimate NIS/NIS+
servers.

password cracking

Obtaining an */etc/passwd, /etc/shadow*, or NIS/NIS+ password map file containing encrypted passwords. An intruder would then run *crack* on these passwords in an attempt to discover account passwords by brute force. See also
dictionary attack.

password guessing

A very low-tech form of *password cracking* where an intruder is trying to guess a user's password by using information the intruder may know about the user (such as birthdays or children's or spouse names). See also *dictionary attack*.

port scanning

Running a security tool such as Satan or ISS against a system (or collection of systems on a network) in order to discover what vulnerable network services are configured on the system(s).

program buffer overflow

Overflowing a program's input buffer in a way that causes executable code to be copied into the stack and subsequently executed. A well-known example is the *fingerd* exploit used in the Internet Worm incident. Refer to the two papers on the Internet Worm cited in appendix D.

session hijacking

Listening to a session between two computers and then injecting forged packets (in one or both directions) in an attempt to alter the outcome of the session in progress. This is also known as a *sequence number attack* because the intruder must try to guess the next sequence numbers in the connection stream in order to quickly forge phony packets with those sequence numbers.

shoulder surfing

Looking over a person's shoulder when that person is typing in a password. This is why it is proper etiquette to literally turn one's back when another is entering a password. This is a subtle form of *social engineering*.

snooping

Using a program such as *snoop* in order to capture and record network packets containing passwords and other sensitive information. A fine example can be found in chapter 9 in the section on using *Snoop*, where a *telnet* session account password is being captured.

social engineering

Using the phone, e-mail, or other means to convince an unsuspecting individual to yield sensitive information or commit a foolish act. For example

> Intruder, calling the Helpdesk: "Hello, this is Phil Jones. I'm out of town and need to dial in to get a report. I had a noisy line or must have fat-fingered my password—could you reset it for me?"

> Helpdesk: "Sure, no problem. I've changed it to 'martini.' Be sure to change the password to something else once you log in."

Intruder: "Thanks a lot. This really helps. Good-bye."

Intruder, calling department admin: "Hello, this is Phil Jones. I'm out of town and need to dial in to get a report. I've lost the access number, can you give it to me?"

Admin: "Sure, it's 801-555-1234."

With just a couple of phone calls, the intruder was able to get the remote access phone number and get a user's password changed to a known value. Within minutes the intruder will be logged into the system with a legitimate user account and password.

time bomb

An otherwise legitimate program is contaminated with a section of code designed to do something nasty when a specific date or time occurs. See also *logic bomb*.

trap door

See *back door*.

Trojan horse

A program containing a (usually nefarious) purpose other than its perceived or intended one. For example

> A fake *su* program is placed in */tmp* or some other world-writable directory. If root's *PATH* is set incorrectly to include "." (specifically, if "." appears before */usr/bin*), and if the UNIX administrator executes *su* while in that directory, then the fake *su* program will be the one executed—not the real *su* in */usr/bin*. The fake *su* would ask for the root password just like the real *su*, but instead of *su*ing, the fake *su* would just e-mail the password just entered to the owner of the Trojan horse. Then the Trojan horse *su* would execute the real *su* as a means of concealing what happened (the UNIX administrator would probably think he just mistyped the root password the first time).

virus

A program that inserts itself into an executable program, makes copies of itself, and through its design is able to be moved from computer to computer. Viruses are found on unprotected operating systems such as MacOS or MS Windows and do not pose a significant threat to the UNIX community. See also *worm*.

war dialing

Setting up a computer and modem to sequentially call every phone number in a given prefix, recording instances where computers were reached.

wire tap

The act of physically attaching connectors or other devices to a communications wire in order to intercept communications traffic.

worm

A program that runs on a system, makes copies of itself, and through its design is able to move (or be moved) from computer to computer. Unlike a virus, a worm does not change other programs. The most famous worm is the Internet Worm of 1988. See the references *The Internet Worm Incident* and *The Internet Worm Program: An Analysis* listed in appendix D.

SECURE SYSTEM CHECKLIST

This appendix contains a checklist of steps to perform on a new or existing system to ensure it is as secure as possible. Each step references one or more sections in the book (the chapter number is given first, then section title).

1. (For new systems) Load the OS directly from an official Sun release CD-ROM.

   - Save hardcopies of all *mkfs* output when building filesystems by hand. Make sure the system's partitions are large enough for patches and OS upgrades. See 16, "Filesystem Geometry." A complete record of all filesystems built during OS installation can be found in the file */var/sadm/system/logs/install_log* .

   - Do not install CDE, OpenWindows, or ToolTalk on servers. These packages have security holes that are better left off a server.

   - Before connecting the system to the network, install and run Tripwire in order to baseline the system before tampering can possibly occur. See 4, "Tripwire."

   Warning: Baselining an *existing* system with Tripwire is considerably more difficult because the system may already have been compromised. This is because Tripwire can detect tampering only *after* a system has been baselined. The only reliable solution is to reinstall Solaris and all of the system's applications from original manufacturer media (not from local backups, which may also be compromised!).

   - Install all required patches and security patches. See appendix C, "Obtaining and Applying Solaris Patches."

279

- Back up the system twice. Store one backup set on-site (in a secure location) and send the other set off-site.

2. Make the system as physically secure as possible. See 3, "Theft and Access Prevention."

3. Set the OpenBoot security level to *command* or *full*. See 3, "Protecting OpenBoot by Setting Security Parameters."

4. (For fileservers) Consider implementing filesystem quotas. See 4, "Filesystem Quotas."

5. In environments with complex file and directory permission requirements, consider implementing access control lists. See 4, "Filesystem Access Control Lists."

6. Disable all unnecessary accounts: daemon, bin, sys, adm, lp, uucp, nuucp, listen, nobody, noaccess. See 5, "Which Administrative Accounts Should Be Locked."

7. Allow root to log in only at the system console; set *CONSOLE=/dev/console* in the file */etc/default/login* . See 5, "Direct Root Login."

8. Make the *su* command available only to UNIX administrators. See 5, "Restricting Use of Su."

9. Log all *su* attempts. See 5, "Su Logging."

10. Set up root (and other administrative accounts) so that the system name is part of the shell prompt. See 5, "Include System Name in Root Shell Prompt."

11. Use secure settings in */etc/default/login* . See 5, "Default Login Environment."

12. Use screen locks when running X-Windows. See 5, "X-Windows Security."

13. Restrict access to *cron* and *at* to accounts that truly need them. See 7, "User Access to *cron* System", and 7, "User Access to *at* System."

14. Turn on logging of failed login attempts. See 8, "Loginlog."

15. Alias *ls* and *rm* commands for root and other administrative accounts. See 8, "Alias the *ls* Command to Show Hidden Files and Hidden Characters in Filenames," and 8, "Alias the *rm* Command to Prevent Accidental File Deletion."

16. Disable IP packet forwarding. See 9, "Turn off IP Forwarding with /etc/notrouter."

17. Disable all unnecessary network services. See 13, "Necessary and Unnecessary Services."

18. Disable *telnet, rlogin, rexec, rcp* and *rsh*; use *Ssh* instead. See 13, "Secure Replacement for *telnet*, *rsh*, and *rlogin*."

19. Disable NFS server capabilities (unless system *must* be an NFS server). See 13, "How to Disable Unnecessary Services."

20. Disable NFS client capabilities (unless system *must* be an NFS client). See 13, "How to Disable Unnecessary Services."

21. Disable automounter (unless system *must* be an automount client). See 13, "Disable Service Not Defined in */etc/inet/services* and */etc/inet/ inetd.conf .*"

22. Stop running *sendmail* as a system daemon (unless system is a mail server). See 13, "How to Disable Unnecessary Services."

23. If the system is a mail server, strengthen *sendmail* security. See 11, "Mitigating E-Mail Security Weaknesses."

24. If the system is a mail relay, consider replacing *sendmail* with SMAP or postfix. See 11, "Replace *Sendmail*."

25. Disable e-mail message source routing. See 11, "Prevent Message Source Routing."

26. Remove all unnecessary e-mail aliases. See 11, "Remove Unnecessary E-mail Aliases."

27. Implement *Smrsh*. See 11, "Implement *Smrsh*."

28. Implement ForwardPath if this is an e-mail server. See 11, "Implement ForwardPath."

29. Implement *inetd* connection tracing. See 13, "*inetd* Connection Tracing."

30. Install and configure TCP Wrappers. See 13, "TCP Wrappers."

31. Implement public-domain *rpcbind* on a system which *must* be an NFS, NIS, or NIS+ server. See 13, "Public Domain *rpcbind*." Otherwise, disable *rpcbind*.

32. If the system is a NIS client:
    - Move NIS maps out of */etc*. See 14, "Move NIS Maps out of */etc*."
    - Make sure the NIS maps directory is safe. See 14, "Protect NIS Maps Directory."
    - Bind to a specific NIS server (or servers) rather than broadcast for a NIS server. See 14, "Avoid Illicit NIS Servers."

33. If the system is a NIS server:
    - Make the NIS domain name different from the DNS domain name. See 14, "NIS Domain Name."
    - Restrict the systems that can see the NIS maps. See 14, "Implement */var/yp/securenets*."
    - Consider hiding shadow fields. See 14, "Hide Shadow Fields."
    - Do not put root and other administrative accounts in NIS. See 14, "Keep Root and Other Administrative Accounts out of NIS."

34. If the system is running NIS+:
    - Make sure the NIS+ security level is set to 2. See 14, "NIS+ Security Level."

- Back up NIS+ tables at least once per day. See 14, "Back Up NIS+ Tables."
- Make sure NIS+ transactions are frequently flushed. See 14, "Flush NIS+ Transactions."
- Do not put root and other administrative accounts in NIS+. See 14, "Keep Root and Other Administrative Accounts out of NIS."

35. Disable *nscd* Caching. See 14, "*nscd*."

36. See what network services are reachable on the system. Take any corrective action. See 13, "System Accessibility."

37. Implement an intrusion detection product. See 13, "Intrusion Detection."

38. Run Tripwire and baseline the system again. Put the Tripwire database for the system in a safe place off of the system. See 4, "Tripwire."

39. Create an incident response team. See 16, "Create an Incident Response Team."

40. Document the system build and subsequent modifications in an electronic logbook. See 16, "System Event Logbooks."

41. Make sure the system is covered under a Sun hardware and software support contract. See 16, "Hardware and Software Service Agreements."

42. Determine what hardware spare parts should be on-site, if any, and acquire them. See 16, "Keep Hardware Spares."

43. Obtain one or more copies of the system's PROM, particularly if one or more software products are bound to the system's hostid. See 16, "Copies of Critical Server PROMs."

44. Make sure other UNIX administrators are cross-trained on the architecture and all procedures for the system. Obtain working-hours and after-hours contact information for everyone who administers the system. See 16, "Contacts and Cross-Training."

45. Back up the system again; get the media off-site.

46. Get the latest CERT and Sun Security Bulletin reports and check for any last-minute security holes that must be remedied. Subscribe to two or more security incident mailing lists and read all of the advisories that arrive.

47. NOW connect the system to the network!!

INDEX

Numerics

A